TARAN

Taran N. Khan is a journalist and writer based in Mumbai. She grew up in Aligarh and was educated in Delhi and London. She has published widely in India and internationally, including in *Guernica*, *Al Jazeera*, *The Caravan* and *Himal Southasian* and has received fellowships from the MacDowell Colony, Jan Michalski Foundation and Swiss Arts Council Pro Helvetia. From 2006 to 2013, Khan spent long periods living and working in Kabul. *Shadow City* is her first book.

TARAN N. KHAN

Shadow City

A Woman Walks Kabul

VINTAGE

3 5 7 9 10 8 6 4 2

Vintage is part of the Penguin Random House group of companies
whose addresses can be found at global.penguinrandomhouse.com

Penguin
Random House
UK

Copyright © Taran N. Khan 2019

Taran N. Khan has asserted her right to be identified as the author
of this Work in accordance with the Copyright, Designs and Patents
Act 1988

First published in Vintage in 2021
First published in hardback by Chatto & Windus in 2019

penguin.co.uk/vintage

A CIP catalogue record for this book is available from the
British Library

ISBN 9781784708023

Printed and bound in Great Britain by Clays Ltd, Elcograf S.p.A.

The authorised representative in the EEA is Penguin Random House
Ireland, Morrison Chambers, 32 Nassau Street, Dublin D02 YH68.

Penguin Random House is committed to a sustainable future for our
business, our readers and our planet. This book is made from Forest
Stewardship Council® certified paper.

MIX
Paper from
responsible sources
FSC® C018179
www.fsc.org

For my parents

Khwab-e-nausheen-e-baamdaad-e-raheel
Baaz daarad piyaada raa ze sabeel
Harke aamad e'maarat-e-nau sakht
Raft-o-manzel ba deegare pardakht . . .

Sweet slumber on the morn of departure keeps the traveller from the road.
Everyone who has come here has built a new structure; each departed, turning over his dwelling to another . . .

Gulistan by Sa'adi Shirazi
Translated by Wheeler M. Thackston

CONTENTS

MAPS x

FOREWORD xii

1: RETURNS 1

2: WRITTEN ON THE CITY 36

3: ABSENCES 70

4: MAP OF MOVING IMAGES 107

5: WALKING WITH THE DJINNS 140

6: VEILED CITY 177

7: RETURNS 216

Acknowledgements 241
Notes 245
Bibliography 256
Index 264

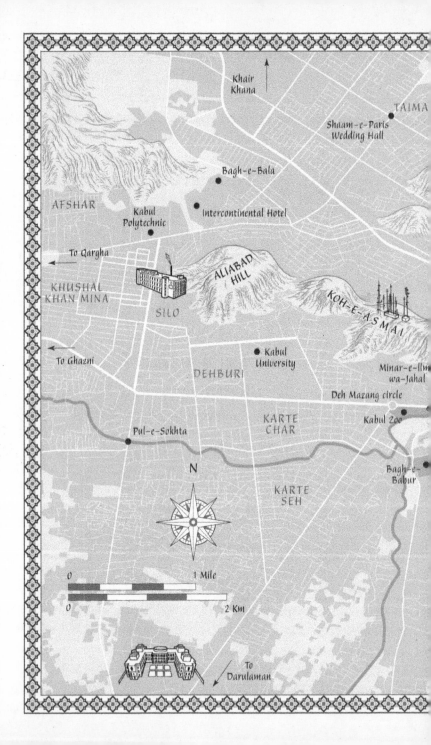

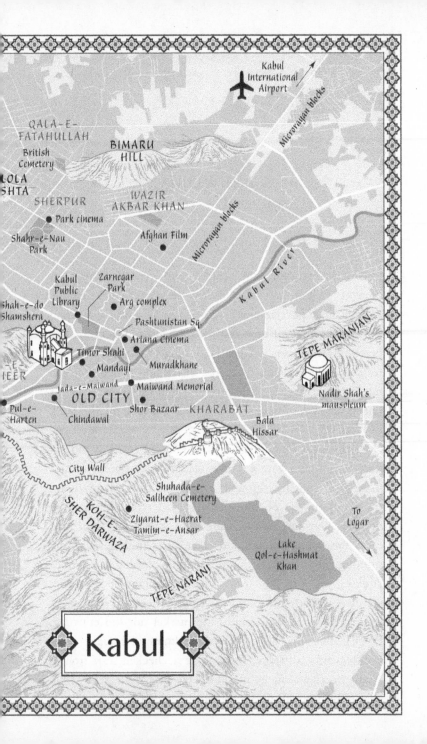

FOREWORD

One of the first things I was told when I arrived in Kabul was never to walk. It was early 2006, five years after the overthrow of the Taliban government by US-led coalition forces, around the same amount of time that the Taliban had been in power before 2001. Winter was just beginning to fade and, like the seasons, Kabul was on the verge of turning, though we did not know it then. As spring transformed the surroundings, I joined the rush of bodies on the street and took my first walk in the city.

My memory begins from a place I almost certainly did not start from. I must have got there somehow. But in my mind I first recall moving through a bazaar called Mandayi, on the southern side of the Kabul River. I remember making my way through narrow lanes and shops that extended onto the street. Traders and their carts spilling onto the thoroughfares. Stepping around the piles of dried fruit, tins of cooking oil, soap. The way the dull sunlight of that rainy spring day filtered through the canopies erected over some shops. The earth was muddy, the market not too crowded; familiar, like the bazaars of cities I knew in India. I recall walking onto a bridge, and buying a checked scarf from a young man standing by its railing. His face was barely visible behind his stock of fluttering fabrics, which he had tied to a wooden frame resting on his shoulders. He smiled when I took his picture. Behind him were the mountains that encircle Kabul – the Koh-e-Sher Darwaza on my left, the Koh-e-Asmai to my right. Between them, below the bridge, was the river – sluggish with some water, some rubbish. I moved across the bridge, and in the process I spanned the city's history, from the Shahr-e-Kohna, or the old city, to the Shahr-e-Nau, or new suburbs, ahead of me.

Memory returns in fragments. I remember walking through the half-empty streets feeling the sun on my back. I heard snatches of song on a radio, passed a group of young men lounging on a broken sofa they had pulled onto the street. I saw walls with bullet marks, and barriers across gates, and the glass panes of shopfronts painted with calligraphy. Under my feet was the slush of the spring. There was smoke rising from the chimneys, and evening colouring the snow on the peaks of the Paghman range on the horizon. Birds on the bare branches of trees, singing songs of the approaching dusk. Back in my room, I had tried to brush the mud off my shoes, my clothes, but it had clung stubbornly. I had looked out of the window. Beyond the walls that enclosed the courtyard, the city had changed. It shimmered like a promise, far larger than I had thought. The more I walked, the larger it revealed itself to be.

In the bluster and immensity of war – the one that began in 2001 and the ones before it – it is easy to forget that Kabul existed 3,000 years ago. Years after I arrived, I read a passage in a history of the city that seemed to ring true. 'Like some people, certain cities suffer from amnesia,' it said. 'Not that they have no past. Rather, this past, no matter how glorious it may have been, will have left so few reminders, so few architectural vestiges, so few visible traces, that it remains something obscure, if not completely invisible.'[1] In this 'amnesiac city', I found that walking offered a way to exhume history – a kind of bipedal archaeology – as well as an excavation of the present.

Over the years these walks deepened and the streets changed. My journeys to Kabul unfolded between 2006 and 2013, and each return yielded fresh transformations. During this time, I moved through a city of memories – stories and fragments of Kabul recounted by others. I wandered through myths and fables, took routes of the imagination, ventured into dreams and poetry. Like vast bridges, they connected different eras and places. In these wanderings, I found a city of hidden abundance.

To call Kabul an amnesiac city is to refer to its physical landscape, where the ruins of the past lie below the surface. But it could also refer, I realised, to its obscured culture, the vanishing of the very idea of Kabul as a city with history; with a specific, cosmopolitan way of life. These expeditions into Kabul's parallel terrains were like chasing the shadows that flickered across its streets.

This happened to be exploration of a kind I was familiar with.

I have a complicated relationship with walking. This has a lot to do, I suspect, with having grown up in Aligarh, a city in northern India, where walking on the streets came with intense male scrutiny, and the sense of being in a proscribed space. As a woman stepping out into its thoroughfares, I needed a reason to place my body on the street. I learned to display a posture of 'work' while walking, and to erase any signs that may hint at my being out for pleasure, for no reason at all other than to walk. All this means I see walking as a luxury, not something to be taken for granted. It is an act of autonomy and mobility I learned early to seize as a form of pleasure. I also grew adept at the allied skill of reading my terrain, looking out for signs that told me if it was open, or off-limits.

Being told not to walk was another way in which Kabul felt familiar. To map the city, I drew on the same knowledge and intuition that had helped me navigate the streets of my home town. Which is why, unlike the maps of guidebooks that seek to make checklists and establish authority, the routes I took were wandering and idiosyncratic. They were not trajectories of efficiency leading to a predetermined destination, nor were they maps of authority or delineation, offering control or explanation. These were routes of discovery – maps of being lost. To be lost is a way to see a place afresh, a way to reimagine a terrain that feels known. To be lost in Kabul is to find it – as a place of richness and possibility.

Exploring Kabul, I found, required the same principles that help in the reading of mystical Persian poetry, in the relationship between the *zahir*, or the overt, and the *batin*, the hidden or implied. This works on the tacit understanding that what is being said is an allegory for what is meant or intended. To talk of the moon, for instance, is to talk of the beloved; to talk of clouds across the moon is to talk of the pain of separated lovers; to talk of walls is to speak of exile. Such wandering leads through circuitous routes to wide vistas of understanding. Like walking through a small gate into a large garden. It is also a useful reminder that in this city, what is seen is often simply one aspect of the truth. What lies behind – the shadow city – is where layers are revealed.

The stories we tell are often crafted from imperfect memory, drawing on what we remember, forgetting the rest. This is also true for cities, where what we see is only that which is recalled, what is apparent. Sometimes this forgetting is unwittingly inflicted, caused by the convulsions of war or the eroding passing of time. At other times it is deliberate, a conscious strategy of erasure. I sought out what was forgotten in Kabul as a way to map this *batin* city.

In the amnesiac city, other versions of the city shimmer in the distance, below the surface, from the penumbra between remembering and oblivion. 'There are a multitude of cities hiding under the white lie of a single name,' writes Darran Anderson, 'and they articulate themselves in secret significances, unwritten memory maps, daily orbits.'[2] Walking was a way to encounter these cities within the city. This book is the story of these walks.

1

RETURNS

Stories in Kabul begin with the phrase '*Yeki bood, yeki na bood*' – 'There was one, there was no one'.

The phrase corresponds to the 'Once upon a time' of fairy tales elsewhere. Whichever way you choose to read this expression, it is a good place to begin this story of Kabul, a city that was, and never was. Or to use the trick of fables: there it is, there it is not.

The story of Kabul begins with bridges, roads appearing on water. In one legend about its origin, it appeared as a magic island in the middle of a large lake. To reach the island, a king built a bridge – *pul* – made of straw – *kah*. The combination of the two words that created this bridge – *kah* and *pul* – gave the city he made on this magic isle its name.[1]

Kabul is an island, or so it appears to the outsider standing on one of its nondescript, potholed streets. It deceives you with its high walls streaked with brown mud, punctuated by steel-topped gates. It hides behind the fine mist of dust that hangs over its streets and homes, so that the city appears as though from the other side of a soft curtain. Like a mirage, a place that is both near and far away.

But walk through the small opening in an entrance gate and everything changes. You enter lush gardens and beautiful homes, their rooms filled with books, carpets, photographs and music. In the older quarters of the city, the flat mud roofs of tightly packed homes form a different kind of thoroughfare, an elevated path across secluded spaces that is protected from the public gaze. Elsewhere, there appear landscapes of homes clinging to the hills, their windows half reflecting the sky, half revealing glimpses of life in the rooms within. The city appears with the shift in perspective.

As a child, I was fascinated by a tiny kaleidoscope my father bought me. It was a plastic tube with a transparent cap at the end, filled with pieces of broken bangles, coloured glass of different sizes. I was riveted by this transformation of everyday objects into the fragments of a magical landscape. And I was drawn to how a simple shift of my wrist, or even of my eye, would make the pieces rearrange themselves into a new picture. Walking in Kabul is like looking through the kaleidoscope. Fragments fall into place, the familiar appears new.

There it is. There it is not. Kabul appears where you don't expect to see it.

***

Before I ever saw it, Kabul was a place I knew. Or more precisely, it was a place that felt known.

My father's family is descended from Pashtuns, or Pathans as they are called in India. My paternal forebears were part of this diaspora that put down roots in the fertile plains of northern India over the centuries. By the eighteenth century, as the Mughal Empire declined, the smaller kingdoms that emerged included states of Rohilla Pathans (the term deriving from 'Roh', the mountainous region of their origin) in the area now known as Rohilkhand.[2]

These kingdoms were eventually crushed by British colonial expansion. Just one *riyasat*, or principality, of Rampur survived in the 1770s; by the nineteenth century it was a 'princely state', nominally ruled by an Indian *nawab*, but effectively under British control.[3]

The first ancestor I heard of – my great-grandfather – was employed in this court, and my family lived there until my own grandfather moved to Aligarh. It was Rampur that provided the template for what I knew of Indian Pathans – from the light eyes and sharp noses of my relatives there, to the wry humour and loud emotions they carried like badges of honour.

I grew up in Aligarh, a university town near Delhi, in a rambling house where I shared the rituals of adolescence with a large number of cousins. Barely ever leaving the confines of our home, we relished the thrill that came with our exotic origin story. It was our favourite explanation for many things, from our fiery tempers and love of good food, to our proprietary claims over Indian movie stars of Pashtun origin. Or our delight in telling the joke about a stubborn Pathan who began bargaining with a fruit seller for a melon. Exasperated by his persistence, the man eventually begged him to just take the melon for free. 'If it's free I will take two,' the Pathan replied.

This tenuous link to the rocky land we had never seen was made more alluring by the fact that it was a distant place of the imagination. We could mould it in any way we wanted. 'We are Pathans,' we declared, 'we think with our hearts. We are brave and emotional.' In part, we had gleaned these ideas from the adults around us, in part from Indian films that depicted Pathans as golden-hearted friends and fierce foes. So when I announced to my family I was going to Kabul for work, there was some concern but also a lot of excitement.

The flight I boarded from Delhi on that winter day in early 2006 was full – mostly packed with foreign aid workers and NATO personnel. There were a few Afghans too, returning home. As we flew over the Safed Koh or 'White Mountain' range to the east of Kabul, the peaks sparkled with snow, and the wings of our plane seemed to almost scrape their summit. We crossed into a valley, and Kabul lay below us. Thin grids of houses, the city's limits ringed by mountains. On the tarmac, we taxied past rows of old fighter planes and smaller aircraft belonging to humanitarian agencies.

I remember being enraptured by the azure sky, the beauty of the surroundings. My more seasoned travel companions knew better than to waste time gaping at the sights, however. Within minutes of the plane coming to a halt, they were marching down the tarmac towards the ramshackle airport building, the women pulling headscarves out of their bags and tying them briskly as they walked. By the time I made it to the immigration desk, the queue ahead of me was long and chaotic. In the arrivals hall, I could see porters holding up bags for passengers to identify from a stationary carousel ('This one? That?') and flinging them on waiting trolleys. My turn eventually came in front of a bulky official, who flicked over the pages of my passport casually. 'Khan?' he asked quizzically, gazing at my name. 'Yes,' I replied, eager to tell my story. 'My ancestors were from here.' 'Then what are you doing there?' he demanded in good Urdu, amused by my excitement. He stamped the page with a flourish. 'Welcome back.'

In fact, my enthusiasm for this 'return' was based on a fine disregard for the actual history and geography of my imagined ancestral land. Not only was Kabul's population and heritage far more diverse and complex than I had imagined, I found that my own forebears could well have hailed from the other side of the Durand Line, the British-era border that divides the Pashtun-dominated regions of Afghanistan and Pakistan. This didn't bother my new Kabuli friends too much, however. Successive governments of Afghanistan had not recognised this boundary over the years. 'We piss on the Durand Line, sister,' they told me generously. 'You're one of us.'

***

My arrival coincided with a season of returns. Before I came to Kabul, I had met Afghan refugees who had fled during the Taliban rule to Delhi. They had been part of an exodus that commenced in the 1970s, at the onset of the country's spiral of conflict. By 2006, however, the direction of movement was reversed. Nearly 3 million refugees had come back to the country in the years following the defeat of the Taliban.[4] Many of them were drawn to the capital for its relative security and the opportunities it offered. The majority were subsistence farmers returning from Pakistan and Iran. There were also labourers, entrepreneurs, politicians and professionals. Along with these came foreign aid workers, consultants and journalists. All these arrivals were to a city in flux.

In retrospect, it was a troubled spring; but at the time there was still space for cautious optimism.

Even as the war in Iraq floundered, Afghanistan was still considered the 'just war'. It had been five years since the Taliban government had been overthrown by the US and its allies, along with the Afghan military coalition called the Northern Alliance. It was believed that al Qaeda had been chased out of the country. The International Security Assistance Force (ISAF) – a UN-mandated, NATO-led mission – was established in December 2001 to safeguard the capital. In 2003 its mission was extended beyond Kabul. There was a rush of foreign aid to rebuild the ruined country after decades of war. Afghans, tired of conflict and lawlessness, had responded with hope and optimism. The 2004 elections had replaced the Transitional Authority established during the Bonn Conference with Hamid Karzai as president of the Islamic Republic of Afghanistan.

From the relative security of Kabul, it was possible to discern the gains made in education, women's rights and infrastructure. But already there were signs of unravelling: the resurgence of Taliban factions across the country, as well as rising discontent with the corruption and cronyism of the government. Aid funds were poorly utilised – even the capital had little access to water, electricity and transport. More ominously, it was becoming a target for suicide bombings, explosions and kidnappings. In February 2006, *Foreign Policy* magazine and the US-based Fund for Peace released their second 'Failed State Index'. Afghanistan was placed at number ten on the list.[5] It was a time that was not quite war, and certainly not peace.

The cycle of conflict that began in 2001 was underlaid by previous years of ethnic strife and sectarian violence, which resurfaced after the defeat of the Taliban. And there was more to it than military gains or losses. It was fuelled by the glut of weapons in the country, and the absence of a strong central government in the 1980s and 90s. It was shaped by the shadow economy of the opium trade, and the competition between different factions to control its gains. Across the country, there had been displacement and erosion of civil society institutions and networks. The cities had poor infrastructure, the countryside had few livelihoods. Within the government, there were high levels of official graft,[6] and a legacy of war crimes and impunity. And there was the tsunami of aid money that brought corruption in its wake. As the capital, Kabul was the centre of many of these forces, the city where all the gains and all the changes of the era arrived first and hit most powerfully. It was where worlds collided: the new with the old, the old with the ancient, the Afghan elite with the provincial migrants, the expats with the Afghans, the civilians with the government, the village with the city.

On this first journey, I was accompanied by my husband and a friend. Our assignment was to teach video production techniques to employees of a radio and TV station run by the Afghan government. We arrived full of ideas, certain we would have the time of our lives.

As I watched, the city transformed. Bare branches of trees gradually grew denser with blossom, infusing the air with a heady smell. Small streams and rivers filled up with water. From behind the ruins of mud walls, I saw new homes rising. The debris of war was everywhere. In places, the bodies of old jeeps and tanks were used to build houses. The door of a vehicle became a bridge, the metal became sheltering walls. The fragments of the past had been rearranged into a new landscape.

Each day, we drove to work through the chaotic traffic of Kabul. Amid the snarls were large SUVs, their bodies emblazoned with the logos of different aid organisations, their radio antennae waving like irritable tentacles. There were also grey minivans called Town Aces, pronounced 'Tunis' by the Afghan commuters who packed into them. The drivers would beat out the names of their destinations to a rhythm on the door without pausing for breath. '*Karte Seh Karte Char Barchee Barchee Jada Jada Chowk Chowk Chowk*,' I heard. Yellow-and-white Corolla taxis nosed in, along with cyclists and pedestrians. Sometimes, the military convoys of ISAF soldiers would be stuck in the traffic too, and being by their side meant being uncomfortably aware that while they may be the intended targets of attacks, it was often the civilians beside them who bore the brunt of the explosions. At every *charahi*, or crossroads, Kabul's army of street children sold magazines and chewing gum and phonecards, or washed the windscreens of the cars waiting to move ahead.

In our commute of about an hour from Kolola Pushta to west Kabul, we crossed several landmarks and changing terrain, glimpsed in flashes through our car windows. It was only once we reached our workplace, and were in the company of our colleagues, that we walked.

* * *

A walk through the history of Kabul would begin where the city itself began – a settlement by a river, at the heart of which is a citadel.[7] Inside the walls of this Bala Hissar, or High Fortress, was a city in itself, with barracks, homes and bazaars. Over time Kabul expanded along the southern bank of the river that flows between the Koh-e-Sher Darwaza and the Koh-e-Asmai. The remains of Kabul's thick wall radiate over the sprawl of the Sher Darwaza; they are said to date back as far as the fifth century.

The citadel stands on a ridge that lies to the east of the Koh-e-Sher Darwaza, and has been occupied by different armies over the centuries. In the sixteenth century, it accommodated the forces of young Zahiruddin Babur, a prince in search of a kingdom. After being ousted from his native Ferghana by family rivalries, and a period of wandering around the Hindu Kush, Babur succeeded in annexing Kabul in 1504 with a small group of followers. He went on to establish Mughal rule over India, but never forgot Kabul, a city that claimed his affections completely.

Walk further by the river from the Bala Hissar towards the north-west, and a domed monument surrounded by a garden appears. This is the mausoleum of Timur Shah, the first king to make Kabul his capital and the centre of the Durrani Empire. This empire was established by his father Ahmad Shah as the 'Land of the Afghans', and forms the basis of the modern Afghan state. By the 1830s, Kabul had spread along the south bank of the Kabul River, and had a diverse population that, according to historians, 'left on all visitors of the period an impression of amiable cosmopolitanism'.[8]

We cross the river in 1880, with the rule of Amir Abdur Rahman Khan (1880–1901). At this time, Afghanistan was part of the power struggle between the Russian and British Empires, who each sought to dominate Central Asia. The British fought two wars in Afghanistan in the nineteenth century, attempting to extend their influence in the country. The last of these ended in 1880, with the departing British forces leaving Amir Abdur Rahman Khan on the throne. The 'Iron Amir' has a mixed legacy of unifying Afghanistan along with a reputation for despotism. He expanded the city that had been damaged during the conflict, towards the north, moving his court and all associated offices to the left bank of the river. These were contained within one complex called the Arg, now the presidential palace. This was part of the amir's efforts to build a strong, modern Afghan state. The shift away from the historic old city would continue in the future, as Kabul spread further and further towards the north.

Abdur Rahman Khan was a prolific builder, constructing palaces (that he designed himself), parks, public buildings and workshops. He also introduced a different architectural style across his capital, taking inspiration from Central Asian traditions as well as European influences. His son Amir Habibullah (1901–19) continued this trend. But it was his grandson, Amir Amanullah (1919–29), who embraced most fully the zeal for modernising Afghanistan.

In 1919, his first year on the throne, Amanullah initiated what is called the Third Anglo-Afghan War, and declared Afghanistan to be independent of Britain's control over its foreign policy. But he was also deeply enamoured of the modernity of the West, and sought to emulate it in his own nation. Amanullah was influenced by his father-in-law, the intellectual, author and publisher Mahmood Tarzi. Tarzi had spent years in exile before being allowed to return to his own

country. Under his guidance, Amanullah set in motion several
far-reaching reforms, like promulgating the first Afghan
constitution.[9] He pushed for the education of women and
discouraged polygamy. Queen Soraya, Amanullah's beautiful,
well-read, well-travelled wife, was the perfect partner in these
endeavours. She rode on horseback with the king's hunting
parties, and wore dashing Western-style clothes.[10]

Walking to the south-west of the city, it is possible to see
traces of Amanullah's most ambitious project, a new
administrative capital called Darulaman. This was planned to
celebrate Afghanistan's 'entrance into the community of sovereign
nations' after his declaration of independence from the
British.[11] Amanullah's vision was of a modern (meaning
Western-style) city plan with European-inspired buildings. At
its heart was the Qasr-e-Darulaman, a massive 'government
palace' that was to serve as a secretariat.[12] Designed by French
architect and archaeologist André Godard, the domed building
echoed the splendour of eighteenth-century Europe.[13] Even
its flower beds grew blooms from imported European seeds. A
wide avenue lined with poplars led to the new quarter, and
soon became a fashionable place to be seen. But to ride on its
admirably straight path, Kabulis had to pay a fee, while 'all the
promenaders had to wear European style clothing and women
were invited to remove their veils'.[14]

In 1928 Amanullah and Soraya embarked on a seven-
month tour of Europe. Besides their official engagements,
they shopped for furnishings for their new residential palace
in Darulaman. On his return, Amanullah announced an even
more radical programme of reforms. But by January 1929, his
government was overturned by a rebellion. Adding fuel to
the fire of the king's controversial modernising measures
were photos from his travels, particularly a portrait of Queen
Soraya in a sleeveless dress.[15] The couple fled to Italy, and

Amanullah returned to Afghanistan only after his death in 1960 to be buried in Jalalabad. His dream of a modern new enclave bearing his name was never fully realised. Its centrepiece, the Qasr-e-Darulaman, was damaged – first in a fire in 1969, and then during the civil war of 1992–96. Its ruined frame at the end of the avenue watches over the changing city.

Kabul was captured by the Tajik rebel leader Habibullah Kalakani, who was derisively called Bacha-e-Saqao (son of the water carrier) because of his humble roots.[16] Kalakani's reign lasted only nine months. By October 1929, Amanullah's cousin Nadir Khan had managed to retake Kabul. He was declared king, and attempted to introduce more measured reforms. But he also met a bloody end and was assassinated while attending the graduation ceremony of a high school in Kabul. His son Zahir Shah took the throne in 1933. He was to be the last king of Afghanistan, ruling for forty years.

Through these political changes, Kabul continued to spread further on the north bank of the river, with the suburb of Shahr-e-Nau laid out in the 1930s. Its orderly grids of houses, surrounded by gardens and high walls, contrasted with the congested lanes of the Shahr-e-Kohna. Embassies and foreign missions of the nations that were establishing relations with Afghanistan through the 1940s were set up here, beside the residences of Kabul's upper and middle classes.

Through the 1960s and 70s, the capital grew steadily, due in part to migration by rural families from the provinces. Walking through its streets, it would have been possible to see houses and shops expanding the city's edges, spreading to both sides of the Koh-e-Asmai, climbing over the slopes of its hills. By the early 1970s, Kabul was the mostly peaceful capital of a small country, home to around half a million people.[17] And then everything changed.

In July 1973, Zahir Shah's cousin Muhammad Daoud Khan mounted a coup while the king was in Europe. He declared Afghanistan a republic, and himself the president. Five years later in April 1978, the Afghan Communist party – called the People's Democratic Party of Afghanistan (PDPA) – overthrew the government of Daoud Khan in another coup, ushering in what is known as the Saur (April) Revolution. This established the Democratic Republic of Afghanistan. Following infighting and purges among factions of the PDPA, the Soviet army entered Afghanistan in 1979. The war of resistance that followed their entry played out as a Cold War proxy battle. Afghan guerrilla fighters – called the mujahideen, or holy warriors – battled the Soviet-backed Afghan government, with support from the United States, Saudi Arabia and other nations. Afghanistan had entered a spiral of violence.

In 1989, the USSR withdrew its troops, while continuing to support the Afghan government, then led by President Najibullah. To the surprise of both friends and foes, the administration managed to survive for a further three years. The collapse of the Soviet Union in 1991, however, resulted in its overthrow by the various factions of mujahideen. This marked the beginning of a dark era for Kabul's population, who had until then been spared the worst of the conflict. Now the front lines came to the city.

Between 1992 and 1996, mujahideen fighters battled each other for control over the capital in a brutal civil war, rocketing residential areas indiscriminately and forcing widespread displacement. Atrocities were committed by all sides, and large parts of the city were laid to waste. About 80 per cent of Kabul's historic core was destroyed.[18] By the time the Taliban gained control in 1996, much of the city was in ruins.

The Taliban's social restrictions added to the desolation of Kabul's shattered infrastructure. There was widespread hunger, and many residents depended on assistance from aid agencies to survive. The US-led air strikes, aimed at ousting the Taliban, contributed to the even greater physical destruction of the city.[19] By the winter of 2001, Kabul was a barely functioning capital of 1.7 million inhabitants.[20]

In 2006, when I first saw the city, it was in the throes of another transformation. The population had almost doubled to around 3 million, drawn by the promise of peace and economic opportunities.[21] On the slopes of Kabul's mountains, thousands of families built and rebuilt their war-damaged homes, using whatever they could salvage from the ruins. At night the light from these informal settlements lit up the horizon, a city above the city, unauthorised but growing, providing shelter to the majority of the population and becoming more entrenched every day. As far as the eye could see, Kabul was spreading.

* * *

Each day, I found a different aspect to this growing city.

On the road to work, I passed large areas that showed evidence of previous town planning, in the strict geometry of the streets. Elsewhere, the growth was more haphazard. I crossed the Silo, a massive granary and bakery built with assistance from the USSR in the 1950s. Its tall yellow walls and chimneys were perforated with holes – relics of the civil war. The area beyond, called Khushal Khan Mina, was laid out over what had been farmland, now occupied by multi-storey apartment buildings, business centres, institutions and ministries.

The radio and TV station where we worked was at Dehburi, in an area that had witnessed fierce fighting during the civil war. In a photograph I had seen from the time, the streets of the neighbourhood were deserted, and the bloated corpse of a soldier floated in a roadside gutter, an ammunition belt still around his waist. The building we occupied had also been damaged during the war. It had later been shut during the Taliban government and was rebuilt in 2003 with foreign assistance.

It was a good place to work, and our colleagues filled our early days in the city with warmth and enthusiasm. Next door was the National Institute of Music, and often our routine would unfold to a muted soundtrack of flutes and drumming drifting across the wall.

I remember early afternoons out with colleagues walking along the green avenues of Kabul University, to see an art show or shoot segments for their programmes. They guided me to nearby restaurants for kebab lunches, helped me pick out the nicest *kulcha*, or biscuits, from the bakery.

One day a colleague invited me to her home, where her family was preparing for her brother's wedding. We left together after work and I followed her through streets with houses in various stages of repair or destruction. The roads got narrower, the walls came closer. My colleague stopped in front of a wooden door, separated from the road by a small drain flowing with water. It opened into a large courtyard, enclosed by mud walls. In the middle of the patch of brown earth, the family had planted pomegranate saplings. From the window of the bustling living room, I watched her brothers cook *samanak*, a dessert made of wheatgerm, stirring it in a large pot set on an open fire. The family had returned to Kabul after 2001, having spent years in Pakistan as refugees. This was the first wedding back under their own roof.

And I remember a more fraught walk one afternoon with a male colleague to a house in an 'informal' hillside settlement. Migrant families had built homes in these areas, now as earlier. The simple structures echoed the houses they left behind in the village, bringing the countryside to the city. We walked up the steep slope on a narrow path, bisected by an open drain. Looking up made my head spin. Along the way, we passed children carrying yellow plastic containers of water up the slopes. There was no water supply in these settlements.

To get to the house, my colleague had guided me along a path marked by small white stones, indicating the area that had been cleared of mines, or unexploded ordnance. This was the legacy of decades of conflict, rendering Kabul one of the most heavily mined cities in the world. A few metres below us, a de-mining crew was at work, sweeping the surface of the earth with their wands. 'Red stones mean danger,' I repeated in my head nervously as I walked on the path that dozens of families took every day. 'White stones mean safety.'

These were my days. My evenings were often spent walking down to the buzzing heart of Shahr-e-Nau market, the commercial hub of modern Kabul. Lights blazed from the many shops that lined its streets, and young men and women walked down dressed fashionably, engaged in the age-old ritual of checking each other out. The street was a mix of the old and new at the time. There were some smaller shops on the ground floors of residential apartments. There were larger department stores like the Chelsea Supermarket, with its slogan exhorting passers-by to 'Be Happy All the Time'. A popular spot with expatriates, it's aisles were stashed with expensive imported pasta, cheese and snacks. At the counter, the owner had tacked black-and-white photographs of Kabul from an idyllic past – showing women in skirts, and families enjoying picnics. Further ahead was the newly built Kabul City Centre, one of the first shopping malls in town, its facade covered with glass, its glamour still fresh, its steps swarmed by children hawking packets of chewing gum for a dollar.

Soon we began venturing out further, visiting the homes of friends, exploring bazaars. The choppers flying in formation overhead provided the steady rhythm to which we woke each morning and took walks each evening. Before dinner we walked to the bakery down the street, returning with warm bread tucked between newspapers, crisp and with black seeds sprinkled on top, fragrant enough to speed our steps home. On Fridays we joined the crowd of Kabulis heading to picnics in the mountains near Qargha, a scenic reservoir just outside town. The road would be packed with cars, and each car seemed to be packed with children, large pots filled with food, melons rattling in the boot and mattresses to spread by the riverside.

***

As I walked Kabul, I found myself accompanied in thought by my maternal grandfather, my Baba. From my father's family, I inherited a map for arriving in Kabul. But it was Baba who was my real guide when I got there, his ideas and his voice guiding my steps across the city. An Urdu scholar and translator himself, he had helped me interpret the world in this way before.

Baba had been raised in a large cosmopolitan family that valued education: temperament as well as training had led him to an assured intimacy with Persian texts, English literature, as well as folk music, poetry and mythology. He was drawn to activism and the Indian freedom movement as a student, and had moved to (then) Bombay while in his twenties. In the metropolis, a dazzling constellation of Urdu writers and poets had congregated during the 1940s, as part of the Progressive Writers' Movement. Baba was a part of this ferment. Many of his friends went on to achieve prominence as poets, writers and artists. It was this creatively charged and ideologically committed world that my grandparents inhabited. They lived most of their lives in Delhi; a few years after I was born, they moved to Aligarh to be near us. My earliest memories of Baba are of him seated at his desk, writing and reading, enveloped by the fragrant mist of his pipe.

My grandparents' home reflected the kind of simplicity that is an active choice, a way of life. The only thing of value for Baba was his large and varied collection of books, which dominated the decor and crept into nooks and crannies freely. I learned reverence for the written word early in life from him. That, and the art of moving through life unburdened by possessions. On my birthday each summer, instead of the ostentatious presents I would have preferred as a child, he wrote me a few whimsical verses in Urdu, addressed to 'Bibi July', Little Miss July.

I thought of Baba on one of my earliest walks through Kabul, as I caught the movement of a bearded old man in a green *chapan* coat, his eyes crinkling with pleasure and his hand moving in a gesture of accustomed grace, rising in greeting and coming to rest on his heart, as he passed a friend on the street. An unconscious symmetry of gestures between the two men, sparking off a memory I had not known I carried, of Baba walking along the streets of his small town near Lucknow, returning salutations with the same focused abstraction.

Baba inhabited Kabul more fully than I could hope to, though he had never been there. In part, this was because of his fluent knowledge of Persian and of the canons of literature and thinkers who defined the region. The rest was intuition, an unconscious immersion in the shared cultural matrix that had shaped the region. He often had something new to tell me about Kabul, an observation or backstory to add to an anecdote I shared with him. He revealed paths in its terrain for me.

When I returned from my first visit to Kabul, I walked through the city again with him, while sitting in his book-lined study in Aligarh, trawling through avenues of poetry and prose. When I went back to Kabul that same autumn, Baba gave me a copy of *Baburnama*, the memoirs of the young emperor, Babur, who had conquered Kabul at the age of twenty-one and who had made the city his own, asking to be buried there.

With Baba I read the poem Babur quoted for the city in his memoir.

> Drink wine in the castle of Kabul and send the cup round
>   to entertain;
> For Kabul is mountain, is river, is city, and is also a plain.[22]

Each time I left for Kabul, Baba sent me off with words that now seem like a path linking my destination to him. I can see him now, standing at the door. His hands on my shoulders, the road behind us. '*Hazar baar boro,*' he said in Persian. '*Sadd hazar baar biya.*' Go a thousand times. Return a hundred thousand times.

* * *

On my first trip, I lived in a house that echoed the spaces of my home in Aligarh. This guesthouse was in Kolola Pushta, a neighbourhood on the edge of Shahr-e-Nau. Until the 1940s it had been an agricultural area dotted with mud forts, where Kabul's middle class built their homes. My guest house too had been carved out from the residence of an affluent family that had moved to Europe sometime during the decades of conflict.

It followed a design distinctive to the time, with large windows and decorative timber ceilings. In some houses, the walls curved to form a graceful *gulkhana*, or conservatory – where owners could soak in the bright winter sunshine amid rows of potted plants. They had wooden doors and concrete floors, dark interiors, cavernous kitchens and inner sanctums. These spaces connected with an architectural logic that was familiar to me from Aligarh: turned away from the street, intimate, looking inwards. The gardens were planted with fruit trees and trailing grape vines.

Like in Aligarh, my room in the guest house was in an extension built around an inner courtyard, a space that was cold and barren when I arrived. Behind our compound's walls loomed a hill topped by a ruined mud fort. Soon, the colours in the courtyard and on the hill turned to various shades of green, and lavish sprigs of almond and cherry blossoms appeared on the trees outside my window. As the evenings got warmer, I sat out and watched spring illuminate the surroundings.

My days and nights settled into a rhythm of restful languor that seemed both intensely known as well as unexpected. It soon became apparent that the house I returned to during those first few weeks was a bubble of luxury in a stretched city. It was also a place that crackled with rapid arrivals and departures. Sometimes guests came and left too fast for me even to exchange hellos. There were contractors from Uzbekistan overseeing construction projects, Indian engineers working on installing software for different firms, aid workers from Germany and Japan. The speed with which this population flitted in and out of the country was not unusual. Among the first questions I was asked at dinners and work gatherings were: 'When did you arrive?' and 'How long will you stay?'

The city was being rebuilt in part by the kind of people I saw around me. Ironically, they rarely got to experience much of the place they had come to reconstruct. For many of them, Kabul was simply the blur of streets glimpsed from their moving vehicles. They were told, like me, never to walk.

Midway through our assignment, we decided to find our own quarters and rented the top floor of a nearby house built in the 1970s. We moved in soon after Nauroz, the festival that heralds the Persian new year, and the arrival of spring.

Across the road from our new place was a compound that housed Indian staffers working at the Safi Landmark, an upmarket hotel housed in the Kabul City Centre. Many of these young men were waiting to move to Dubai. Some of them had been waiting for over a year. On Fridays, they would play cricket together, and the afternoon peace of the holiday would be shaken by the familiar sound of bat meeting ball, punctuated by loud cheers and robust curses, all from behind the high walls of their compound.

Our landlord was a retired pilot who lived on the ground floor with his family. I had some early run-ins with 'Ismail Sahab,' as I called him ('Sahab' being a respectful form of address), especially regarding my ineptitude in the kitchen. But in his house, and through his expansive personality, I got my first glimpse into Kabul as a city with a particular culture and way of life, populated by people who were familiar with its codes and manners. Like the cities I knew in India. Or simply, a city I knew.

It was also an initiation into life outside the charmed circles of *khareji* – or foreigners' – residences. At the time, Kabul had power cuts each evening. In the guest house, we could disregard these thanks to the massive generator that was switched on for our benefit. But Ismail Sahab did not own one, and refused to invest in one for our sakes. As a compromise, he let us use his electric battery to run one light and our laptops. But even this would be switched off after his own early dinner. As far as he was concerned, we now lived in a house, not a *guest house*. And the distinction was particularly clear each evening: as night fell, one part of the city lived with the darkness while the other powered up generators.

After several evenings spent bathed in the ghostly glow of our computers, we gave up and got our own generator, at a suitably inflated *khareji* rate. From our balcony too emanated a note that joined the symphony of thudding machinery. And our rooms joined the squares lit up across the city, brazenly shining between the paler light of lamps and candles, or just darkness.

Ismail Sahab was a collector, and spent most evenings in a little study that overlooked his garden, a space packed with his artefacts. Some days he invited us over to look at photographs, or his stamp albums. Sometimes he shared the music that he enjoyed: Afghan as well as Indian musicians like sitar virtuoso Ustad Vilayat Khan, or the singer Begum Akhtar. This was the music that I had first heard on the cassettes in Baba's house. In our own living room stood Ismail Sahab's gramophone, and over the weeks we worked our way through his collection of classical Indian ragas and jazz. We avoided one room in our part of the house. It was filled with Ismail Sahab's collection of prayer beads. They were hung up across the walls, occupying virtually every inch of space, like thousands of unblinking eyes watching the empty room.

His greatest passion, however, was his garden. He lavished care and attention on it, arranging flower beds and rocks and water channels according to various theories of landscaping that caught his fancy. It took a closer look to realise that many of the planters were empty rocket shells, or that the bell hanging by the garden door was made of a discarded bullet casing. Ismail Sahab spent most days shifting his chair from spot to spot in his lawn, examining his plants and fruit trees – like a ruler of a small kingdom, with similarly arbitrary whims.

Our standing with him varied like the spring weather. On some days he would grumble about our loud steps and the 'dancing' on his roof. Other days he would summon us to

dinner, where his wife patiently and smilingly heard out my
faltering salutations in Dari (the kind of Persian spoken in
Kabul). When I'd introduced myself, she'd realised that my
name was a version of one often heard in Kabul. 'Nastaran,' she
told me firmly, waving away the Indian-inflected version I had
offered. 'You are Nastaran.' And Nastaran I stayed for her, the
tiny white flower so common in Kabul, and which lined the
hedges of Ismail Sahab's garden. I could see them growing
from my kitchen window.

We settled in and invited friends over for a housewarming
dinner. I have a photograph from that evening. The people in
it are mostly young – expatriates or Afghans who had grown
up abroad – working on different projects to rebuild Afghanistan.
Everyone is laughing, their faces full of energy and camaraderie.
Many left soon after that picture was taken, others a little later.
But at that time, it seemed like Kabul was where it was all
happening, where everyone wanted to be.

***

One summer afternoon I walked through Shahr-e-Nau
with my friend Wazhmah to her family's apartment near the
park that lay in the middle of this neighbourhood. We
crossed streets fragrant with kebabs, trailed by children
who tried to sell us magazines and maps, and copies of
Nancy Dupree's *An Historical Guide to Kabul*.[23] The English-
language tourist guide to the city, first published in the
1960s, enjoyed a renewed rush of popularity after 2001. Its
charming and precise descriptions of Kabul's sights, and its
itineraries of walks across the city's shrines and monuments,
made it a poignant, as well as informative, read. Not far from
where we were walking, a suicide bomber had claimed
several lives a few weeks earlier. The injured had included
street children.

From the window of the apartment, Wazhmah showed me the spot where her father's family home used to stand. It had been sold and demolished, to make way for apartments or a mall. On the other side of the park was her mother's home, which had been taken over by families with connections to powerful warlords turned politicians, she told me. Her relatives were trying to prove their ownership in court, but were unlikely to succeed. Wazhmah's parents had fled Kabul during the civil war. Her father had stayed on in Afghanistan, and then moved to Pakistan. Her mother and sisters had left for the US. On a previous trip, Wazhmah had hoped to return to Kabul in some lasting way, had even dreamed of bringing her family back together in this city that had once been their home. She told me this as we gazed at the hole in the ground next to her apartment. Watching the earth being shifted from the foundations of that house, I learned how complicated returns could be in Kabul. It was a gamble to call this city your home, where the earth could literally move from under your feet.

As Kabul changed in the years after 2001, the very idea of home was recast too. By 2009, Kabul's estimated population was between 3 and 4 million people, and a construction boom reshaped the geography of the capital.[24] People needed shelter, and the suburbs expanded or were rebuilt to accommodate them. One Friday afternoon I attended a Quran-reading ceremony to mark the completion of a colleague's new place in Sar-e-Kotal, not far from the older suburb of Khair Khana in northern Kabul. The neighbourhood was populated by salaried workers, who had bought plots of land and were constructing homes on them. In the sun-drenched rooms of a three-storeyed building that seemed barely finished, we had lunch with my colleague's extended clan. I looked out of one of the windows. All around the house were bulldozers and cement mixers.

Kabul was churning up its earth in an orgy of seemingly limitless construction.

Entire neighbourhoods were being rebuilt from the flattened landscape of the civil war and the Taliban's rule. Some of these houses – like the one I was in – represented a measure of prosperity and stability for families that had faced earlier cycles of displacement. But not all constructions were meant to provide shelter for ordinary Afghans.

Kabul's real estate prices boomed from around 2007 to 2010, forming a bubble buoyed by aid dollars and profits from the opium trade. Older apartments, like those in a Soviet-era housing colony in east Kabul, fetched a sale price of around $150,000, up from a 2001 rate of close to $15,000. New constructions rose across Shahr-e-Nau, where many of the older homes – like Wazhmah's father's house – were torn down and replaced with apartment blocks. These were built from glass and concrete – material imported from Pakistan and China – and gave an edge of hard glitter to Kabul's landscape. In the changing appearance of Kabul's streets, these structures reflected the quick gains made by the powerful, as well as the aspirations of many of the new Afghan elite. They were poorly designed – turning cold in the winter and overheating during the summer. But at the time, they offered speculators good returns on investment.

The building boom also led to the creation of 'poppy palaces' across parts of the city – ostentatious mansions named for the likely provenance of their finances. These were often owned (directly or indirectly) by politicians, warlords and the newly rich entrepreneurs of Kabul's wartime economy. Built in an architectural style that resembled wedding cakes, often painted in lurid pinks, greens and yellows, these mansions displayed Roman columns, curved balconies, lavish domes and glittering tiles on the outer walls. They were based on ideas of luxury and modernity seen elsewhere, like Peshawar (where there is a large Afghan refugee community) or Dubai, and translated into reality by local masons. Sometimes they had a board displayed prominently on their gate, declaring 'Mashallah', to ward off the evil eye.

The disconnect between these mansions and the city they occupied was striking. The elaborate balconies overlooking the streets and the roof terraces remained empty – few Afghan families would relish being seen from the street. Instead, most of these buildings were rented out as offices and residences to the NGOs, aid agencies and businesses who could afford the exorbitant rents they commanded, from \$15,000 to \$20,000 a month. This was in 2007, when the annual per capita income in Afghanistan was around \$350.[25] The brightly coloured buildings that towered over the narrow streets from behind concrete slabs and sandbags gave the city a giddy, wanton air.

* * *

With my husband I returned to Kabul on journeys over the next seven years, working on different media projects. Each return was to a different house, and the various rooms we inhabited shaped my personal map of the city. One of these was a house we shared with two Afghan friends, both of whom had left Kabul early in life, and had come back in different ways, over different times.

I had met Khalid on my first trip, when he had been working with the UN, and had supervised our training sessions at the radio and TV station. From beginning as a colleague, he soon became a good friend. Short of stature, he bristled with unpredictable tempers, sometimes exploding with laughter, other times with wrath. His personal history was a reflection of the flux that marked the lives of so many of his contemporaries, born near the end of Afghanistan's era of peace. His father had been a general during President Daoud Khan's government – an army engineer who built roads across the country. He had

vanished on the day of the Saur Revolution, when the coup
by the PDPA overthrew the republic in April 1978. President
Daoud and his family were massacred. Khalid's family waited
for his father to return home that evening. His mother, Khalid
told me, never stopped waiting.

In the years of Communist rule that followed, Khalid's
family left the country, one after the other. He himself left as a
child in the 1980s. He lived in Pakistan for some months before
joining his siblings in California. There he acquired the name
he called himself by, part of his now hyphenated identity: Kal.
He had returned in the 1990s, he told me, when he had spent
four years between Afghanistan and Central Asia working as
an aid worker and photojournalist.

A few years later, he got married and moved back to the US,
living the quiet life of an immigrant with a regular job, raising
a family in California. He returned to Kabul after 2001 to work
with the UN, and then started a media production company.
Some of my early returns were to work on projects with him.

In his office, a beautiful old house near Shahr-e-Nau, I met
several actors, among them movie stars of a previous generation.
Sometimes I conversed with actresses and crew members.
Other evenings I sipped green tea on the stone porch and
watched foreign donors come over to inspect the facilities –
guns at their hips, vast budgets at their disposal. These were
the bizarre constellations of ISAF-era Kabul.

In 2007, the capital was abuzz with the energy of a gold
rush. There seemed to be no end to the kind of trade you
could do in Afghanistan then, few businesses that would not
make a profit. Restaurants and real estate, construction and
social messages – with Khalid, I met people who were
launching enterprises in all these areas. The economy, according
to the World Bank, was posting an average annual growth rate
of 9 per cent from 2003 onwards.[26] Much of the impetus came

from the transient currents of foreign aid and foreign military bases. The prosperity of this 'violent peace' was to prove neither broad-based nor sustainable.[27] But at the time it was an atmosphere flush with dollars.

The house we shared with Khalid a few years later in Qala-e-Fatahullah was smaller than the one in Shahr-e-Nau. The scaling down represented a shift both in Khalid's life as well as in the city. The new place lay eastwards from Ismail Sahab's house in Kolola Pushta; a walk through a series of small streets that gave way to the edges of a bazaar. Along the way were offices of men who held important posts in the government or the police, barricaded behind walls and checkpoints. It always seemed to me a gamble to be living close to such powerful figures. While some felt reassured at the extra security, I was alarmed by the possibility of ending up as collateral damage.

The road wound past the panorama of the mud fort that framed the locality. Along the route were small *chaikhanas*, tea houses, with elaborate calligraphy and images of kebabs and teapots painted on their glass fronts. There was a real estate agency and a series of staid-looking pharmacies, then shops selling wedding clothes for women and tailors whose windows were covered with posters of sharply dressed young men with gelled hair.

Until the 1970s, the area was a deserted stretch on the northern edges of Shahr-e-Nau. It was so far off the map that no buses ran there, and many of the streets I knew had not yet been built. It had once been a wetland that drained the spring rains and became a meadow in the summer. The water in the area was brackish, Khalid said, and would never let me drink it. He also made sure I acquired his Kabuli habit of shaking out my shoes before wearing them, to avoid the scorpions that lurked in corners.

The house was shielded from the street behind a large, newly built mansion that was rented out at a far higher price. A narrow drive led to our rooms, which were edged by a small garden. This feature gave the house a good security billing. When friends who worked with large aid agencies came to visit or stay, or when a visiting journalist needed an impressive backdrop for a report, our cook Masoud would be asked to 'patrol' its length carrying a Kalashnikov. When the performance ended, he would prop the gun back against the wall, slip on his apron and resume cooking. Behind us was a girls' school, and my day began with the sound of students singing patriotic songs during morning assembly. After the festival of Nauroz, Kabul's roads would be filled with uniformed children returning to class after the long winter vacation. I would see their figures trudging along our street in the mornings, holding hands and eating ice cream, kicking pebbles along the path.

It was a house full of men. Besides the people I lived with, many others passed through. Some had homes and wives and children in Europe or the US, some would stroll over from homes in the city. They would come for business or family visits or simply to shoot the breeze with their buddies. Some just stayed for the evening, others spent days or weeks in our spare room. Living in this house meant living with a sense of limbo – our daily routines were determined by my housemates' distance from their families, and from the responsibilities of family life.

This meant I occupied a male subculture with all its trappings and rituals. On Friday mornings, for instance, Khalid and a few selected helpmates would unleash aggressive cleaning operations that usually involved large quantities of bleach being splashed around the kitchen. In the evenings, they would sink into sofas in front of the television. The talk would go on deep into the night. Often it was about the years of jihad, about the extended tracks that war brought into the years of uncertain peace, about the cycles of departures and returns that had shaped their lives. They cursed and laughed at old acquaintances or friends, now transformed (like everything else in their country) into men of responsibility and power, either in government or business. The atmosphere in the house was part frat party, part Ramboesque fantasy.

Some days I would need a break from the masculine vibe and would seek out different company. I went bargain hunting at the Lycée Mariam market, or I explored shops where my smartly dressed female colleagues revealed their secrets to dressing on a budget. I found a good tailor a short walk down the street, and a little further, at a second-hand shoe store, I found a pair of red walking shoes that I slipped on with delight. '*Ba khair beposhi*,' said the owner to all the girls walking out of his shop, many (like me) wearing their new purchases already. 'May you wear them with joy.' At the house, we celebrated birthdays with barbecues, plotted escape routes with the neighbours in case of an ambush, remembered not to sit down too abruptly on the couch that had the box of grenades under it.

Our garden flourished or perished depending on Khalid's moods. It was there that I heard the story of two men who were his frequent visitors. One was a former mujahideen commander from Kandahar, who had been a figure of repute during the anti-Soviet jihad of the 1980s, before the factions turned on each other. The other man had served in the Afghan army under the Communist government at that time. The army man had been given the task of assassinating the mujahideen commander. He had planted a bomb in the latter's car. It would go off when the car hit a dirt track, activated by the movement and jolts of the road. Barely a kilometre before they reached the track, by some combination of intuition or plain luck, the commander had changed cars. The man who took his place was killed.

I heard this story from Khalid as the two men sat on plastic chairs in the garden, guns by their side, sipping vodka together. At that time, they had been on different sides of a clear line. Over the years these lines had blurred and shifted, pushing different men into different battles, until at last they were sitting across a table from each other, watching the sun set and the NATO choppers cleaving their way across the glorious Kabuli sky. To me, they seemed to be like ghosts of Kabul's difficult past, exchanging memories.

Encounters like these were an effective antidote to a tendency to be romantic about Kabul. They brought with them the awareness that to talk of war in the past tense in this city was a mistake. War did not come to Kabul, nor did it leave. It ebbed and flowed, and what people learned to watch out for was how it affected them.

Our other housemate, Dr Shah, was a path into a different iteration of Kabul. An economist by training, he had worked in development aid around the world. When I met him, however, he was a consultant with a private company. 'Doctor Sahab', as we called him, was older than Khalid, and carried himself with an air of gravity and reserve. But soon I realised that his conversations glinted with wry humour.

Doctor Sahab had left Kabul for Europe for the first time as a teenager, in the early 1970s. The departure had turned out to be more lasting than anyone had foreseen. A few days before his first journey, he told me, he had cycled around the city and taken pictures of all the landmarks with his camera. Why he did this, he still cannot fathom. After all, photography was rare and expensive then, and slide film even more so. But for three days, he had ridden his bicycle to tombs, palaces, parks and historical spots, capturing their images in a rare catalogue.

These slides of the Kabul of his boyhood were carefully preserved at his home in Germany. 'I will show them to you,' he told me often, but he never did. Instead, over many evenings in our shared house in Kabul, he talked those pictures to life.

His stories conjured up the vanished world of the Kabuli elite that he belonged to. He spoke of a crockery shop by the river called Shakir *Chainak-faroush* that stored the best china teapots. Of the fine fabric covering cushions in every home that he knew, and the subtle simplicity of the rooms of these houses. On his way home from school, he would stop at Pohine Nindare, or 'Screen of Learning', a cinema that showed educational films. He talked of a city from a more confident era, where the future was unclouded by the prospect of conflict.

Sometimes in the flow of his reminiscences, it seemed that Doctor Sahab forgot he was talking to me and his words and anecdotes would become a story he told himself. From his accounts I grasped a fuller understanding of what I had glimpsed in Ismail Sahab's garden — of a culture specific to Kabul, a sophisticated way of life that was defined by its setting.

Like many of his generation, Doctor Sahab possessed a fine understanding of this Kabuli culture. He also had a front-row view to its vanishing from the city. Each day, he would find new elements of this transformed city that angered him. The power cuts, the opulent narco-mansions, the potholed streets, the corruption of the government. The confectioner who overcharged him for sweets. Children being made to clean the gutters. All these causes elicited a rage so persistent that it permeated every aspect of his life, and was simultaneously impossible to articulate with any clarity or precision. In conversations, Doctor Sahab transmitted this emotion through frequent and versatile use of the word 'animal'. Into this word he channelled all the shades of his feelings, casting it as adjective, adverb, preposition, punctuation and expostulation. He overused it magnificently, to describe everything from the ('animal') politicians to the ('animal') providers of the Internet services, the ('animal') electricity supply and the ('animal') hosts of ('animal') TV shows. From him I learned the bitterness of a homecoming touched by loss, the helpless rage at being an outsider in your own home. For Doctor Sahab, Kabul no longer existed within Kabul.

'This is not my city,' he would tell me sometimes at the end of one of these conversations. 'These are not my people.' The words both mystified and annoyed me. In some ways, there was nothing new about Doctor Sahab's situation. War creates ruin, cities are formed by movement. And Kabulis, like residents of many other cities, have been complaining for centuries about how the place has been ruined by 'outsiders'. But what struck me about Doctor Sahab's experience was this: the city of his youth had been destroyed by war. But it was in the reconstruction of peace, in the remaking of Kabul after 2001, that it had been erased again, this time from memory. The very idea of Kabul as a city of history and learning, beauty and culture, seemed to have vanished below the surface of the newly raised city. The irony that it took a Kabuli who had spent most of his life abroad to introduce the city's past to me was, however, lost on Doctor Sahab.

Urdu poetry has a genre that addresses such loss of place. The works in this genre are called '*shahr ashob*', verses that lament the decline and ruin of a social order. These poems are often elegies to a lost way of life. Like the compositions that describe Delhi after the turbulent events of 1857, when a widespread uprising begun by Indian sepoys challenged British authority before being suppressed. Such poems bemoan the destruction of the city's court, its beauty and culture, its grace and its everyday courtesies. I thought of the stories told each evening by Doctor Sahab as his versions of *shahr ashob*, laments for the city he had lost.

Which was why I thought of him a few years later, when I saw a series of videos that had been shot in the 1990s.[28] In one sequence, perhaps taken at the cusp of the Taliban era, a man stands in the courtyard of his ruined home somewhere in the Afghan countryside. Everything is destroyed, except the door, and one corner of a room on the first floor. This corner contains a carved wooden panel, simple and elegant. There are flowers engraved in the wall, and borders and embellishments. There is also a niche, a *taaq*, a feature familiar to me from my own home in Aligarh. It is a small ledge to place mundane household items on. Perhaps a lamp, perhaps some books. The lower parts of the wall are covered with soot and the intersecting walls end abruptly to expose the mountains behind them.

The image was of an ordinary corner in an ordinary home, a place of beauty and function in the everyday, which now seemed like a shrine. Embedded in these walls was the memory of Afghanistan as a place where home was valued and looked after with care. Where it was possible to sit by the *taaq* and gaze at the mountains, perhaps. It was all that remained of the home that once stood around it. On the screen, I watched the solitary figure of the man move the rubble from his ruined courtyard. And I thought of Doctor Sahab walking to work each morning, picking his way through the debris of his city.

Despite my best efforts to share Kabul in his company, Doctor Sahab resolutely kept his walks to himself. The closest I got to wandering with him was on his night-time rambles through the city of his memories. He remained our personal Scheherazade, spinning tales of a doomed city, always beautiful, always in the past.

Sometimes, however, he let us share his wanderings in oblique ways. Some evenings he would bring us back baklava from a small restaurant run by a Turkish baker whose family had lived in Kabul for generations, the only place (he said) where they used fresh walnuts to line the pastry. Other evenings he would treat us to ice cream frozen in creamy layers, which came packed in tiny tinfoil boxes. He refused to reveal where he got these delights from, in a city that he claimed to no longer recognise.

And then there were evenings when we would serve as handy targets for his wrath about everything that was wrong with Kabul. If the network connection during the Skype calls he made to Germany proved shakier than usual, he would eye us tetchily as we sat hunched over our laptops. 'You people,' he would drawl, in his English tinged with French tinged with Dari. 'You are taking all the power of the Internet.'

***

Over the years, my family's response to my travels to Kabul changed. It became harder to explain my reasons to anxious relatives and friends each time I packed my bags. 'Why do you want to go back?' they asked.

It was only when I was there I felt I had answers. Being in Kabul was like entering a room in my family's home in Aligarh in the middle of a blazing summer day. From the bright sunshine you move into darkness. As your eyes slowly adjust, the room begins to take shape, dim interiors opening up slowly, expanding with each step to reveal furniture and nooks, objects you recognise. The longer I looked, the larger Kabul became, revealing depths and spaces, with details emerging behind what was first apparent. And as I walked its streets over the years, Kabul felt increasingly like home.

The only person who never asked me why I went back was Baba.

So it was typical that I found something like an answer one evening in his study in Aligarh. We were talking of poetry, and Baba asked me, 'Do you know what it means to be *ghareeb*?'

Yes, I said, in Urdu it means poor. But in Arabic, he said, it also means outsider, or stranger. And in Persian poetry, the idea of *ghurbat* often refers to the state of being away from your own land. A kind of exile or distance from home that is also poverty. An idea that I later realised was echoed in the songs of *birha*, separation, that were sung by the indentured labourers from Bihar, shipped across the dark sea to the sugar plantations of the Caribbean.

In his absent-minded way, Baba then went on to quote a few lines from the poet Muhammad Iqbal, who wrote in both Persian and Urdu, and whose books I often found in Kabul.

> *Ghurbat mein hon agar hum*
> *Rehta hai dil watan mein*
> *Samjho wahin humein bhi*
> *Dil ho jahan hamara*

> Even in exile
> Our hearts dwell at home
> Think of us as being there
> The home where our hearts live [29]

Where this home that Iqbal refers to is located, Baba told me, is a fluid idea. It may be where you were born, or it may be a place that claimed you. It may even be a place of the imagination, but it is where you are whole.

When I had left Kabul for the first time, my friends had scattered water on the ground behind me. May it light up your path, they said. May it guide you back. This road was both tenuous and bright, revealing itself by a trick of looking. Like a bridge to a magical island, or a passage to many stories. It illuminated the earth.

2

WRITTEN ON THE CITY

The road to Kabul is made of stories.

A fragment of a memory leads me to the afternoon when I first read about the city, in a book I found on Baba's shelves. The adults were deep in sleep; the house filled with the kind of stillness in which fables begin. The short story I perused was written by the legendary Bengali writer Rabindranath Tagore in 1892.[1] It sketched the anatomy of an unusual friendship set in (then) Calcutta, between a little girl called Mini and a 'Kabuliwala' – a trader from Afghanistan. He brings Mini treats of almonds and raisins in his big bag. They play and laugh together. Each time he visits her street, she calls out to him: 'O Kabuliwala!' We learn that the Kabuliwala loves Mini because she reminds him of his own daughter, back in his faraway home. In his pocket, he carries a piece of paper with his child's tiny hand printed on it. This is the closest he has to her image. As I remember it, this was the first time I had heard of Kabul – through the story of an impoverished pedlar, seeking the familiar face of his child while wandering a distant land.

Growing up, I read a lot. Partly because I loved it, and partly because there wasn't much else to do as a teenage girl in Aligarh. Given the tacit boundaries of my conservatively liberal Muslim family, the world outside my door was as distant as a faraway continent. I ventured into it like a tourist. To school, family outings to the cinema, a few social events with friends. All of these expeditions were monitored and supervised. Crucially, they all required reasons – a sanctioned purpose that permitted my presence on the streets, which could never be aimless. My male cousins roamed the thoroughfares of Aligarh freely, spending late nights at buzzy tea shops, leaping over walls, gazing at the stars. I cultivated a fluency in occupying interiors. Reading, then, was a path into possibilities; it offered a parallel terrain which I could stride through boldly.

Books were thus my private continent, providing both excitement and safety. They were my maps to navigating the world, and also the way I created a sense of belonging, of being at home. They opened up worlds for me, without my leaving the house.

The rambling bungalow I grew up in was full of books. Most of the volumes in the cupboards lining the high-ceilinged, dimly lit bedrooms had belonged to aunts and uncles, marking their passage through the boarding schools of northern India during the 1950s. These included wholesome volumes handed out as prizes for moral science, English elocution and attendance. Musty and haphazardly stocked, these cupboards always contained something new to discover, or something familiar to return to. This was where I found my first copies of P. G. Wodehouse and developed a taste for the romances of Georgette Heyer. I read Anton Chekhov and Isaac Asimov, Daphne du Maurier and Ayn Rand. I read through afternoons with power cuts, peering at the printing by the light of a window open just a crack, one hand turning the pages and the other swirling a fan over my grandmother's sleeping form. I read through long winter evenings when there was nowhere to be but home. Books were all the social life I got, and all that I ended up needing.

Years later, I found this upbringing to have been perfect preparation for life in Kabul. The carefully cloistered routines of my adolescence corresponded seamlessly with the rhythm of the city in 2006. Expatriate workers banded together in guest houses that were often converted bungalows, their high walls enclosing lush lawns, creating the perfect zenana. In my own guest house, the room I occupied overlooked the inner courtyard, just like it did back in Aligarh. So the things other women from abroad found difficult about the city often seemed quite natural to me.

'*There's nowhere to go out in the evenings.*' We never did anyway.

'*What do you do for fun here?*' I answered by rolling my eyes, and turning to my books.

Reading was how I learned to inhabit Kabul, a large part of how I made myself at home there.

Until one trip, when I realised I had forgotten to pack my usual stock of reading material. Without books, I was lost. The evenings loomed dark and frighteningly long unless I found myself something to read.

I began looking, and asked for help. The responses I got from people like myself – expats who had come to work in Kabul – ranged from amused disdain to baffled attempts at helpfulness. It was as though I had set out to look for exotic fruits or designer swimwear in a Kabuli market. (Except that *those* would probably have been available in the swish shops of Shahr-e-Nau, or the sprawling 'Bush Bazaar' market, named after the US president who ordered the invasion of Afghanistan in 2001.) Friends who often travelled offered to bring something back from Dubai on their next visit. Others gently suggested that I prepare better for hardships the next time I packed for Kabul.

What began as a light-heartedly desperate search for books to fill my evenings turned into a series of walks through spaces that were shaped by the written word. As I wandered its streets in search of something to read, I began to read Kabul like a story, cast in a script that is embossed onto its alleys and stones. Like a palimpsest: heavy with inscriptions and erasures, written over and over again.

Walking showed me a way to read the city, just as reading guided my walks through the city.

***

During my first trip to Kabul, I had walked through my neighbourhood of Kolola Pushta to a nearby guest house rented by an international NGO. The locality is framed by the 'round hill' that gave it its name, topped by a mud fort on the summit. That spring day, after a shower of rain, it stood clear against a blue horizon, free of Kabul's notorious dust.

This fort was a key location during the revolt against King Amanullah in 1928. It was captured in December by the rebel leader Habibullah Kalakani, who then gained control of Kabul in January 1929. As Amir of Afghanistan, Kalakani rolled back Amanullah's controversial modernising measures. Many of the court elite switched loyalty to him for his brief reign.[2] But by October 1929, Kabul had fallen once again, and Amanullah's cousin was proclaimed king. Kalakani surrendered against a promised amnesty, but was executed along with his close associates in November. The silhouette of the fort above the wide, pleasant streets I wandered on was a reminder of this interlude of tension: between city and countryside, between the desire for modernity and for tradition.

My destination lay off the main road that was framed by this vista, and I turned onto a side street, catching a glimpse of old

Kabuli homes and the towering trees on their lawns from behind the walls that sheltered them. The area lay on what used to be the edges of Chaman-e-Wazirabad, a meadow that was flooded in the winter to form a lake for migratory birds, 'much to the delight of numerous hunters', noted Nancy Dupree.[3] Here, Kabul's middle-class families built houses with large gardens from the 1940s onwards. Much like Ismail Sahab's house, with its well-tended lawn.

In the years after 2001, many such residences had performed the particular metamorphosis of the time, and turned into guest houses or coffee shops or restaurants. I walked past offices of aid agencies and residences of foreign workers. The area accommodated parts of the apparatus that powered post-2001 Kabul.

In the NGO guest house I visited that day, the cupboard lined with reading material reminded me of my home in Aligarh. It had wooden doors fastened with a latch, and was located by the mantelpiece. What seemed out of place were the lurid colours and paperback spines of the books inside it – 'comfort reads', one resident told me, to help escape their 'difficult reality'.

Trying to get your hands on books – specifically, English-language books – was an education in hierarchy in this intensely rank-conscious part of the city. These were books sequestered behind layers of security, allowed access to with the right ID cards. Books that were tucked into handcrafted bags and taken along on long drives in SUVs through Kabul's traffic-choked roads, as the people behind the international reconstruction effort went to work. These were not books for everyone.

As I wandered through Kabul looking for something to read, I found that often the closest I could get to these riches were the book swaps at Kabul's chic coffee shops, where

patrons were offered the pick of whatever books they liked off
the shelves, and were requested, in turn, to leave behind
whatever books they could when they departed. It was an
elegant intervention in the carousel of expatriate life in Kabul,
where imminent departure was a large part of the reality of
being present.

I made my way through several of these cafes. Some had
signs prominently displayed on the street, and windows painted
in Mediterranean colours to attract passers-by. Others were
situated in quieter neighbourhoods, advertised only with small
hand-painted boards. They did not erect barricades or post
security guards outside, in the hope of slipping under the radar
of potential attackers. On the shelves of each of these coffee
shops I found the accumulated debris of departed journalists
and aid workers – a collection of names so ubiquitous as to
resemble a pantheon. Pakistani journalist Ahmed Rashid's
book on the Taliban turned up often, as did Steve Coll's *Ghost
Wars*, a useful introduction to how truth can be far stranger
than fiction in Afghanistan.[4]

There were books by war reporters talking about reporting
wars, books on war photography by war photographers, stories
of sewing circles and beauty schools and tailors and booksellers
of Kabul. There were a few glossy Lonely Planet guides, and
many volumes of that ode to Afghan innocence, *The Kite
Runner*.[5] In hushed bowers just off the pitted streets of the city
the world forgot, and then came to rebuild, the shifting titles
and subject matters of these books seemed like beacons of
passing eras.

I walked away empty-handed from these book-swaps,
turning instead to my copy of the *Baburnama* – the candid
diary of the youthful 'padshah' that had been given to me by
Baba back in Aligarh, in its English translation.[6] The memoir,
written originally in Chaghatai Turkish, is held to be one of

the classic autobiographies of world literature. It is also, as I
found, a guide to Kabul like no other.

Babur had been ousted by his uncles from his own kingdom
in Ferghana, now in modern-day Uzbekistan. The *Baburnama*
begins when he is twelve and recounts his repeated attempts to
capture the fabled city of Samarkand. He succeeded in holding
this prize only briefly. In 1504, after a series of military defeats,
he turned his sights to Kabul and managed to gain control over
the city. Babur was captivated by his new territory, and his
memoir abounds with descriptions of Kabul's wondrous
climate, the sweetness of its fruits and the beauty of its
surroundings. 'In the Domain of Kabul, there are hot and cold
districts close to one another. In one day a person may go out
of Kabul town to where snow never falls, or he may go in two
astral hours to where it never thaws.'[7] He wrote lyrically about
its bazaars and described expeditions of bird catching. He
praised the fine quality of its firewood, visited its shrines and
counted the varieties of tulips he saw growing on the foothills.

Wandering through the city in his company, I read about
Babur's love for running water and the gardens he laid out in
and around Kabul, fed with streams. When his descendants, the
rulers of Mughal India, visited this edge of their kingdom, they
would use these spots for picnics. As would modern Kabulis,
centuries later.

The *Baburnama* is a candid account of an eventful life, with
the author's voice retaining its immediacy over the centuries.
Nothing was taboo or off-limits for Babur's royal quill. He
documented his bashful hesitation in consummating his
marriage with his first wife and his infatuation with a young
man named Baburi. He recorded incidents of carnage and
decapitation. He described epic drinking sprees during his
years in Kabul, and in anguished detail listed the after-effects
of an excess of alcohol and maajun (a mix of opium and other

substances). 'A maajun party never goes well with an araq or
wine party. The drinkers began to talk wildly and chatter,
mostly alluding to maajun . . . Try though I did to keep the
situation under control, nothing went well. There was much
repulsive bedlam. The party became intolerable and I disbanded
it.'[8] In the midst of Kabul's expat life, the *Baburnama* read as an
accomplished memoir of life in a war zone, with drugs, booze
and desperate love affairs.

Babur continued his diary as he turned his sights towards
India. He laid claim to the throne of Delhi and won a key battle
in 1526. The victory led to the establishment of what would be
the powerful dynasty of the Mughals. Ironically, it is after these
gains that the *Baburnama* takes a melancholic turn. Forced to
spend most of his time maintaining his grip over his new realm,
Babur pined for the familiar landscapes of Kabul. He wrote
anxious letters asking after the gardens he had planted. He wept,
like many an exiled Afghan after him, when he sliced melons
and thought of the fruits he had left behind. To his absent
companions who had returned to the cool climes of Kabul, he
penned verses titled 'Lines Addressed to Deserting Friends'.[9]
Perhaps he dreamed of the running water, the channels he had
created in his favourite gardens, like words etched into the earth.

His fifth incursion into India was to prove his last. Babur
died in December 1530 in Agra, at the age of forty-seven. His
memoir ends a year earlier, in mid sentence. He was buried in
India, but his remains were moved to Kabul, where he had
asked to be laid to rest, some years later.

His grave lies on a slope of the Koh-e-Sher Darwaza, south-
west of the old city. For the mausoleum of the founder of a
great dynasty, it is remarkably lacking in ostentation. It is,
however, located in a large garden laid out by Babur himself.
This garden was damaged during the civil war of 1992–96,
like much of the city. In 2002, the Aga Khan Trust for Culture

began the task of restoring it, using Babur's description in his memoirs as a guide. I walked there on a warm spring day in 2006, which also happened to be when the newly reconstructed central water channel was being tested. As the water gushed down, the watching workers broke into cheers.

I walked up the fifteen terraces of the garden, looking at the later additions like a small marble mosque built by Babur's great-great-grandson Shahjahan, a swimming pool and a pavilion. On each level, the trees that Babur mentions in his memoir had been replanted – including cherry, apple, peach, walnut, mulberry, apricot and *arghawan* (Judas). This was a garden resurrected through words.

At the top of the hill, between other graves, is Babur's resting place. It is surrounded by a delicate marble *jaali* (latticework screen) – a replica of the original – which was being installed by craftsmen from India when I visited. The grave is open to the sky, as Babur wished. The view was magnificent, encompassing the valley of Chardeh, bound by the snow-capped Paghman mountains. On the slopes of the hill behind the garden's boundary wall rose traditional mud houses. A group of children filled containers of water from the taps in the garden to take to their homes on these slopes.

Standing at this terrace, I discovered Kabul opening for me through words on a page, written by a long-ago king. On the flyleaf of the book, Baba had inscribed for me the famous dictum usually attributed to Babur, words to use as a lodestar as I wandered this familiar-unfamiliar terrain. '*Babur ba-aish kosh, ki alam dobara neest.*' Babur enjoy and be merry, for the world will not come again.[10]

***

The *Baburnama* was one of the books I found on the shelves of the Shah M Book Co. The iconic corner bookshop of Kabul is located at an intersection called Charahi Sadarat, a crossroads that to me seemed to be poised between the gleaming modernity of Shahr-e-Nau and the unyielding plainness of the various government offices and ministries round the corner. To walk there from the direction of Shahr-e-Nau, I took the Sher Ali Khan Road, a busy thoroughfare flanked with wide pavements. I walked past high walls, with some sections pasted with election posters, and the ubiquitous graffiti that I saw across Kabul, advertising *azogam*, or sealant. The divider in the middle of the road was planted with plane saplings – one of Babur's favourite trees. Their soil was moist from recent watering, their leaves dense with Kabul's ubiquitous dust. It was the end of spring.

The route passed the Iranian Embassy, with its perennial queue of visa applicants outside – Afghans hoping to find work in the neighbouring country. Further down the road the plain walls gave way to shops – a row of stationery sellers and printers, advertising their services in colourful fonts. As the road turned, the facades of the buildings turned unexpectedly graceful, topped with cream-coloured turrets. The snow-capped peaks of Kabul's encircling mountains came into view. In the middle of this intersection was a small patch of green, flanked by beggars in wheelchairs and slow-moving yellow taxis. This crossing would often be closed to allow convoys of politicians and military officials to pass. The area experienced some of the worst traffic jams in Kabul, and the crossroads reverberated with the voices of traffic policemen, bellowing 'Corolla Corolla' on their loudspeakers, urging the taxis to move along.

On the other side of this green patch, the street curved with a series of photographers' studios, displaying brightly coloured pictures of Indian actresses and scenic locales. The bookshop lay just before these studios. Its relatively small size – a mere sliver compared to its wider neighbours – made it easy to walk past. But its green walls and bold red lettering announced its presence: Shah M Book Co, declared the sign on top, in English.

I walked into the relative silence of the shop from the street, and started browsing. The shelves near the door were stocked with English books on Afghanistan, the titles echoing those I had seen in the cafe book swaps. The high prices on these volumes raised my eyebrows and my parsimonious instincts. I may well have walked out again, but the owner Shah Muhammad Rais was at the counter that day. When he heard that I was from India, he offered me tea. As we sipped from dainty cups, Rais told me how he had started the store. Years ago, he said, he had travelled to Iran on a vacation to get his first glimpse of the sea, but had ended up in a city nowhere near the coast. On his first day, he wandered onto a road filled with bookstores, sat down in one and got through half of *Othello* by the evening. He bought the book and finished it overnight, returning to the bookstores the next day, and the next, and every day after that for the rest of his holiday.

By the time he returned home, he knew he wanted to sell books for a living. The bookshop he started has remained open through each of Kabul's shifting eras: Communist, Mujahideen, Taliban, ISAF.

Besides selling books, Rais had another passion. He wanted to create a collection of publications on Afghanistan, as a way of documenting his country's literary heritage. As part of this effort, he had preserved pamphlets and almanacs, gazettes and souvenir booklets from different periods of Afghanistan's turbulent recent past. Over the years, his work had led him to fall foul of the shifting diktats of successive governments. During the Communist era, he said, he had been jailed for a year for keeping mujahideen propaganda magazines. When they came into power, the Taliban had burned a large pile of his books and postcards, objecting to the images of living things.

From under his desk, Rais pulled out some of the materials he had managed to salvage and showed them to me. These included a series of souvenirs released by successive governments of Afghanistan over the 1970s and 80s. At the beginning of these brochures were chronologies showing the rulers of the country, punctuated by gaps. In some, for instance, the monarchy was blotted out, their names coated with thick black lines. In others, the Communist rulers skipped over certain years and regimes. These erasures marked years of bloodshed, families splintered over the globe, endless intrigues across palaces that now lay in various degrees of ruin. A never-ending series of conflicts, concisely reflected on a few yellowing pages.

Rais is proud of the bookshop he has built, and as I walked around the stacks with him, I saw the sweep of his English stock – from Pashto–English phrase books for beginners to academic studies of ethnic groups in Afghanistan. There were lushly produced accounts of Afghan women leaders as well as memoirs of statesmen on their years in Afghanistan. There were books on Sufism, poetry and Islam, as well as the *Afghanistan Investors Directory*. The one book Rais refused to keep in his store was the one written about him by Norwegian journalist Åsne Seierstad, *The Bookseller of Kabul*.[11] Seierstad lived with Rais's family for several months in 2002, soon after the overthrow of the Taliban government. But the thinly disguised portrait she created of his life was contested by Rais. The protagonist in her book, called Sultan Khan, is outwardly liberal, but tyrannical within the home. He denies his son an education, and his second marriage to a much younger woman grieves his wife. The book became an international bestseller, and the clash between Rais and Seierstad got attention across the world. Rais took legal action against Seierstad in a Norwegian court (she was later cleared on appeal), and also wrote and published a rebuttal, *Once Upon a Time There Was a Bookseller in Kabul*, which was proudly displayed in his shop window.[12]

I told him I was looking for a large-print edition of Bedil's poetry for my grandfather, and Rais led me upstairs, to where he kept his Persian stock. Abdul Qadir Bedil is one of the most challenging and renowned Persian poets. Born in the Indian city of Patna in the seventeenth century, his verses are imbued with Sufi thought and Indian colloquialisms. Ironically, he is now mostly forgotten in India, but revered across Afghanistan and Central Asian nations like Tajikistan and Uzbekistan. Delighted to hear of a Bedil reader in Aligarh, Rais showed me around the collection on the upper floor. The prices were significantly lower than the English books below. And the titles I browsed through represented a pantheon of a different kind, familiar to me from Baba's study: poets like Jalaluddin Rumi and Muhammad Iqbal, Mirza Asadullah Ghalib of Delhi and Sa'adi of Shiraz.

Rais helped me find a collection of Bedil's poetry published in Iran, with print large enough for Baba's failing eyesight to decipher. Downstairs, as I settled the bill, he brought out a slimmer volume – a copy of tales from the *Shahnama*, the epic poem by Abul Qasem Firdausi, familiar to Persian speakers across the world.[13] He waved away my offers to pay, and wrote an inscription on the flyleaf with a flourish. 'For Mehdi sahib of India,' he wrote in a precise Persian hand, 'from one book lover to another.'

* * *

Heartened by my success at Rais's bookshop, I decided to visit the book market on the Koh-e-Asmai, the mountain that divides Kabul nearly in half. This lay southwards from Rais's shop. The road crosses the security fortifications of various government offices, and then an expanse of *attari* (apothecary) shops, with Sikh traders sitting in front of their tiny stalls selling turmeric, pungent asafoetida and other medicinal herbs. A little further is Ju e Sheer, which literally means 'river of milk'.

The name of the locality, I heard from some residents, comes from a stream that used to flow down the Koh-e-Asmai. The water was so pure that the reflection of the moon in the stream made it look white, like milk. It was on these ancient slopes that various currents of Kabul's diverse past ran together. At the bottom of the hill is a temple dedicated to the goddess Asmai, the deity who is said to have watched over the city since the era of the Hindu Shahi kings of the ninth century, and whose name has stuck to the peak through the ages.[14] It is possible that the stream ran to this temple. Others say the name came from the milk poured into the river by Zoroastrians, who built temples even earlier on the slope of the mountain. One afternoon, I made my way to this hillside, where books gleamed behind the glass fronts of stores that clung to the craggy earth like stubborn mushrooms.

Some stalls were basic and exposed to gusts of wind that deposited dust on their stock; others were equipped with computers and heating. Some of the stalls had been painted brightly, and the splashy colours appeared as a contrast against the adobe mud houses that clustered a little above them. I approached the market from the main street, and within a few steps was lost in the labyrinth of narrow book-lined gullies. Shops led into shops, and little boys ran up and down alleys or disappeared up ladders, coming back breathless but triumphant with a book that I had asked for, or just one they felt I should have.

I walked up further, past soldiers choosing pens for their children, past enthusiastic booksellers trying to thrust Indian folk tales printed in Persian at Peshawar's Taj Mahal Press at me, past row after row of printed sermons in Pashto by Zakir Naik, a Mumbai-based preacher who was enjoying a wave of popularity then. I asked a boy at a stall for his English stock, and he unearthed a slim paperback copy of *Saving Private Ryan* in a specially abridged version to help readers learn English. I flipped over to the list of questions at the back. 'What is your opinion of the idea mentioned in the book that war makes men into brothers?' it asked.

I ended up browsing at a tiny stall manned by Arash Ahmady, working my way through his eclectic collection. He told me he worked at a hospital in nearby Karte Seh, but spent his weekends on the mountainside, selling books, just because he loved them. With fingers slowly numbing and backs hunched against the chilly breeze of Kabul's unpredictable spring, we went over finely embossed maps of Kabul; a copy of Omar Khayyam's poetry translated by Edward Fitzgerald, bound in soft blue leather; several biographies, including one of M. K. Gandhi. 'Where did you get these?' I asked, and he replied matter-of-factly, 'Kabul.' Then he saw the look on my face, and added quickly, kindly, 'Of course, you won't find them here any more.'

Later, I learned from a friend the story behind this unlikely wealth. In the 1990s, as the civil war moved from the countryside to Kabul, most families who could leave, did. A lot of the books of the kind at Ahmady's stall were from embassies and cultural centres that hastily shut down, he said, and from the houses of Kabul's remaining elite. 'You won't find them here any more,' my friend said, his words an echo of Ahmady's. He described his own wanderings by the booksellers near the Kabul River during those years, picking up volumes that no one else seemed to want, and that he could barely afford, but bought anyway. We were silent for a while, and I thought of a Kabul where the books of Bedil and Tolstoy, Khayyam and Gandhi were passed down over the years. Like the books in the cupboards in my home in Aligarh – inherited from a previous generation, visited and revisited over long evenings.

Ahmady's books cost too much for me, so all I walked away with was an English–Dari phrase book and a cheap copy of the fables of Mulla Nasruddin. The wisecracking buffoon who offers homespun wisdom and speaks truth to authority is a beloved figure across India, Central Asia and beyond. Baba often told me stories about Mulla, whose cheeky irreverence he found endlessly endearing. I was perhaps thinking of Baba when I bought the book. It was only later that I realised I could not read the stories in Persian; the unfamiliar language in the familiar script I knew from Urdu evaded me in a delicate deceit. Like a screen hiding an image I knew, its shape glimmering from behind the curves and graceful arches that obscured it.

But the book stayed by my bedside. I would pick it up every so often, as though expecting it to suddenly become comprehensible to me. Perhaps I found in it a familiarity that transcended language. It reminded me of the kind of knowledge possessed by the illiterate pavement booksellers by the banks of the Kabul River, or the now vanished bookshops that sprawled over Mumbai's pavements. These booksellers would unearth volumes for customers, share recommendations and sort through titles and authors with complete confidence, finding in the texts an intimacy beyond words. Watching the flow of their hands as they moved books around was like walking along a well-worn path, known even in your dreams.

***

My early forays through Kabul were accompanied by a conviction that Baba would have been at ease there, certain of his way through its streets and the trappings of its culture. He would often describe aspects of it to me, saying 'Some cities I have never visited, but I know well.' Much of this intimacy came through books and reading, forged by Baba's knowledge of Persian, learned as a schoolboy in Bhopal. This was not unusual for the time – Persian used to be part of the education of elite Indians, across faiths. The language had taken root in India around the twelfth century, linking parts of the country in a loose linguistic embrace with regions like Iran and Central Asia, extending to the eastern state of Bengal.[15] It was the language of administration and of refined cultural expression, until it was replaced by English under the British Raj – the language that I used to explore the world.

Perhaps this was the difference in our approaches to the city. While I discovered Kabul mostly through Western accounts, Baba's path lay closer at hand, through the shared heritage of the region. He knew, for instance, to look for Kabul in the *Shahnama*, and told me that one of the heroines of the epic was a princess of the city. He knew that the celebrated Sufi poet Jalaluddin Rumi had been born in Balkh, in northern Afghanistan, rather than Turkey, as I had assumed. (Which was why in Kabul I often heard him referred to as Maulana Jalaluddin Balkhi.) He prompted me to find Bedil in a place where he was revered, and to seek out the sights of the city in Babur's centuries-old memoir.

From all this came his understanding of the codes of the city; a fluent awareness of its complexity and nuances. It was as though he could, even from a distance, discern the layers of Kabul's streets more clearly than me. It was why I turned to him repeatedly to guide my wanderings through these alleys, which he did so effortlessly, from his study in Aligarh.

I thought of Baba in particular one afternoon when I heard the names of two adjoining palaces in Kabul, which used to lie near a park called Zarnegar, meaning 'edged with gold'. The park was built by Amir Abdur Rahman Khan, who constructed palaces and pleasure gardens on the left bank of the river as part of his drive to modernise and expand Kabul. The sites of the palaces – Bostan Serai (Orchard Garden) and Gulistan Serai (Rose Garden), the latter built for the queen – were chosen for their seclusion and their beautiful views.[16] Some of the buildings that marked these complexes have been lost, others survive in a different role. The twinning of the names, however, reveals a more lasting reference: to the famous texts of the thirteenth-century Persian poet Sa'adi Shirazi, called *Bostan* and *Gulistan*.

A long poem and a collection of prose and poetry respectively, the works are among the most significant in the Persian canon. They were part of Baba's school lessons; traditionally, the education of most students of Persian on the subcontinent began with these works. Their influence spread among Western writers too, including Voltaire and Henry David Thoreau. *Gulistan*, I read, was the primary text of Persian instruction for officials of British India in the early nineteenth century.[17]

With the shift in language, the city appeared differently, written by a calligrapher's pen in the graceful angles and curves of Persian letters. And much like this script is held together by subtle signs and dots, Kabul's terrain revealed itself to be punctuated by names and allusions that bind the streets into a text.

To see Kabul in this way was to read it like a poem.

On the streets of Kabul, poetry shines forth from a range of surfaces. The rears of Corolla taxis and the backs of trucks are eloquent with verses, from modern ditties to the words of long-dead poets. Walls record pithy comments, like the phrase scribbled opposite a military compound: 'Stop singing songs of broken love.' And poetry recurs in conversations with Kabulis, who love to pepper references with a few choice verses. In this city, the words '*sha'ir mega*', or 'the poet says', are often argument clinchers.

Poetry illuminates the everyday with its lustre, and it colours memories.

It rings out in the voices of street children, who burn '*spand*' – small seeds – in their tin boxes as a charm against the evil eye, in return for a few afghani notes. They twirl the fragrant smoke over cars and people, reciting the verses that seal them from harm.

> *Spand balaa band,*
> *Spand nazarband.*
> *Ba ishq e Shah-e-Naqshband,*
> *Ba dokhtara-e-Samarkand.*

> Spand, lock away the demons,
> Spand, turn away the evil eye.
> For the love of the king of Naqshband,
> and for the beauty of the girls of Samarkand.[18]

The king of Naqshband referred to here is a renowned Sufi mystic Sheikh Bahauddin Naqshband Bukhari, founder of one of the most influential schools of this philosophy. Embedded in these few lines, recited at breakneck speed by ragged children, is a link to Kabul's own deep past, and its place in the shared history of the region.

It is also a reminder that while most Afghans cannot read or write, they are steeped in an oral tradition of storytelling.[19] Their ears are attuned to tales that are fluid and change in the telling, like the accounts that would arrive in the ancient bazaars of Kabul, borne by merchants from distant lands. Including from India. I had read earlier of the fabled Chahr Chatta bazaar,

built in the seventeenth century. The name referred to its four
vaulted roofs that covered four arcades. Its walls were decorated
with mirrors and a special solution mixed with mica that made
them sparkle.[20] At night, it was ablaze with the light of lanterns.

I thought of the accounts of fabulous cities and adventures
that would have made their way to this bazaar, and of how
listeners would have made sense of them in the only way
possible: by melding them into their own stories. By seeing
in the tales of faraway places the echoes of their own lives.
By seeing the distant cities as reflections of their own home,
casting them into endless versions of Kabul. Eventually, these
stories would have become part of the story of Kabul
itself, become one of the tales told about Kabul in other
cities far away.

The *spandi* children joined this chain of storytellers. As they
moved down the road, their tiny figures twirled the containers
round and round, car by car, person by person. They bound us
with their magic, aligning bodies into a path held together by
smoke and poetry. Like a line of verse appearing on the street.

*　*　*

Following another such path made of words, I ended up in
Kabul's Public Library. I was guided there by the outraged
ire of my Afghan friend Nazira when I provoked her one day
by asking with casual condescension, 'Does Kabul *really* have
a library?'

When we met, Nazira was working at a video production
company. To me she seemed to be the embodiment of a chic
young Kabuli woman. She dressed with style and moved with
an air of efficiency that made heads turn. Her family had
migrated to Pakistan when the Taliban had captured Kabul.
They had returned after 2001, in time for Nazira to begin
college at Kabul University. She had chosen to study French,

and had lived in France for a few months during a language course. As she began to accompany me on my expeditions, her feisty presence by my side often opened up new vistas of Kabul. Like the visit to the library, which she arranged as a response to my ignorance.

The library building is located at one end of Charahi Malik Asghar, at the point where it connects to a wave of traffic flowing down a one-way street. It has stood here since 1966, and in this time its surroundings have transformed a great deal. The one-way street is one of the busiest thoroughfares in Kabul – even its horizon appears crowded, with giant billboards advertising mobile phones and powdered milk. A few steps away is the Lycée Esteqlal, established by King Amanullah, and run with French cooperation. Many prominent figures from recent years studied at this elite institution, and were referred to by their less polished contemporaries as '*murgh-hai-ye Francewi*', or 'French fowl', for their affected ways and accents.

Towards the right lies a leafy road that houses the Foreign Ministry, set behind a beautiful, large garden. In the years after 2006, the profusion of buildings which were high-risk targets for attacks meant that this road was slowly hidden behind concrete barriers and sandbags and was closed to regular traffic. So to visit the library, we didn't walk down its familiar if absent pavement. We drove through the one-way route, around the Zarnegar Park and the ever-expanding security barriers for the luxury Kabul Serena Hotel. We got out at the gate of the seemingly tiny space on which the library was squeezed, between a stream of cars and towering buildings.

Despite being open to the public, the library was difficult to enter. We were stopped first at the gate and then at the door, and questioned by security guards. These interrogations continued until we crossed the threshold. And then, everything changed. In one of those contradictions that Kabul pulls off so neatly, from that point on we were honoured guests, greeted with great enthusiasm and hospitality wherever we went.

The library building followed the template I found so often in Kabul's official buildings, which in turn reminded me of entering Delhi's government offices. The library had long dark corridors, punctuated with little nooks where large kettles were placed on the boil. One of these corridors opened into the General Hall, a reading room with neat wooden bookshelves and large tables, which was flooded with the late-afternoon sunshine. The collection was a mix of texts – from *The Other Half of Gender* to *The Little Data Book*. Of the average hundred users who visited the library every day, most headed to this hall.

We went first to meet the director, Hamidullah Shahrani, an energetic man in his thirties who had been appointed to his post just weeks before. He took over a collection that had seen large losses over years of war. Many books had been stolen during the civil war, he told us. Others were lost to the shifting currents of political masters. He told a story that I had heard different versions of during my time in Kabul – about a minister during the Mujahideen government who confiscated a large number of books acquired by the previous Communist government, labelling them 'propaganda'. 'We hear about Changez Khan destroying the library of Baghdad, but he was an outsider inflicting damage to a country he had conquered,' Shahrani said. 'Here, we have done this to ourselves.' (When I had recounted this conversation to Doctor Sahab later, he had chuckled and wagged an admonishing finger at me. 'We have all done it to each other. Don't. Point. Fingers.')

From the window of the director's office, I could see the dome of Amir Abdur Rahman Khan's mausoleum, which during the 1920s had housed a public library. In 1929, during the brief rule of Habibullah Kalakani, many of the books and manuscripts that had been placed there had been looted or had disappeared.[21]

Unlike some of his colleagues in other Kabul institutions, Shahrani was full of plans. We talked of his vision for larger buildings and online access, of digital archives and connecting to libraries across the world. We talked giddily in the future tense with a sense of recklessness, revelling in the optimism of our conversation. He offered to take us around and we walked through the dark corridors with him, watching as they seemed to light up in the face of his enthusiasm. This was fuelled perhaps by a refusal to admit the uncertainty that faced not only the fragile books on the library shelves, but the entire enterprise of running a library in a country marked by decades of war. As we met staffer after staffer, however, I realised that perhaps his approach was not entirely unfounded. Most of the people working in the library had held their jobs for over thirty years, giving their careers a longevity unmatched by the shifting regimes that had administered them.

One of the oldest employees of the library was Haideri Wojodi, who worked in the manuscripts section. We found him seated in a sunny spot by the window, wearing a short-sleeved sweater against the spring chill, poring over a newspaper. This first glance of Wojodi reminded me of Baba, seated in the winter sun in his Aligarh study, examining the English newspapers first, and then the Urdu ones. When we met, Wojodi was around seventy-six years old and had worked in the library for over forty-eight years. There was respectful reverence in the way his colleagues approached him – Wojodi is one of Kabul's foremost living poets, and a leading Sufi mystic and thinker. The links that tie Sufi Islam to poetry are deep and diverse, as can be seen in the verses of Jalaluddin

Rumi. Wojodi's poetry is one such strand in the romance between the writer and the Creator. On Thursday nights, he conducted discussions with his disciples on faith and life. Poetry was at the heart of these discussions.

Born in the valley of Panjshir, that lies north of Kabul, Wojodi was the son of a preacher. He attended a village school, where lessons were held under the trees. Life was impoverished and peaceful, and he grew up listening to and reciting poetry. He wrote his first verses when he was still a boy; words that appeared to him in a dream. 'I saw a beautiful girl in a garden who invited me to sit by the spring and wait for her. She climbed over a wall and vanished, I waited but she never returned.'

> What were you
> Who showed your face
> You stole my heart
> Made me without heart

When he was around thirteen, Wojodi was forced to quit school because of a financial crisis in his family. This was not an unusual occurrence; children from poor rural homes often left to work on farms. But he continued his education through his own reading. He made his way through Sa'adi's *Bostan* and *Gulistan*, the works of the poet Hafiz and the epic *Masnavi* of Jalaluddin Rumi. In 1954, still a teenager, he moved to Kabul.

In the capital Wojodi found spiritual and literary mentors, and there he made his home. It must have been an exciting moment to be a young writer adrift in the city. By the 1960s, education had created a spurt in literacy, and Kabul was changing at a rapid pace, particularly for its educated elite. The literary works produced at this time were influenced by Eastern philosophers as well as Western writers. Wojodi discovered his voice among the new Afghan poets and writers of the time.

In 1964, he began working at the Kabul Public Library, while writing poetry on themes that included life in his city as well as greater questions of peace and spiritual striving.

Though his poetry was inaccessible to me, I could see plainly his love for the library, where he had spent almost five decades amongst the pages stacked on shelves behind his desk. These included copies of some of the oldest newspapers and magazines produced in Afghanistan. Wojodi showed me some pages, printed in Turkish, Arabic, Persian and Urdu – the different languages a testimony to the range of words that Kabuli readers could access. The first newspaper produced in Afghanistan, the *Shams al-Nahar*, or *Morning Sun*, was part of this collection. It was established by Amir Sher Ali Khan in 1873 on his return from India.[22] There were some publications produced under the aegis of Amir Amanullah's father-in-law Mahmood Tarzi, known as the father of Afghan journalism. (The modernist Tarzi also undertook translations of fiction writing into Dari, beginning with the work of Jules Verne, from the Turkish translations rather than the original French.)[23] It also had copies of two journals printed during the reign of Amir Amanullah: *Aman-e-Afghan*, which served as the key organ of the government and was published in Dari from Kabul, and *Tolo Afghanistan*, which was published in Pashto from Kandahar. The greatest time for publishing and for writers in Afghanistan, according to Wojodi, was during the country's 'democracy decade' of 1963–73, when King Zahir Shah instituted a constitutional monarchy. There were state-backed publications, as well as privately run magazines being produced then. This era ended in 1973 with the coup by the king's cousin, Daoud Khan. Soon after, Afghanistan was to enter decades of conflict.

These early journals and magazines in the library were fragile – they were visibly falling to bits, their cardboard bindings filled with dust. But they were that rare instance in Kabul of a collected memory of writing. It was difficult to miss the connection that stretched between Wojodi and the pages in their folders, which somehow continued to survive against the odds. He seemed like a deceptively frail guardian of Kabul's literary legacy, bound to it with a deep belief: that words are important through the darkest times. Words to bear witness, to stay human, to keep alive belief in beauty, even as the city was destroyed and remade over and over again.

There were many things I wanted to ask Wojodi, but didn't want to tire him with my questions. There was also the palsy he was affected with, which made his body tremble with the effort of talking. I told him this and he laughed and recited a couplet in Dari for me. 'Though my body is shaking, inside I am a mountain.'

Wojodi had lived in Kabul through the tumultuous years following the Saur Revolution, which overthrew Daoud Khan's republic in 1978. He stayed even as part of the city's elite emptied out after the USSR invaded Afghanistan in 1979. During these years, he continued to work at the library. The job was no mere sideline, something to pay the bills while he pursued his real work as a poet. 'I was fortunate to have spent my youth here, surrounded by books. The smell and feel of them was like a *nasha* (intoxication), and I would stay here for hours after work, soaking in the pleasure of being around pages, stories,' he said. And now, he added, he was like a bird in its cage, the library the only environment he was familiar with, one he would perish without.

Watching Wojodi walk around his bookshelves was like seeing a path into a forgotten Kabul. Talking to the poet, I thought of the phrase I had heard often as I searched for books: that the city had 'nothing to read'. This idea, I realised, had more to do with the reader than Kabul itself.

The darkest times for the library, Wojodi said, came with the civil war. The building was in an area that saw heavy shelling, and 'the sky would be raining rockets. The library was shut down for some periods. People were looting the collection for what they could find.' Even on those days, he would try to get to work, because the thought of all those books being destroyed was too difficult to bear.

I remembered a video a friend had shared with me of this time, showing a young man reciting verses while standing in the middle of a ruined building.[24] This was Qahar Asi, a prominent Afghan poet who wrote during the 1980s and 90s. I had not come across his work, but my friend also sent me the poem Asi was reciting in the video. Written in 1992, it spoke of Kabul's destruction, invoking its past and its blood-soaked present, embracing despair and anger and love all at once. Asi was killed in a rocket attack two years later, another victim of the civil war. Wojodi's story recalled to me Asi's voice, echoing over the broken courtyard, flinging verses into the roar of war.

Wojodi left Kabul only when the Taliban came to power in 1996, and returned soon after 2001. Since then, he had been coming to work in his old office, settling down for the day in his favourite spot by the window. It was both his sanctuary and his reality. But after the years of war, Wojodi's passion for the pages that he had sandbagged his life with faced a fresh challenge: the zeal of the new librarian to move the archive to another location, where it would be digitised. The idea had not found complete approval with Wojodi, who was worried about the effect the treatment would have on the fragile pages.

I watched as he abandoned our conversation to move into a deep discussion with the director, urging the younger man not to move the manuscripts until there was an appropriate space for them. They made an arresting contrast, the director with his eyes fixed firmly on the future, and the aged poet-philosopher, gently whispering to him of the need to handle the past with care.

After bidding us goodbye, Wojodi returned to his sunny spot by the window. Behind him flowed Kabul's sluggish, noisy river of cars. And behind that shimmered the domes of the mausoleum that used to be a library. In this tableau, I saw the shifting vistas of Kabul, framed by two constant streams – war and poetry.

* * *

We descended into the library's basement. The books here were English titles, written about the country by visitors from across the world, during different eras.

The *Baburnama* turned up in its English translation, as did the less candid memoirs of his descendants. There was a volume titled *Scenery, Inhabitants & Costumes of Afghaunistan* by James Rattray, a lieutenant in the British army, containing sketches he made during the first Anglo-Afghan War (1839–42). It was published in London in 1847, and provided a hungry Victorian public with images and stories from an exotic, faraway land. His drawings were made into lithographs, including pictures of the elite ladies of Kabul (who he believed exercised greater control over their husbands than the women of India) as well as of warriors in elaborate headdresses.[25]

On my request, the librarian in charge of this section pulled out a large map of Afghanistan and unrolled it on a wooden desk. It had been published in (then) Bombay in the 1860s. I pored over its unfamiliar borders as Nazira pelted the librarian with questions. Like many of her contemporaries, Nazira had returned after 2001 to a city she called home but had never really known. 'Did people come here during the Taliban years too?' she asked in tones of astonishment. 'Yes,' replied the librarian, adding gently, but with a touch of reproof, 'people read even then, child.'

Much of the ruined library building, he said, had been repaired by Taliban officials, who mostly left the books alone after burning all the pictures they could find of humans and animals. Intriguingly, they had left the pictures in the anatomy textbooks intact, for students of medicine. 'They didn't have money, but they protected whatever remained after the civil war.' He pointed to the bookshelves around us. 'They put up these stands and painted the shelves.'

We went in search of the poetry section, which we found perched on the top floor of a different building. On the shelves was a mix of poets from all over the Persian-speaking world, but I gravitated to the names I recognised – Bedil, Ghalib, Firdausi. I took out a few of these volumes, and found that they had been published in pre-Partition India, in the presses of Peshawar, Lahore, Lucknow.

On one shelf I found the books of Muhammad Iqbal, catalogued under the name Iqbal Lahori. But the librarian who looked after this section showed me the handwritten card he had stuck into the volumes, with his own preferred appellation of 'Iqbal Hindavi', or 'Iqbal of India'. We laughed over this, even as we insisted that such labels were irrelevant. Poets have no borders, we assured one another.

Steeped in the traditions of the East but fluent in Western thought, Iqbal viewed poetry as a call to action, a guiding force to create change.[26] For the poet-philosopher, Afghanistan was an inspiration: the free nation across the borders of

British-ruled India, unsullied by the slow corruption of spirit that came with Western domination. A key theme in Iqbal's poetry is the need for Muslims everywhere, but especially in the Indian subcontinent, to shake off indolence and servility and embrace self-respect and modernity. In this conception, Afghanistan was a model for Eastern leadership, and Kabul shone with the promise of regained purity and rugged strength. Iqbal described it in one poem as 'the heart of Asia'. To me, this was a new way to see this country – as the heart of my own part of the world.

Iqbal had visited Kabul in the autumn of 1933, driving across the Khyber Pass with two companions, at the invitation of King Nadir Shah.[27] The monarch and the poet admired each other greatly, and Iqbal's journey was made to support Nadir Shah's project of modernising Afghanistan, and to help with plans for the newly established university in Kabul.

With his companions, Iqbal made his way through different cities. His long Persian poem from this journey is called *Musafir* (*Traveller*), and recalls his travels like a pilgrimage, evoking several historical figures buried in Afghan soil, as well as paying homage to mystics and thinkers. The poem includes verses he wrote at the mausoleum of Babur, which addressed both the king and the city so close to his heart.

> How fortunate art thou to sleep on this land
> It is free of the ruse of the West.[28]

I had read travelogues of Europeans who had come to Afghanistan during the interwar years. They celebrated the simplicity of the landscape and its people, and their perceived distance from the corruption of industrial societies. Iqbal's verses recast this terrain in a way that embraced both its history and the promise of rejuvenation through modernity.

Reading about his journey was another path into Kabul. From being a place on the margins of my imagination and experience, it shifted to a place that felt proximate, part of a wider cultural continuum. It was another thread that seemed to run from the familiar books on my grandfather's shelves to the streets I was now walking, binding them across the years, across distance.

Iqbal's Afghan-inspired poem was overtaken by harsh reality even before it was completed. A few weeks after the Indian delegation departed from Kabul, Nadir Shah was assassinated. His son Zahir Shah took the throne at the age of nineteen, and Iqbal dedicated *Musafir* to him.

In the *Javed Nama*, an earlier Persian poem dedicated to his own son, Iqbal wrote these lines:

> Asia is a body of water and clay,
> Of which the Afghan nation forms the heart.
> The whole of Asia is corrupt,
> If the heart is corrupt,
> Its decline is the decline of Asia;
> Its rise is the rise of Asia,
> The body is free only as long as the heart is free,
> The heart dies with hatred but lives with faith.[29]

In Kabul, poetry can be read as the past, and as prophecy.

* * *

As in the rest of the library, the books in the poetry section were kept on open shelves, with no protection from the elements. Slowly, inevitably, they were also falling apart. I asked the librarian if many people still visited his section. 'In the entire day today, there were three visitors,' he said in a mock-tragic style. 'Nobody cares for poetry, or for this library any more.' And then he added more soberly, watching my young

Afghan companion walking around the room, trailing desultory hands over the dusty shelves, 'Poetry has fled Kabul.'

In 1977, I read, before the spiral of conflict began and the population of the city was only 500,000, the library had 14,000 registered members. In later years, the number had fallen to around 1,300 Kabulis, from a city of over 5 million people. Among the uncounted costs of war must be tallied the vanishing of books from the lives of readers, and of readers from the repositories of books.[30]

As we left, I noticed a van parked next to the small sliver of green that flanked the building. It was a wreck, with cracked windows and boarded-up doors. The librarian, who had walked out with us, said it had been intended as a mobile library, to take books into different parts of the city, or perhaps into the provinces. It had only been used a few times when a suicide attack at the shopping centre across the road in 2010 blew out its windows. It had been standing parked against the wall ever since. We walked over the grass, crossing dandelion clocks and stone benches ideal for quiet reads, to a small statue set in the corner of the park. On the stone was inscribed a Persian verse from Firdausi's *Shahnama*:

> *Tawana buwad har ke daana buwad*
> *Ze daanish dil-e-peer barnaa buwad*

> Who has knowledge, has power
> With education, an old heart can become young

Surrounded by the roar of traffic and sentries crouched behind sandbags, the text seemed dated in its idealism. But it had endured, even as Kabul had changed.

Before leaving his section, I had asked Wojodi for a poem that he felt represented something special about Kabul. He had quoted a famous *qaseeda* (panegyric) by the seventeenth-century poet Sa'ib-i-Tabrizi, who was summoned to the court of the Mughal emperors in Delhi. On his return, the poet wrote this ode to the city:

> Oh, the beautiful city of Kabul wears a rugged mountain skirt,
> And the rose is jealous of its lash-like thorns.
> The dust of Kabul's blowing soil smarts lightly in my eyes,
> But I love her, for knowledge and love both come from
>   her dust.
>
> . . .
>
> Every street in Kabul fascinates the eye,
> In the bazaars, Egypt's caravans pass by.
> No one can count the beauteous moons on her rooftops,
> And hundreds of lovely suns hide behind her walls.[31]

It is a beautiful poem, which I had read in my copy of Nancy Dupree's guidebook to Kabul, and yet I had felt disappointed when Wojodi quoted it. Over time the verses had become a literary shorthand for Kabul, often used to round off articles or travel blogs about the city. It is in the spirit of courtesy in Kabul to offer to a guest the response they think is desired, rather than what they may feel is accurate. I felt the *qaseeda* to be one such instance of the poet showing me not his city but the one he felt I wanted to see.

But then I encountered a continuation of these lines in the work of a young poet, Ramazan Ali Mahmoodi. The poem addresses the seventeenth-century lines and is also titled, quite simply, 'Kabul'.

> Flowers are falling on Kabul's skirt from the sky,
> Like God is giving wedding dresses to a new bride …
> Every moment gives a blossom of hope from God,
> Men and women softly smile in Kabul.

How well you have described, o 'Sa'ib', the blooms on its
    mountains and slopes,
But what if you had seen the beauty of the winter of
    Kabul?
'Mahmoodi', let us now share the glad tidings with our
    friends,
A green spring is coming to the green garden of Kabul.[32]

Read together, the two poems formed a path into the city,
bridging the centuries. Like the path that had opened for me
by reading the story of the Kabuliwala in Baba's study all those
years ago.

3

ABSENCES

Kabul appeared, from the road or the sky, announcing its proximity with the unfolding of graveyards.

First as vast, panoramic swathes that covered entire hillsides. Later, as the city grew closer, passing in smaller flashes, squeezing into the gaps left by the living. Or perhaps it was the other way round, and the city had insinuated itself into the spaces between the tombstones. Either way, the dead were as much a part of the landscape as the living, providing one of the few points of stability in a constantly changing terrain. Standing in the middle of Kabul's streets, I could look up and see, like waves rising on the horizon, layer after layer of its dead, lost in their eternal sleep as the city expands around them.

Paths emerged through these markers, like secret passages leading across the hills and in between homes. As I walked the streets of Kabul I saw women taking shortcuts through graveyards. Children carried water to their homes in the mountains following these lanes. People stopped to exchange salutations in the shade of the trees that spread over gravestones. There were graves next to houses and in the middle of markets, forming an island in the middle of a busy thoroughfare or providing a respite in the upward climb to dwellings on the hills. They were a part of the city's terrain, its everyday rhythms, in a way that was unfamiliar to me.

In Aligarh, the graves remained within the orderly spaces allocated to them, and any interaction with these spaces was governed by strict protocol. For instance, as I was taught as a child, it was polite to offer greetings when crossing a cemetery. To be disrespectful invited retribution. If you walked over graves, the dead lamented as your steps sounded over their heads, my cousins told me. Then their spirits would appear in the mirror in the middle of the night, and whisper to you until you went mad. 'If you step on graves you go blind.' 'If young girls cross over graves at dusk they get possessed by evil spirits.' 'They curse you so loudly that if you could hear them you would faint.' All these were stories I grew up on in Aligarh, and in Kabul too I heard similar tales. But in practical life, walking through the streets often meant stumbling over some kind of grave.

I learned to distinguish the different ways in which these markers punctuated the earth – from a brief ellipsis of small headstones between densely packed houses and shops, to the longer dashes of elevated tombs that appeared up the mountains. The simplest graves were plain mounds of earth marked with small stones. Others were more lasting, with carved headstones. Some were clustered together into family plots, ringed by an iron fence. Some were marked by a green cloth tied to a flagpole. Green is the colour of martyrdom in Afghanistan, and these flags marked the resting places of *shaheeds*, martyrs of one of the country's many conflicts. Often, they were the only splash of colour on the bare slopes of hills. It was ironic how picturesque they looked, touched by the mellow sunshine of the Afghan spring, or even whipped by Kabul's notoriously dusty summer winds. From a distance, they resembled some strange and terrible variety of tree, evergreen and hardy, that flourished particularly well in this soil.

And then there were the grander *ziyarats*, or shrines, often located within graveyards, or sometimes as solitary mausoleums.

These were the graves of Kabul's patron saints, holy souls who watch over the city. Many Kabulis offer *aqeedat*, devotion, to one or more of these saints. They are visited to seek cures or blessings, to drive away troubles or to secure joys. Several such *ziyarats* dotted the mountains around the outskirts of the city, or were hidden away in the narrow streets of its old quarter.

These varying formations of graves across the city eventually pulled my steps towards the cemeteries themselves. The rise and fall of markers and memorials in these spaces seemed to offer a story written into earth that could only be read by walking.

Over time, this web of memorials turned out to be far larger than I had supposed. I found the paths I wandered in these cemeteries were like veins – leading to the many shades of loss that run through Kabul. The city is marked by absence, of which a plot in a cemetery is merely the simplest manifestation.

***

One of the more orderly graveyards in Kabul lies in a locality called Sherpur, in the shadow of two colonial-era wars. Because it is the only burial ground for Christians in the city, it is a spot occupied largely by those who came from elsewhere. Within its walls lie soldiers as well as hippies, engineers as well as explorers. People who came to Kabul for various reasons, and never left.

The Qabre Gora, or 'Graveyard of Foreigners', as it is colloquially known, is located a short walk from the Sherpur crossroads. The name of the locality carries the memory of a shadow city. In the 1870s, the Afghan ruler Amir Sher Ali Khan had planned his new capital Sherpur here, away from the already crowded old city.[1] The new dwellings were to be centred around a fortress (a 'New Bala

Hissar'), and would house the court elite and administration. As it happened, only the military installations were built before the second Anglo-Afghan War overtook the amir's plans in 1878. The British troops used these very installations for shelter that winter. Years later, Amir Amanullah flattened the remains of the constructions to build Kabul's first airfield.[2]

After 2001, this land – belonging to the Ministry of Defence – acquired commercial value as Kabul's real estate prices boomed. In 2003, bulldozers demolished mud houses and evicted the families who lived there. The land was parcelled out to powerful figures and their relatives, which included former militia commanders, senior government officials and ministers.[3] This alleged 'land-grab' caused protests among citizens as well as the Afghanistan Independent Human Rights Commission. But the international community and representatives of foreign embassies – which lay a short walk from the site – mostly remained silent. For many Kabulis, these events were an early indication of how things would go wrong in the coming years. They also signalled how this new cycle of change was underlaid by the old patterns – impunity for the powerful, and silence from their foreign allies.

Soon, massive mansions came up in Sherpur, which were rented at exorbitant rates by the people who could afford them – foreign contractors, aid organisations or consultants, media houses. In magazines and websites aimed at expats, I would come across advertisements for these poppy palaces: 'Forty rooms, underground parking for twelve cars, good security.' The scale and brazen style of these structures made them architectural displays of impunity. Many Kabulis referred to this area as 'Chorpur', the village of thieves. Each time we took that route to get to work, my driver Abdullah would say, 'Look, Taran, very bad place, full of *badmash* [crooks].'

Abdullah knew these streets well. Before he started driving for expats like me (that is, after 2001), he had been a taxi driver. And he had never left the city. Not even for a night, he said in reply to my persistent questioning. The only trip he had taken in nearly forty years had been to Ghazni, to attend a wedding. He had returned to Kabul the same day.

Each time I was in his car, I would listen to the only station he tuned to – Radio Ahmad Zahir – which played the legendary Afghan singer's repertoire day and night. Once I asked Abdullah what the biggest difference was now from driving during the Taliban years. 'The silence,' he said. 'The streets were completely quiet then.' There were few cars around, and Abdullah's taxi was often flagged down by the guards stationed at crossroads, and examined for cassettes and other contraband. If they found any, they would pull out the spools and throw them on the road. That was the only sound you heard, Abdullah said. The rustling of the magnetic film that had been extracted from the disembowelled tapes, sighing as they were thrown around the streets, hanging off the trees and electricity poles. Maybe they looked like the flags fluttering over graves.

The day I visited the Qabre Gora too, Abdullah took the route via Sherpur. We turned into a narrow street and slowed down in front of a high wall. Only the massive black doors made of wood were unusual, as was the empty space behind them – an oddity in an increasingly built-up neighbourhood. On the wall, a small sign in English said 'British Cemetery'. I stepped inside the gates and felt like I had crossed into a pastoral graveyard in a little English village. There were shady trees and trimmed grass between the gravestones. Only the snow-topped peaks circling the walls marked the spot as unmistakably Kabul.

The cemetery is located in the area where events played out during the Anglo-Afghan wars in the nineteenth century.[4]

These were motivated by the British desire to curb Russian influence in the region – part of what was called the 'Great Game' – as both empires sought to increase their power in Central Asia. The first conflict began in 1839 when the British attempted to replace the ruler Dost Mohammad Khan with the more pliant Shah Shuja. After facing a violent uprising in Kabul in 1841, the retreating British forces were ambushed and massacred on the road to Jalalabad. Shah Shuja was killed a few weeks later. This disastrous retreat left a profound impression on the British imagination at the time. Returning in 1842, the avenging British army burned and looted the city for two days. They particularly targeted the beautiful Chahr Chatta bazaar as a symbol of retribution.[5] After securing the release of their prisoners, the British eventually withdrew, and Dost Mohammad Khan returned to reoccupy his throne.

The second instalment of this conflict unfolded nearly forty years later. Another British invasion in November 1878 had forced the Afghan Amir, Yakub Khan, to accept Britain's control over the country's foreign relations, and to receive a permanent envoy at Kabul. In September 1879 this envoy was murdered, along with his staff, at their quarters near the Bala Hissar. In response, British troops occupied Kabul in October. They used the Sherpur cantonment as a convenient and warm retreat while they waited for reinforcements over the winter.

A brief idyll followed this spate of conflict. 'Once settled in their cantonments at Sherpur,' wrote historian Nancy Dupree, 'the troops set about enjoying the valley; bamboo punts, flat bottomed canoes and row boats skimmed along on Wazirabad Lake, cricket and polo teams met in contest, and there were many competitions at horseracing. The city, returned to its former prosperity, continued to fascinate: "Towards the afternoons the main bazaars present a most lively and animated appearance, and are densely and incongruously crowded: camels, elephants, mules, horsemen, Afghans and Englishmen all jostling along in a busy stream".[6] But this seemingly placid coexistence masked undercurrents of resentment. By December 1879, the Sherpur cantonment was besieged by thousands of rebellious Afghans. After several days of tense waiting and battles, these Afghan troops dispersed, leaving the British back in control of the city. Keen to end the campaign, the British army withdrew in 1880, having recognised Amir Abdur Rahman Khan as the ruler.

Many of the fallen soldiers of this era were buried in the British Cemetery, with some graves dating back to the first conflict. When I saw it, the tombstones had been repaired of the damage of preceding years, rose bushes flourished and the grass had been recently cut. From behind the enclosing walls, apartments and houses crowded the horizon. On the slopes of a hill visible behind the wall, another graveyard was spreading, unrestrained by walls.

The caretaker for the British Cemetery was called Rahimullah. Like Abdullah, he had stayed in Kabul during the civil war and Taliban rule. 'I never asked for this job,' I watched him tell an interviewer in a video shot in 2010. It had instead found him. Rahimullah had started coming to the cemetery during the 1980s to graze his cow. One day, the gardener who was in charge of the place had left him with the keys and vanished. Rahimullah ended up caring for the graveyard for the next twenty-eight years. He continued this work during the Taliban government, weathering a visit from Mullah Omar himself, he said. With his charmingly wrinkled face and long beard, Rahimullah was sought out by the community of expatriates as well as international reporters. But in the same video interview, he talked about the criticism he faced from his own community for caring for the graves of 'infidels'. 'I don't care what those people say,' he declared. 'I need the money to feed my family . . . What foreigner, what Afghan? I deal with dead bodies.'[7]

The dead bodies that Rahimullah dealt with were not all British, nor is the graveyard a military cemetery. Frozen in this enclosure of the 'Graveyard of Foreigners' is the ebb and flow of different currents into the city over the years. So it is possible to read this graveyard as a compendium of the many times the city has served as a crossroads, and the many ways in which people made it their own.

Among the tombstones, I spotted the resting place of Aurel Stein, the Budapest-born, Hungarian-British archaeologist and explorer. Stein devoted his life to studying the history of the Silk Road, the movement of technologies, ideas and culture between East and West. He spent decades trying to gain permission to enter Afghanistan so he could continue his study of the region. He finally succeeded in 1943, but within a few days of his arrival in Kabul, he fell ill and died, just weeks short of his eighty-second birthday.

On other graves, I saw passages from the Bible inscribed in English and Persian. '*Dar eenja nest, oo zinda shud,*' reads the script on one, a translation of the biblical phrase, 'He is not here, He is risen.' The smaller graves of children ('Bianca Ruthnick 7.5.1955–11.8.1955 Gulbahar'), more common in other parts of the city, were unusual here. There were inscriptions commemorating people who died on the job, far from home: an engineer from Poland buried in 1942, a Jesuit priest from Mumbai in the winter of 2004.

Some inscriptions were tributes not only to the departed, but also to the land that claimed them. A plaque dedicated to Raffaele Favero caught my attention with the faint but unmistakable calligraphy of 'Allah' above the name, and with the Afghan appellation ('Raphiulla Khan') that appeared with it. The inscription on his headstone, in Italian, read, '*Morto a Kandahar, nella terra che amava e che noi tutti abbiamo amato*'. Died in Kandahar, in the land he loved and we all loved.

In one corner, a beautifully carved headstone rested at a dizzy angle, declaring that 'Billy Batman loves Joan, Jade, Hassan, Caldoania & Digger'. The 'hippy stone' memorial, embellished with hearts, marks the cemetery as an outpost of the counter-culture movement that passed through Kabul in the 1960s and 70s – around the same time the Beatles were spotted in Afghan coats. From the soldiers of colonial armies to the wave of 'flower children', the British Cemetery is a rare record of Kabul's obscured past.

Perhaps the most unexpected headstone was of 'Com Zou Xing Zhi', which identified him simply as of 'The Chinese Embassy in Kabul'. Above the inscription was a star, once red but now hollowed out and blurred around the outlines. The date of his death is marked as December 1982. I had read that no Communists were buried in the cemetery over the years of Soviet presence in Kabul.[8] None except one, it seems.

The Soviet soldiers who were killed in Afghanistan were sent back home in zinc coffins to be buried. I learned this from Svetlana Alexievich's wrenching account of the Soviet war in Afghanistan, which I read in my bedroom in Kabul. *Zinky Boys*, a collection of testimonies from this war, is also an account of a great elimination of memory, examining how the Afghan war was erased in the USSR. Mothers of dead Russian soldiers talked of how they were not allowed to open their sons' coffins. Then how could they be sure, they asked, that someone else had not been buried in their place? Some families got nothing back of their children – not a piece of clothing, not a cigarette lighter. The news carried no mention of the dead or the injured. Veterans were forbidden from discussing the events they had lived through. The hardest burden to cope with, one soldier confided to Alexievich, was how it felt to be simply wiped off the consciousness of the nation. He spoke of his friend who had died of a bullet wound to his head. 'He was a quiet boy and no "Hero of the Soviet Union",' he said, 'but all the same, he shouldn't have been forgotten so immediately and completely'.[9]

Close to 15,000 Soviet troops would be acknowledged killed over the years of the Afghan conflict.[10] They form the biggest absence in the British Cemetery, where a whitewashed wall is embedded with memorials to fallen soldiers of different eras. The surviving markers from the oldest graves have been relocated here, with a plaque in the middle that reads 'This memorial is dedicated to all those British officers and soldiers who gave their lives in the Afghan wars of the nineteenth and twentieth century. Renovated by the officers and soldiers of the British Contingent of the International Security Assistance Force in Kabul February 2002. We shall remember them.' On the same wall, other countries of the ISAF military coalition have also erected their own markers.

I read through some of the tributes to the British soldiers: 'In memory of Major John Cook 5th Gurkha Rifles Who died on the 19th December 1879 . . .' 'In Memory of Cecil H. Gaisford, Lieut. 72nd Highlanders, Killed in Action on the Asmai Heights, 14 Dec. 1879 . . .' 'In memory of . . . Private Jonathan Peter Kitulagoda. The Rifle Volunteers. Killed in action in Kabul 28th January 2004. Aged 23 years.' 'In memory of . . . Lance Corporal Darren John George', I read. '1st Battalion The Royal Anglican Regiment (The Vikings). Kabul 9th April 2002 Aged 22 years. A loving husband and father. His name liveth for ever more.' The words sprawled over the wall, spilling across stones, across the centuries and across wars.

The plaques with the names of soldiers killed since 2001 were kept updated. But like the Soviet soldiers killed in Afghanistan, the bodies of these men were absent from the cemetery. They were carried away and laid to rest in quiet graveyards in their own countries. Only those who chose to stay were buried in the Afghan soil.

The more recent graves that I saw in the British Cemetery, therefore, were of aid workers. Like the Americans Dan Terry and Tom Little, who had led a medical expedition to Nuristan, and were among a group of ten international and Afghan NGO staff ambushed and killed by gunmen in August 2010. The FBI, I read in news reports, had wanted to take all the American bodies to the US for investigations.[11] But the families of Terry and Little had insisted they be buried in Afghanistan. While Terry's resting place is marked with a simple wooden cross, Little's tombstone is etched with verses from the Bob Dylan anti-war ballad 'Let me Die in my Footsteps'.

Before coming to the cemetery, I had read through various newspaper articles about it, including one from February 2002, which was shortly after the Taliban government had been defeated. Early in that winter of hope, the British forces had held a remembrance ceremony in the cemetery they had repaired. Music was provided by a Gurkha band and the assembly sang 'God Save the Queen'. In the shadow of the cantonment where British officers had punted on lakes and battled with rebellious Afghans, in the shadow of a city dreamed of but never built by an Afghan king, a chaplain had spoken of the soldier's duty of safeguarding his country. 'Lord God, we are soldiers in order to protect peace and freedom; the nation would have known them little but for us,' he read. 'What safety could there be in quiet lands, or in the homes of simple men at night, if we soldiers were all asleep or gone?'[12]

Around the same time as this ceremony, the British Embassy took over the maintenance of the cemetery. Rahimullah was paid for the first time in years, which must have made him, like his employers, optimistic about the future. In the years that followed, however, he gave interviews complaining that the money was not enough, how times were hard. He seemed disillusioned with how things had turned out.

Rahimullah died in 2010, and was buried in the Muslim cemetery on the other side of town. His son took over his job. When I met him, he simply exchanged greetings, and continued working at clearing away leaves from the ground. The graves were still well tended, but in silence, a quiet of the kind that would fall over the retreats of expatriates and aid workers, over words like freedom and 'just war', and many of the promises that were raised here, like stubborn ghosts, all those years ago.

* * *

Once I began looking for graves, they appeared everywhere.

For instance. On the wall of my friend Khalid's office there was a black-and-white picture of a man in military uniform. It was a little grainy but clear enough for most people who walked in to do a slight double take, and ask, 'Is that you?' Only a few people turned around and said, 'You look so like your father.' The man in the picture – Khalid's father – had disappeared when President Daoud Khan's government was overthrown by the Communist-led coup in April 1978.

His family scattered across the globe in the years following this disappearance. Tracking their trajectory is like tracing the path of shrapnel scatter. And yet they remained bound to a central absence, one that still looms over Khalid's life.

In the early days after his father went missing, Khalid told me, his mother would go and join the crowd outside the Ministry of Interior in Shahr-e-Nau. Everyone there was waiting for news

about disappeared family members. After seizing power, the
PDPA went through infighting between two factions – the
Khalq (Masses) and the Parcham (Flag). By October 1979, the
Khalqi leader Noor Mohammad Taraki was assassinated and
replaced by his former protégé, Hafizullah Amin. Khalid told
me that the new president released a list of thousands of people
who had been killed during the previous administration. The
gesture was supposed to be a distancing from the mistakes of the
past, a purging and an absolution. But for Afghans like Khalid
and his family, such distinctions between the factions were too
fine to matter.

Usually Khalid's sisters accompanied his mother to the street
outside the ministry, but on one occasion he went. He
remembers the large crowd, and the stalls selling *shola ghorbandi*
– a roadside food. He remembers the officials with the list
seeming relaxed, making jokes as they looked up names for
families. The whole exercise seemed banal, entirely routine, for
them. Khalid doesn't recall this, but another friend who lived
in Kabul at the time told me that the list of the dead was also
pasted on the wall outside the ministry. People would read row
after row, trying to find their missing loved ones. I had walked
past that wall several times, without suspecting that its surface
held this memory of disappeared Afghans.

Khalid's mother never accepted that her husband was gone.
'She kept looking all those years. Even when she moved to
California, she didn't stop waiting for him to return. We lived
with that ghost. And then she died and *I* started looking for
him, because I thought: What if he is still alive, what if he is an
old man somewhere and everyone has stopped looking for
him but he's waiting to be found? This thought haunted me, it
drove me crazy. Living with the uncertainty was the hardest
part.' He filed cases with humanitarian organisations and
looked extra carefully at men of a certain age. It was a burden

made somewhat easier by the knowledge that he shared it with thousands of other families. 'This happened to so many people. It's part of being a Kabuli.'

By the time I met him, Khalid had halted his efforts to find what had happened to his father. A few years earlier he had learned of a possible mass grave that may have held his father's remains. It was now below several feet of concrete, he was told, and formed the foundation of a new military building. Khalid had stopped then. 'I didn't have the courage to go on,' he said simply. A picture on the wall, an empty place at the table, smiling faces seen only in fading family albums, an ageing woman awaiting a return. These are the graves that are embedded in virtually every Kabuli home.

Walk out of the houses and the streets are just as haunted, dotted with tombs that defy identification, and with landmarks that shift shape to reveal loss of different kinds. To walk through Kabul is thus something of an education in recognising these mausoleums of the everyday. Like a monument I heard about from Doctor Sahab, called 'Sipahi Gumnaam', tomb of the Unknown Soldier. It was located at Jada-e-Maiwand, he said, a wide avenue built in 1949 as part of King Zahir Shah's drive to modernise the city. It had been created by knocking a path through the narrow, crowded alleys of the old city, linking it with the new settlements on the west of the river. Jada, as the avenue is colloquially called, had a facade of two- or three-storey shops and offices and apartment blocks on either side. But its sparkling modernity was a ruse, a flimsy veil. Behind the veneer of these buildings, the dense urban fabric of the old city continued unchanged.[13]

But when I tried to find this memorial, I was lost. The people I asked for help had not heard of it, or offered conflicting directions. I wandered uncertainly on this shifting terrain, thrown around between different accounts and contradictory memories. Eventually, I mentioned the difficulty to Doctor Sahab. 'Nobody calls it that any more,' he told me. 'Nobody knows the old names.'

The monument that Doctor Sahab referred to as Sipahi Gumnaam was what I had heard called 'Maiwand Memorial' – a black and blue column in the centre of a roundabout, built to commemorate a famous Afghan victory at Maiwand, near Kandahar, over the British army in 1880. The structure had been damaged during the civil war, and was repaired after 2001 with foreign aid. In the amnesia that afflicted the reconstruction of Kabul, the old landmarks had transformed; even the memories behind them had taken on new shapes.

For me, the monument some remember as the tomb of the Unknown Soldier recalled many other graves – hidden or revealed – for unknown, unnamed soldiers. The column that stands in the heart of Kabul can be imagined today as a prescient mausoleum to a vast absence – that of a generation of Afghans lost to the war against the Soviets, and then against each other.

In December 1979, the Soviet army entered Afghanistan.[14] Hafizullah Amin was assassinated and Babrak Karmal, of the rival Parcham faction, was placed in power. This incursion was probably intended to be a short-term measure, with troops withdrawing once stability was restored. Soviet soldiers instead ended up fighting a guerrilla insurgency for a decade.

These mujahideen were scattered under different leaders, but the aim of expelling the Soviets united them. Afghanistan became a proxy battlefield for the Cold War, with the US and other nations backing many resistance groups. The conflict resulted in the death of close to a million Afghans, and four million refugees fled to Pakistan or Iran,[15] from a total population of sixteen million.[16] Millions more were displaced internally. A significant section of Kabul's elite also departed soon after the Soviet invasion, taking part of the city's social and cultural capital with them.

Ten years later, in the winter of 1989, the USSR withdrew its troops, ending an increasingly unpopular and expensive war. It left President Najibullah in charge of the Afghan government, and supported his administration with food, fuel and aid. (The resistance too continued to be supported by their foreign backers.) With the Soviets gone, Najibullah made efforts towards reconciliation with mujahideen factions. But in 1991, the Soviet Union collapsed. The resources and aid it had been sending to Afghanistan came to an abrupt end. In April 1992, Najibullah agreed to step down. The ensuing power vacuum led to the beginning of a new spiral of civil war in Kabul.

As the power-sharing agreement between mujahideen groups fell apart, each tried to capture territory for themselves. The newly created Islamic State of Afghanistan effectively went to war with itself. Different parts of Kabul fell under the control of different commanders, usually along ethnic lines. These commanders fought and formed alliances over the next four years.

During the 1980s, people fleeing the war had sought refuge in cities. Such migration had swollen the population of Kabul to nearly 2 million, from a mere half-million in the 1970s.[17] This was the population that came under attack in the following months.

Between April 1992 and December 1994, around 20,000 people were killed.[18] (Afghan friends told me the number was closer to 50,000.) Nearly three-quarters of the survivors were forced to leave their homes, either within the city or for the refugee camps in Jalalabad, adding another layer to the population displaced by the Soviet-era war.[19] Each side committed atrocities. Rocketing affected much of the civilian population, with the hills used as vantage points from where to indiscriminately target residential areas. Crimes against women were commonplace, as were disappearances and executions.[20]

So the memorial to the Unknown Soldier in the centre of Kabul could even be read as a monument to these losses experienced by the city – a monument to its transformation.

The area around Jada-e-Maiwand faced heavy destruction. Families who lived in the historical old city escaped from their homes during breaks in the shelling and rocket fire. Making their way across Jada, some of them recalled to me years later, had been the hardest part of their journey, akin to crossing a border. In videos of Kabul shot around this time, I had seen wide stretches of avenues with their pavements shattered, and the surrounding buildings in ruins.[21] In the same videos I saw families making their way out of the city. Men and women shuffled down the street, with as many of their possessions as possible loaded onto handcarts. A teenage boy in military fatigues sat on a chair in the middle of the street, clutching a gun and watching this pitiful exodus.

I walked down Jada in 2011, when its pavement had been repaired and taken over by roadside hawkers making a living. My steps wound around haphazard piles of Chinese-made goods – toys, umbrellas, packets of detergent, soaps and shoes. Some were on the ground, others arranged in wheelbarrows. Knots of shoppers stood and bargained, examined the wares and eventually carried away their purchases in powder-blue plastic bags. An old man walked slowly past these crowds, his bent shoulders covered with layer upon layer of coats and jackets that he was trying to sell. Taxis tooted past merrily, picking up passengers sharing a ride to the old city, or to the suburban expanses of Karte Seh. I heard the Tunis shuttles beat out their familiar songs as they stopped, and started, and stopped again for passengers. At the back of one of the yellow Corollas, I read a sticker that said 'I am a moving coffin'. Over this everyday bustle of the street loomed empty buildings, and when I looked up I could see right through their windows. They seemed to be small squares of darkness that gazed at the world like vacant eyes in a tomb.

Where do the graves end in Kabul, and what innocuous landmark does not reveal itself eventually to be yet another kind of gravestone? Under the pulse and busy rhythm of this city, there is a hush; unremarked but never forgotten by those who belong to its streets.

***

Names without graves, graves without bodies.

Even before coming to Kabul, I had read and heard a lot about the atrocities committed during the Taliban era. But it was only when I got there that I learned in detail about the war that had preceded their rule. My ignorance was not unusual. With the collapse of the USSR, the attention of the world had moved away from Afghanistan. The civil war, despite figuring as one of the darkest moments in Kabul's history, had raged in silence.

And yet it was everywhere. Virtually every Kabuli has a story from this time, virtually every family bears the scars. Like the story of Naheed, a teenager who was chased to her death in the summer of 1993 by a group of fighters affiliated to a warlord who held sway over her locality. For Kabul's residents, the story of this young girl's death is a parable for the savagery of the civil war. It is also an example of the silence that veils events in this era; a silence that is, in fact, a form of deliberate erasure. Her grave, I was told, is now a shrine. To find it, I went to where Naheed had lived – in Microrayan, in north-east Kabul.

The housing colony was built in the 1970s with Soviet assistance, as a self-contained residential area for civil servants. The influence of Soviet-era design is clear in the neat layout of the apartment blocks that are interspersed with community gardens. Inside the complex were health centres, kindergartens, shops, playgrounds and schools. The construction was earthquake-resistant and the apartments had facilities like central heating, modern kitchens and toilets. All this, along with the paved streets and wide pavements, made it a modern, safe place to live.

This changed during the civil war. The damage wrought during those years was still evident when I first visited in 2006, in the bullet-pocked walls and destroyed amenities. In 2011, after a decade of the internationally assisted reconstruction of Kabul, the scars were still visible on the buildings, but there was also much that was new and beautiful.

For outsiders, Microrayan would perhaps appear the same as any other neighbourhood – constrained and dense with social restrictions. But to Kabuli eyes, this was one of the most open areas of their city. Certainly Masoud, our cook, who lived in the old city and who accompanied me there, felt this way. 'It is very free here,' he said, gazing at the flow of women and children on the street, with a mix of envy and disapproval.

I joined the flow of pedestrians, onto the streets where families strolled together, and women wearing smart cotton coats clipped past in high heels, their arms laden with shopping bags. In the community gardens, people had planted trees that were just starting to bear fruit. It was Friday afternoon on a mild summer day. The entire neighbourhood seemed to be out.

I went first to Nazira's house – she lived in the area, and had volunteered to help with my search. She had heard of Naheed, but had never seen her grave, and was also curious to find it. Nazira's family had lived in Microrayan before the Taliban's arrival forced them to flee for Pakistan. The apartment they were renting now was close to their original home. But un-expectedly her mother was unhappy about the homecoming.

'She says that all the old people have left,' Nazira told me. 'She says that earlier, there were only Kabulis living here. Now there are people from everywhere.'

We walked through the bustling lanes, stepping over water that gushed out from a pipe as an elderly man washed his carpets on the street, cannonballed into by boys chasing a runaway kite. We reached the block that Nazira thought was Naheed's, and rang a few doorbells, approached a few residents. At each place, we got a different answer. 'We have heard of her, but she didn't live here.' 'Naheed who?' 'Try that house, they are old residents.' 'We were not here then, we came after the war.' 'We are just visiting.' In some places, we got sullen silences, in others barely disguised anger. 'What do you care?' one man sneered. 'Are you trying to make trouble?' 'Why are you going around stirring up that old shit?' asked another. Looking for Naheed was like stepping on the fault lines of history.

Eventually, we found a matronly lady in a ground-floor flat who interrupted her Friday house-cleaning to answer our questions. Yes, she knew of Naheed, and yes, this was the building where she had lived. 'Climb all the way to the top,' the lady said, walking us to the stairwell. 'It's the door on the left.'

We climbed up six floors and rang the bell on the left. No response. We tried the flat opposite. A rosy-cheeked girl of about thirteen opened the door. Her name was Khadija, and she too had heard of Naheed. Her parents had lived in the same flat during the civil war, she said, before she was born, and her mother had been close to both Naheed and her elder sister. Khadija's family had moved to Pakistan soon after Naheed's tragic end. They had returned only a year ago.

Since Khadija was alone at home, she couldn't invite us in. But standing at her door, she recounted Naheed's story for us, across the hall from where it had happened. 'Naheed had a very beautiful sister who was around sixteen years old,' she said, the words coming with the fluency of a familiar tale. 'The mujahideen faction that controlled this area during those years heard of her and came after her. But the sister was not at home. Naheed was alone. She refused to open the door and the soldiers broke it down. To escape them, she jumped from a window.' I had heard various versions of the story, but hearing it from this girl so close to Naheed's own age, so close to her home, made it different. For the first time, I saw Naheed as a flesh-and-blood figure, not wrapped with the bland shroud of her martyrdom. And the flight from the window of a frightened young girl hurts more than the end of a saint.

It is said that when the Taliban captured Kabul in 1996 there were celebrations at being liberated from the excesses of such militias. Maybe in Microrayan, these were prompted by Naheed's memory.

In the years since 2001, stories like Naheed's have come to represent not only such crimes but the impunity with which they were committed. Organisations like the Afghanistan Justice Project, Human Rights Watch and the Afghanistan Independent Human Rights Commission (AIHRC) have tried to document the abuses of this and previous eras. But justice and healing for victims and their families has been a difficult cause to pursue.

The dawn of what seemed to be an era of peace in late 2001 offered an opportunity for an accounting of such crimes. But this was soon overshadowed by other factors. 'US forces allied themselves with commanders who were responsible for some of the worst war crimes committed during the civil war,' said the Afghanistan Justice Project report, published in 2005.[22] 'They did so because they believed these commanders could help the US defeat al-Qaeda and the Taliban . . . The US, along with senior officials in the U.N. and in some other governments, has also opposed efforts to investigate past abuses, arguing to do so would imperil "stability".' In other words, these early efforts were overshadowed by a perceived need to preserve the country's fragile domestic stability, over justice and accountability. As the report also points out, this strategy did not succeed.

All of which meant that the dark era of Kabul's civil war remained largely unresolved, casting a shadow into the present. Several leaders implicated in abuses from the time continue to play a prominent role in Afghan politics, as allies of the international forces. They joined the new era of democracy, donning the role of parliamentarians, or governors, or high-ranking officials. In 2007 the Afghan parliament passed a controversial 'Amnesty Law', granting broad immunity from prosecution to those who had organised or carried out abuses between 1978 and 2001, in the cause of reconciliation and national unity. While individuals are still able to pursue criminal charges against the perpetrators, this leaves them exposed to the risk of revenge from powerful figures.

To justify this reality, some Afghan and international institutions use a single, telling sentence. 'Everyone has blood on their hands.'[23] The words are used like a shrug of the shoulders, a moral stepping away. Perhaps this is the reason why it is so difficult to speak of the crimes of this era. The chain of responsibility and complicity goes too high, too wide. It implicates those in power now, and their foreign allies, and their history of silence.

In the current cycle of war and uneven peace, Naheed has become part of this shadowland – a reminder of what many want forgotten, a symbol of how little has changed.

I asked Khadija if anyone lived in Naheed's old home now. Until last year, she said, even the door hadn't been fixed. But now the owner had had it repaired, and sometimes would come to check on it. An exorcism of ghosts, perhaps, by Kabul's real estate rates.

Naheed had been buried behind the apartment building where she had lived, I had heard. After some searching, Nazira and I found the grave, tucked away in a small garden, hidden by tall hedges, flourishing grape vines and heavy rows of washing. Encircled by this banal equipment of everyday life was a headstone and the green flag of martyrdom. Under the flag, tied to the pole, were scores of knotted handkerchiefs and bits of coloured cloth, representing *mannats* (special requests) and prayers – of the kind that I had seen at shrines across the city. Many were discoloured, covered with dust and cobwebs.

On the headstone was an inscription in Persian, giving Naheed's name and age, and the time of her death. As we stood at the grave, a group of men watched us curiously from one of the windows overlooking the plot. They were painters, getting an apartment ready for new tenants.

Naheed's story does not end with her death. In one version that I heard in Microrayan, when the funeral procession was about to set out for the cemetery, there was a rocket attack, and the mourners were forced to scatter. In the confusion, Naheed's body was abandoned. When they returned, it was nowhere to be found. Perhaps the family buried her in a spot no one knows of. Perhaps her body was lost forever. Perhaps this part of the tale is simply a myth calculated to add to her aura as a pious soul. There are details to Naheed's story that are hazy, or hard to confirm, or contradict each other. Its power is as a symbol of the darkness of that era. Either way, I was told, the grave behind the house is empty. An absence that is like a beat of silence in the roar of the city.

* * *

One evening, I told Khalid the story I had heard in Microrayan. In return, he told me about another Shaheed-e-Naheed, or martyred Naheed. She was a student who had joined a large demonstration by women in April 1980, marching in protest against the Soviet invasion. The Naheed of this tale had reportedly challenged the Afghan soldier who aimed his gun at her as the procession made its way towards the Arg. 'We women will be better at defending this country than you are,' she is said to have told him.[24] She had been shot dead; and her story became a rallying cry, a symbol of the resistance against the Communist government and their Soviet backers. She was the Naheed that Khalid's generation had grown up with. The one he thought of when he heard my story.

The names of these two women, so similar in their fates, came to me like an echo from across Kabul's decades of wars.

***

My friend Lema told me another graveyard story, this one about a strange funeral described to her in turn by her father. He worked as a security guard and commuted from Kabul to the neighbouring province of Wardak every day. One day he passed a funeral procession at a roadside graveyard. The next day, on the same route, he saw the body by the empty grave. This happened a third day. On the fourth day the body was gone. Curious, he asked some questions. 'A lady from the village died abroad,' he was told, 'and her body was flown back to be buried in her *khak*, her native soil. But each time they buried her, they would find her body outside the grave the next morning. The family was distraught, the villagers perplexed. Finally they consulted a wise man, who told them that the lady must have insulted her *khak* at some time when she was abroad. That was why the earth was refusing to accept her. On his advice, she was buried along with a dead dog, to trick the picky soil into accepting her.'

Lema is a good storyteller, and has a fund of such fantastic tales that she insists are true. But even as a parable, the story reveals much about the Afghan sense of *khak*. The term refers to a sense of identity, the place where your ancestors were from, where they are buried. It is the dust that defines you, and that will eventually claim you. To be a true Kabuli meant to be buried in its soil, usually in the largest cemetery in town – the Shuhada-e-Saliheen, graveyard of the 'Pious Martyrs'.

The road to Shuhada runs along the southern edge of the city, some distance from the bustle of its centre. It passes abandoned buildings and unfinished shopping malls, ghostly reminders of Kabul's post-2001 real estate bubble. The road branches and goes past a dense collection of bazaars for bamboo, auto parts and gravestones. Then all these shops vanish, replaced by the edges of a marshy lake, Qol-e-Hashmat Khan, which has attracted duck hunters since the Mughal era. In spring, the slopes of the nearby hills are covered with flowering Judas trees, making them a favourite picnic spot for Kabuli families.

A short distance after this lake, Shuhada begins, but it is difficult to tell exactly where, even if you are watching out for it. Graves start cropping up, and quite suddenly, you are there, in the middle of a virtual city of graves, ringed by a suburb of the living. I visited the cemetery with Doctor Sahab, who had been promising to accompany me here for a long time. Just when I had given up on him keeping this promise, he planned the expedition.

The road drops into a valley encircled by the bare slopes of Kabul's craggy mountains – the Koh-e-Zamburak and the Koh-e-Sher Darwaza. Along the summit run the remains of Kabul's walls, like a ragged seam over the rocks. The valley is a sprawl of graves surrounded by the indefatigable hum of the city, as it spreads outwards, engulfing its former margins.

We walked past houses mushrooming between graves, with flowery curtains in their windows, overlooking tiny gardens that grew suspiciously fine blooms and large, lush grapes. The day was heating up, and the road dipped and fell, revealing the vista gradually. By the roadside, stalls sold tea and *bolanis*, pickles and ice candy. Children rode on the backs of donkeys, or carried canisters of water up and down the slopes, like moving pipelines, supplying the ever expanding settlements on the hills. Under the shade of trees, men leaned against graves, kettles and a generous stock of cups by their side, washing them out for new additions to their party. And in front of a concrete gate marking the Turkish cemetery, a group of boys played cards with ferocious concentration, barely looking up at passers-by. The cheery informality of the relationship Kabulis have with their graveyards was evident in Shuhada.

It is possible to walk to this graveyard through the mountains, on a route running like a memory through Kabul. On Thursdays in particular, the pious used to walk barefoot from the old city on a path that leads through the musicians' quarter of Kharabat into Shuhada. The pilgrimage begins at the *ziyarat* dedicated to two brothers, named Asheqan-o-Arefan, and ends roughly in the centre of the valley, at the *ziyarat* of Hazrat Tamim Jaber-e-Ansar. For some, this is the most sacred shrine in the city.

At the entrance of the shrine, I looked up and saw the face of the mountain etched with a single word in large letters: 'Allah'. Inside, the building gleamed with marble and chandeliers, embellished with large bunches of artificial flowers. The call to prayer sounded, and Doctor Sahab walked into the men's section. I entered the women's enclosure, where two ladies sat with a baby, discussing which *ziyarat* to move on to next. Dressed in their best, they were comfortably sprawled out on the carpets marshalling their strength for their next stop, enjoying their day out. But when I asked if they were having fun, they looked offended, and said that they were seeking the blessings of the saint for the child. 'What can be better than that?' they said tartly.

The congregation in the men's section broke up. One of the men chided us for talking too loudly while they had been offering their prayers. 'It is wrong, we should not hear your voices,' he scolded. '*Khoob*, thanks for setting us on the right path,' said the young woman next to me, her eyes downcast, her words a barb. She spoke just loud enough for the man to hear, but softly enough to let him pretend he hadn't.

The women decided to continue to the shrine of Panje Shah, further into the valley. Perhaps they didn't know it, but they would be following pilgrimage routes that had existed for centuries. Long before Islam arrived in the region, the springs and large *chinar* trees of the valley were revered by Kabuli Hindus and Buddhists. Shuhada has been hallowed land for over 2,000 years.

In his memoir, Babur records visiting the tomb of Cain or Qabil in the valley.[25] He also describes the spring of Khizr, named for the mysterious figure in Islamic mythology who appears to the troubled in times of need. Khizr, who is often depicted wearing green robes, is the protector of travellers. Like Hermes in the Greek tradition, he turns up on streets and crossroads, guiding walkers and wanderers away from trouble. It was quite likely, I thought, that he had been trailing me since I arrived.

On our way into the valley, we had walked past the marble monument that marks Ahmad Zahir's grave. This was the resting place of the 'Afghan Elvis', whose voice was the soundtrack for my view of Kabul from the back seat of Abdullah's car.

Zahir died in mysterious circumstances in 1979, on the cusp of the nation's transformation. For decades, the singer's velvety voice recalled the memory of Kabul's pre-war era in drawing rooms across the world. So great was his legacy and his popularity even after his death that when the Taliban came to power in 1996, they peppered his tomb with bullets. After 2001, the monument was repaired and saw frequent visitors.

Often these included Afghans who had returned to Kabul after years away, and whose most vivid link to home had been the voice of Zahir crooning his familiar ballads. The day I visited, I saw a group of women cutting the grass around the monument and tying it in bundles, to carry away for their livestock.

In the Islamic tradition, the living have an obligation to the dead, and Kabulis take this duty seriously. On Thursdays and Fridays, the Afghan weekend, families visit the graves of their relatives, or come to honour the shrines of saints. Family members sprinkle water on the graves of their relatives, the wet earth indicating the freshness of their loss. It makes it seem like they just buried their loved one. It is a way to say: *I just lost you, I am still in pain, I am still mourning you. You are still remembered*.

With Doctor Sahab, I had walked on to the small shrine of a *pir*, a spiritual guide, who he said had commanded a following in Kabul. I heard Doctor Sahab talk about his many accomplishments, but I was still puzzled about what we were doing there, unable to understand the rare note of devotion in my companion's voice. Until he mentioned that the *pir* had been revered by his own father and grandfather. In fact, the shrine was his family *khanqah*, or centre for spiritual guidance. We were back to *khak*, the elusive bond that linked Afghans.

Doctor Sahab's quiet pleasure at being in this spot was unlike his usual attitude of determined estrangement from the streets we shared. 'I don't know these people,' he would say, referring to the cycles of departures and migration that had reshaped Kabul. 'This is not my city.' He looked like he was at home now.

In a video shot in the winter of 1992, I had seen Kabul with snow falling on its streets, making the jagged edges of ruined homes smooth.[26] I had paused at an image of a palace, its frame partly obscured with white. I had spent a long time trying to recognise it. It was only later that I realised it was the Qasr-e-Darulaman, the grand building I knew so well, made unfamiliar by its relative wholeness. I had failed to recognise it because I only knew it as a ruin. Memory works this way in Kabul; landmarks derive from their destruction.

Sometimes, to see the city completely, we must learn to see what is missing. What has been forgotten, or what lies beneath the surface of the amnesiac city. The other side of the maps of graveyards, which are maps of remembering, are maps of what is forgotten.

Standing with Doctor Sahab in the densely written and rewritten valley of Kabul's saints, with bare feet on its dust, I found a way to address the question that had been following my wanderings through Kabul's graveyards. What was it that I sought there, that the living could not give me? Perhaps my walks were driven by the realisation that it is in such spaces, marked by what is lost, that the city is most fully present.

* * *

This was my last visit to a cemetery in Kabul. Spring was about to turn into summer, and the landscape already seemed more arid than before. I had walked onwards with Doctor Sahab to meet Zafar Paiman, an archaeologist struggling to preserve the remains of a Buddhist monastery he had excavated in the heart of Shuhada. The day we visited was to be the final day of work for his team on the site, at least for the foreseeable future. The next morning, it was to be closed down and handed over to the government. The exposed stones of this ancient structure, I realised, were not only a reminder of Kabul's often forgotten past, they were also a monument to its fraught present. From the moment I saw it, the monastery on the hillside was hanging by a thread.[27]

Afghanistan's Buddhist past is often invoked with hushed pathos. What comes to mind for most are the ruined Buddhas of Bamiyan, destroyed by the Taliban government in the spring of

2001. But for Kabulis of a certain generation, who remember Afghanistan before war gripped their lives, it was a part of their past, something encountered in stories and their own selves. I once met a young man who was named after one of the most prominent Buddhist kings of the region, Kanishka. His father, he told me, had given him that name to reclaim the history of his land.

Kanishka's name links him to the histories embedded in Afghanistan's soil, ranging from the Hellenic influences that followed Alexander's conquest to the Emperor Ashoka's evangelical outreach. Buddhism was an important strand in the web that ties the region together. From the first to about the third century, Kabul was a part of a powerful empire that stretched from India to Central Asia, astride the ancient Silk Route. This period saw a flourishing of Buddhist art forms and patronage to monasteries by rulers like Kushan Kanishka, the 'King of Kings'. The region went on to be ruled by the Hephthalites, or 'White Huns', in the fifth century, and the Hindu Shahi kings in the ninth century. This succession of rich and varied empires left behind vast reservoirs of material remains that are still being uncovered today.

Informal excavations and reports on these sites began in the nineteenth century, at a time when the British and Russian empires were expanding. The explorers of this era usually had mixed motives, and could be deserters, people on the edge of the law, or restless souls beating a path away from respectability. Contemporary Afghan archaeologists have a complicated relationship with the legacy of these early expeditions. They acknowledge their contributions but, as Zafar told me, they also encounter evidence of plundering at certain sites.

Formally, the history of archaeology in Afghanistan began in the 1930s, when Amir Amanullah granted a thirty-year monopoly to the French Archaeological Delegation on all

survey and excavation work in the country. It was only in the
1950s that other nations were allowed to participate, and India,
Japan, the USSR, Italy and others sent missions to work in
Afghanistan. In 1964 the government stipulated that all finds
from these expeditions would remain in Afghanistan, rather than
being divided up with the foreign missions. Thousands of pieces
soon poured into Kabul's small museum, giving it an enviable
collection.

This included exhibits from Hadda, the fifteen-square-mile
complex near Jalalabad in eastern Afghanistan. Hadda was one
of the largest Buddhist temple and pilgrimage complexes in the
world during the first through third centuries. Archaeologists
working there found thousands of sculptures made of stucco,
clay, and limestone of immense variety. From the site emerged
'meditating Buddhas and Bodhisattvas to small heads of
grimacing demons, monsters, penitent donors, helmeted warriors,
noblewomen, heads of lions, elephants, winged tritons, and
bacchanalian scenes'.[28]

Zafar began work as an archaeologist around this era, a few
years after the founding of the Afghan Institute of Archaeology
in 1964. He studied history at Kabul University and, in the
late 1970s, was part of a year-long expedition to study the
caves and sites in Bamiyan. In 1980, soon after Afghanistan
entered an era of war, Zafar left for Paris, where he completed
his higher studies. He went on to join France's national
archaeological association, AFAN, and worked at sites across
Pakistan, Afghanistan, Switzerland and Uzbekistan.

In 1980, soon before he left Kabul, Zafar had been part of
a team of Afghan and French archaeologists who conducted a
survey of sites in southern Afghanistan. When he returned in
2002, soon after the defeat of the Taliban, he undertook a
similar survey of sites in different provinces of Afghanistan –
an exercise which must have been something of an inventory

of loss; a taking stock of what remained, after the long decades of war. In 2004, he began work on the excavation I had come to see.

The site of the monastery complex is on the slopes of a hill called Tepe Naranj, Orange Hill, in the shadow of the Koh-e-Zamburak. The word *naranj*, orange, perhaps referred to the colour the slopes appear at sunrise, tinged with the ochre soil, or maybe to the orange robes worn by the monks centuries ago. We walked to the site from the shrine of Hazrat Tamim Jaber-e-Ansar, finding our way via landmarks of different shrines.

As we approached the hill, I saw Zafar skittering down the slopes – a slight, wiry man in his sixties, sure-footed in rubber slippers. Years of working in the sun had weathered and darkened his face, and when he smiled, his face broke into deep-etched lines that created a striking resemblance to the kind of statues he unearths. When we met, Zafar and his team had been at work for nine years, raising up the remains of a stupa and other structures from between ruined graves and encroaching homes. From the quality of the relics, it is thought that the monastery was likely to have been a space for the elite, with residential quarters for the monks possibly located some distance away.

I followed Zafar up a flight of narrow stairs and onto the level earth of an artificial terrace. A short climb up, I stood facing the surviving base of a small, perfectly proportioned stupa. Tiny details of its columns and stones shimmered in the sun. From this vantage point, Kabul's history lay spread out before me like a map.

To the left was Bala Hissar, the ancient citadel that overlooks the city. The hill that the citadel is on is called Tepe Zamarrod, or Emerald Hill, for the colour it takes with the spring.[29] Opposite was Tepe Maranjan – named, according to one story, for a wealthy magician of pre-Islamic times who was reputed to have turned his riches into ashes to form the mountain.[30] This site has also yielded rich Buddhist material from excavations in the past, and contains the ruins of significant monuments.

At the top of Tepe Maranjan stands the imposing domed mausoleum of King Nadir Shah, who was assassinated in 1933. It is also the resting place of Zahir Shah, and his wife, Humaira Begum. The couple had lived abroad since the coup of 1973. The former king returned in 2002, after the ousting of the Taliban. His wife, however, passed away while preparing to join him in Kabul; she returned only to be buried there. Beside the mausoleum is a large sign in Pashto that reads 'Zhowandai Dawey Afghanistan' – Long Live Afghanistan. Ahead glittered the water of Qol-e-Hashmat Khan, and beyond it the road to Logar, which connected to the historic trade route to Peshawar, another city coloured with shades of its Buddhist past, and further, to India.

I followed Zafar just above the stupa, to another terrace where three chapels stood in a row. During the course of the works, the team had enclosed them with a wall and a low roof to provide some protection from the elements. We entered from the bright sunlight into the dark interiors of the first chapel. Slowly, as my eyes adjusted to the gloom, there appeared beautiful carvings and the remains of huge statues. In the centre was a large pedestal with four niches, each probably intended for an idol of the Buddha, each a different colour depending on the direction it faced. Green for north, Zafar said. Red for west, yellow for south, and blue for east. The central pedestal was likely to have held a four-headed image of the Buddha.

In the second chapel, a large statue of the Buddha in the meditation position dominated the room. His attendants knelt and stood around him, their clothing still partly a pristine white.

The top halves of the entire group had disappeared, and yet there was a completeness to the assembly of warriors, princes and bodhisattvas, ranged around to pay obeisance to the contemplating figure. Zafar scraped off some of the dirt covering a fragment of the Buddha's robes from the top of the figure. They emerged in red, and his locks in blue, cascading to his shoulders.

Zafar is an authority on Afghan Buddhist sites, and as he moved around the spaces he showed off the details on each of the figures as though they were old friends. On the right of the Buddha stood a horseman, his boots and short cloak indicating he was probably a member of the military aristocracy. His *chapan* still had its minute buttons intact. Next to him stood a smaller statue wearing a knotted lungi, the folds of the garment falling in delicate ripples round his feet. The proximity of this statue to the central Buddha figure suggests that he was a person of some importance, perhaps from central India, tied by bonds of commerce and religion to Kabul.

On the left of the group by the Buddha, a figure knelt at his feet. The head of this figure had been found nearby, wearing a crown decorated with three crescents and embellished with pearls. It was likely to represent a Hephthalite king who had adopted Buddhism, Zafar said. But when I looked for it in the chapel, it was not there. Zafar told me that after he had returned from a visit abroad, he had found it damaged.

These relics are fragile – their forms of plaster and clay so easy to break, so easy to return to the earth they emerged from. Yet they are what remind the forgetful world, and Afghans themselves, of what used to be. They embody the confluence of ideas and civilisations that formed this *khak*. Perhaps that's why people like Zafar struggle so hard to save what they can. When I asked him why he does what he does, he replied mock-flippantly, as though avoiding a longer discussion:

'Because I am in love with Buddhism, and archaeology.' If so, it is a fraught romance, and Zafar has learned to be the patient lover, in a relationship with a volatile partner. He cherishes what he has, without asking how long it will stay.

Outside, the wind threw up the sound of prayers and announcements from loudspeakers across the valley. 'Funerals,' said Zafar laconically. 'There are fifteen a day.' The loudest voices came from a newly constructed mosque nearby. Its pink-tiled exterior glowed with the light caught on its reflective glass windows, blinking at us in the afternoon heat. People passed us by – schoolgirls on their way home after classes, a neighbour calling out cheery salaams on his way down the hill. The archaeological site was a rare empty space on the hill, an oasis in the midst of booming construction. A few years ago, Zafar had had a wire fence placed around its perimeter, along with the protective walls and roof. This was intended to keep out people looking to salvage construction materials, those tempted to build their new homes using the remains of ancient structures. But even as the dig wound down to its last few hours, the slender wire fences around the monastery seemed at best a tenuous promise. The site was being excavated and preparing for burial at the same time. It was a place that could easily vanish under the city that circled it hungrily.

Zafar's problems are not unique. Unauthorised excavations and theft feed the international black market for antiques. But on that final day of work at Tepe Naranj, the reason behind the site's closing was more prosaic. Zafar's grants had run out and, despite his efforts at fundraising, he had been unable to find donors. He simply didn't have the money to continue.

There was an edge of absurdity to this, given the large budgets of international donors in the country. For all the attention to other archaeological sites, and for all his experience,

Zafar's work seemed to count for little. The constellation of agendas and donor goals that had shaped his country after 2001 had also reduced him to an isolated figure, fighting against the odds to preserve his finds. I think of Zafar each time I see pictures of the empty hollows in the cliffs at Bamiyan, or when I see images of flattened earth elsewhere, where there had once been pillars or temples. Embedded in their barrenness, I realise, is the fact that it does not always take zealots with rocket launchers or explosives to obliterate culture. At Tepe Naranj, I saw that it is possible to do so simply by looking away.

Walking up to the summit of the hill, Zafar spoke of his dreams for the site if he ever got the money to return. 'I would convert this entire area into an open-air museum, with the monastery complex restored so Afghans can come and see this side of their heritage.' As a clever touch, he proposed to build restaurants at the top *and* bottom of the hill. 'This way, we take their money at both places, when they are thirsty from climbing up, and then again when they are parched from walking down,' he said, smiling at his own acumen. The idea draws from Tepe Shotor at Hadda, which was preserved for a time as an in-situ museum for tourists. The site was looted over the years of the civil war, its pieces destroyed or smuggled. When Zafar himself went to Tepe Shotor in early 2001 to assess the damage, he ended up being thrown in jail by the Taliban. Besides trying to take pictures, his crime was that he had worn white socks, which was deemed an insult to the white Taliban flag.

We reached the highest space in the complex, a circular area with a ledge around its interior, and a central hearth that may have been used for rituals. As Zafar conducted an argument in absentia with other archaeologists about its function – 'And so I will tell them, whether they like it or they don't like it' – I sat on the ledge, taking in the sunlit airiness, and the faint etchings of leaves on the walls. This room was perhaps where the community elders met to take important decisions related to war, or the economy, or for prayers. And the hearth may also have acted as a beacon, added Zafar. I thought of dark nights during the cold Afghan winters, with monks lost in prayer and farmers readying their families for bed, and the sight of a blaze on the Orange Hill.

Around us, the workmen rushed to complete the protective walls around the room, fighting against the ticking clock. They used pails made of discarded rubber tyres, and daubed the walls with mud. We walked back down the slope, and on the way Zafar stopped me at a small enclosure. He lifted the protective covering to reveal a pair of massive feet: the remains of a standing Buddha, facing east. From the size of the feet and the pedestal they stood on, it was clear that the original figure would have been huge, visible from a great distance. At the same time, this particular statue seemed oddly positioned, set apart from the others. To me it appeared aloof, somehow removed from the different parts of the monastery.

Zafar remained looking at the statue after I moved away. I watched them, standing side by side for a bit – the Buddha and his disciple, lost in contemplation on the scrubby Kabul hillside.

On the way down, I asked Zafar once again why he does what he does. Like many of my Afghan friends, Zafar dislikes being cornered, and having to drop civilities for plain speaking. Perhaps that's why he replied so curtly, with an edge of exasperation to his voice. 'Because this,' he said gesturing energetically at the earth, the sky, and the stupa on the hillside, 'all this was Afghanistan also.' He paused and then continued more calmly. 'Because the Buddha was ours also.'

4

MAP OF MOVING IMAGES

One of the first ruins I was drawn to in Kabul was the skeleton of a cinema. Its walls were crumbling and its facade was broken, but a ghostly red sign above the foyer spelt out in English: Cinema Theatre. Above this, in Persian, I could discern part of its name, Barikot. This ruin lay west from the book market at Ju-e-Sheer, on the road that turned with the Koh-e-Asmai and ran for some time with the river. Fruit and vegetable sellers lined the roadside by its slopes, colouring it with seasonal hues. Further down the road is the Minar-e-Ilm-wa-Jahl, the 'Monument to Knowledge and Ignorance', erected by Amir Amanullah to commemorate his victory over an anti-reform rebellion in 1924. The stone column has inscriptions of the names of the victims of this uprising. At its base are carved symbols of education and progress: a book, an inkwell, a pen, above two crossed swords.[1] Five years later, Amanullah would face another revolt, and be forced to flee the country.

Behind the embellished column rise the hills, along which stand the remains of Kabul's defensive walls. In the gorge between the column and the hills is the Kabul River, sometimes dry, other times with a glimmer of water. A few minutes from here are the gates of Kabul's zoo, and then the roundabout of Deh Mazang, named for a village that stood on the location. The slopes of Koh-e-Asmai here are covered with flat-roofed homes, their mud-plastered walls blending into the landscape. The roundabout was a traffic bottleneck, and the long delays here were overseen by the Directorate of Traffic, that was located on the circle. Beyond this is the Barikot. Over the years, it became harder to spot the crumbling building between newly constructed apartments and shops. You had to look for it to see it.

The first time I saw the broken frame of this theatre, I assumed it had been destroyed by the Taliban, given their aversion to films and entertainment. In fact, it was battered by mujahideen fighters during the civil war, when they battled for control of the locality. Nevertheless, some cinemas had stayed open even during those years, I heard from my friend Siddiq Barmak, an Afghan film-maker who lived in Kabul then. 'People would go watch films because there was nothing else to do,' he said. 'It was the only place they could find relaxation, where they could escape the sounds of war.' Cinemas mostly played Indian blockbusters – a lot of action thrillers and a few comedies, he said. I imagined Kabulis escaping to these halls to watch fake explosions and fake blood on the screens, as real rockets fell and real blood flowed on the streets outside. This image is a snapshot of Kabul's relationship with films. It is hard to tell when reality stops and fantasy begins.

***

I had learned early in life that cinema offers many kinds of escapes – a lesson I found useful in Kabul. My earliest experiences of watching movies were also among my first experiences of the world beyond my home. For the girls in my family in Aligarh, outings into town were few and far between. Occasionally these included the high point of watching movies with my aunt, a gynaecologist, who drove us to the late-night show in her powder-blue Fiat. The car would be packed mostly with girls – the boys could watch movies any time they wanted, with their friends. So any men who accompanied us were usually younger cousins, or a chaperone strategically selected for his inability to interfere with our enjoyment.

Even these rare expeditions were bound by strict rules. What you watched mattered, so did where you watched it and who you were with. My adolescence coincided with the phase of popular Hindi films that were preoccupied with rape, revenge and twisted aggression. Most of these were off the cards for us, so the few films we were shepherded to were cherished.

With millions of other viewers of Bollywood films, I learned to suspend disbelief diligently. We were not in the cinema to see reality, but to escape it. These films were high on drama and emotion, punctuated by songs and dances. They seemed to demand suitably emotional responses. When the songs played, the men in the audience (meaning most of the audience) danced and sang along. They hooted in delight at the appearance of women in revealing outfits, and made raucous kissing sounds during the romantic scenes – or whenever they felt like it. They laughed loudly at all the jokes, and yelled when a power cut turned the screen black and switched off the fans whirring by our sides. The women could join in the weeping. One of my lasting memories of watching films in Aligarh is of my aunt at the end of the row, sobbing passionately at the tragic scenes, partly drawn by real emotion, partly from a determination to get her money's worth.

The most memorable part of these outings was the return home, when we zipped down the empty streets after midnight. My aunt would raise the volume on the car's music system as far as it would go and we sang along with the tunes, our voices loud and unencumbered. At the crescendo of the familiar songs, my aunt would fling her hands off the steering wheel in abandon. We would all scream in delight.

I remember seeing the startled looks on the faces of the few men we passed. I remember savouring this unfamiliar sense of licence, revelling in my fleeting power to shock, simply by being there, on the streets of our city at night, where we had no business to be. Such tiny subversions were the milestones of our lives, guided by the principle that having fun was something a bit raffish, not entirely ladylike. It was a commodity to be doled out carefully, certainly not to be indulged in every day. From these teenage nights out to the cinema, I absorbed several important lessons. That films were fun. That cinema halls offered escape. And for these reasons, there would always be people who tried to take them away.

I recalled this when I saw my first functioning cinema in Kabul, in the park at Shahr-e-Nau. There had been rain earlier in the day, turning the light fugitive. I walked there carefully, the mud slippery beneath my feet, avoiding the puddles that had filled up the broken surface of the road. I wound a path through Chicken Street, looking at shops displaying carpets, *chapans*, jewellery and maps of Afghanistan crafted out of lapis lazuli. In one of these shops I bought a bag, and the shopkeeper put a handful of almonds in one of the pockets, as a blessing for the road. I saw a woman cross the street wearing elegant high-heeled boots, her red scarf a rebuke to the grey sky and the muddy brown streets.

I had ended up on the broad road that forms part of the perimeter of the park, lined with stalls selling pizzas with hearty toppings, ice-cream parlours and juice stalls. The air was rich with the smell of wet earth, which mingled with the fumes of passing cars and generators. Small-screen TV sets played inside shops. I heard the soundtrack of a popular Indian soap, its dialogue dubbed in Dari. An ISAF military convoy passed, and from one vehicle a soldier threw packets of food – or maybe toys – to the street children who ran alongside. The soldier's face was hard to see from behind his protective gear of dark glasses and helmet. Behind him emerged a building with a pistachio-green foyer and movie posters on its roof. A sign in English declared 'Cinema Park'. I walked over to check out what was playing. Framed against the tentative greenery of the Kabul spring, I found the familiar images of angry men – their torsos bared and muscles tensed. The titles of the films were full of rage too: *Aag hi Aag* (*Fire and Fire*), *Nafrat ki Aandhi* (*The Storm of Hate*), *Himmatwala* (*The Daring One*). I watched a line of Afghan men queue up for tickets for the next screening. Like Aligarh, there were no women there.

***

A walk through the history of cinema halls in Kabul would begin, as the city does, in the heart of the old city.

Among the first to be built was Behzad, located near Shor Bazaar, a bustling street that ran parallel to the Jada-e-Maiwand. A relative of Barmak's lived in the area, and had watched his first film at this theatre during the brief reign of Habibullah Kalakani in 1929. This relative had tried to sneak into the women-only matinee on a Tuesday while wearing a chadori – the all-enveloping veil that is so emblematic of Afghan women – but had been caught. Cinema Kabul, located across the river, was also built in the 1920s. It catered to the more upmarket audience of the new suburbs, and hence screened both Indian and American films. During the silent-movie era, there would be live performances by musicians on the piano and the violin accompanying the film.[2] Several theatres came up across the capital in the 1950s and 60s, proving the popularity of movie-watching in Kabul. There was even one just for women.

Most of these theatres showed popular Indian movies to a devoted audience. Families who came to Kabul from smaller towns during vacations would watch the same film several times during their stay. In a dizzying subcontinental twist, an older friend who grew up in Pakistan told me that he sometimes travelled from Lahore to Kabul or Jalalabad as a teenager, so he could watch the Indian fare that was banned in his own country.

Park Cinema on the other hand, was part of a constellation of elite establishments that lined Shahr-e-Nau Park during the 1970s. It showed Hollywood films that had been dubbed into Persian in Iran, as well as Italian and French fare. Nearby was a tennis court and playgrounds and a kiosk that sold imported comic books featuring Tarzan and Mandrake the Magician. The cinema was so exclusive, Khalid told me, that people were not allowed to enter in traditional Afghan clothes. You could rent trousers from stalls just outside the hall. From these stories, I learned that in Kabul, like in Aligarh, cinema was an escape. It was also a place of aspiration, a window to a world that was still far away, still full of wonders.

Kabul's cinema halls kept going through the political tumult of much of the 1980s. During the government of President Najibullah, from 1987 to 1992, films produced in Afghanistan were screened once a week. In November 2001, soon after the Taliban government was overthrown, Barmak told me, close to a thousand people turned up at Cinema Bakhtar, behind what is now the luxury Kabul Serena Hotel. 'Even Karzai was not in the city then,' he said. 'The world was watching the Bonn Conference. But in Kabul, we went to the cinema.'

Some of the theatres reopened, but many like the Barikot remained in ruins. Even those that did function were run-down and out of bounds for women and families. Instead, people watched films on video CDs or on TV through newly bought satellite dishes. The return of entertainment to the ravaged city was celebrated as another instance of the Taliban's defeat, and proof of Afghanistan's enduring love for films.

Back in India, I had read about the joyous outpourings that had accompanied the arrival of kitschy Hindi films on pirated CDs. Despite this, I was unprepared for the overwhelming presence of Bollywood in Kabul. The city seemed covered with a veneer of fantasies manufactured in my country. Walking down a street meant encountering pictures of matinee idols at every step. They gazed out from shop windows, stuck between advertisements for powdered milk and telecom services. There were massive cut-outs of actors at gyms, their muscles bulging inspiringly. The glass fronts of beauty salons and wedding halls were covered with images of glamorous actresses, like powerful totems invoking style, joy and whatever else their devotees desired. Hindi film songs formed the soundtrack to Kabul's streets, playing from the TV sets in grocery shops, from radios, from taxis. They chased you like the gusts of wind, picking up dust from the unpaved streets, rising above the mud-walled homes on the mountains. Middle-aged men talked fondly of the memories those songs brought back, of watching popular Indian films on the national TV channel in the 1980s. Conversations on the road – from the men selling CDs on Chicken Street to the *bolani* sellers in Karte Seh to the policemen at checkpoints – often turned to the movies they loved, the actors they admired, the songs they knew every word to.

Privately, I was often incredulous at this wholehearted embrace of popular Hindi fare. Like when I heard about the store owners who smuggled videos during the Taliban government. Braving imprisonment for something as trivial as Bollywood entertainers seemed ill-advised, even a sort of betrayal of the high standards expected from stories of war and repression – secret groups for reading *Lolita*, perhaps, but for watching a romantic drama called *Kuch Kuch Hota Hai* (*Something . . . Something Happens*)?

It was only later that I asked myself why things that are so ordinary elsewhere should make news in Kabul. Perhaps it came from the entrenched idea (one I shared) that conflict zones are spaces of noble suffering, where such frivolous concerns are out of place, even unseemly. In 2006, I met two young women who had grown up in Microrayan during the Taliban government. They had invited me to dinner because they wanted to meet someone who actually lived in Mumbai, the city of origin of their cinematic diet. Through the meal, they quizzed me on plotlines, popular star pairings, the romances of various actresses and the Indian cultural traditions as seen in these films. 'But how do you know all this?' I asked them, amazed at the sheer volume of films they seemed to have watched. When the Taliban took over, they said, they weren't allowed to go to school or to work. So they spent their days in a small room with blacked-out windows, watching films in secret. When the government was overthrown in 2001, they emerged having watched a large number of films and speaking good Hindi, learned from the dialogue of the movies they'd watched. They'd had to be very careful that the soundtrack was never overheard, and made sure they got the videos only from trusted sources. But they had never got caught. Incredible as this story sounds, it is not entirely unusual. The more I asked, the more such stories surfaced. Across darkened rooms, Kabulis had broken the imposed silence by watching Bollywood fantasies.

For the girls locked in their rooms, the flickering images on the TV screens had taken on meaning beyond entertainment. The joy they got from this pastime made these films something worth hiding away, worth taking risks for. They became something like a home, a place where they could be closest to what they used to be.

They were a way of staking a claim to ordinary pleasures, just like people living outside war do.

* * *

In a city where reality is often tentative and brittle, fantasy can offer more dependable terrain. Saleem Shaheen is one of the few Kabulis who not only inhabits this world of make-believe, but also constructs it. Shaheen is the country's – self-proclaimed – most popular actor, director and producer. He has spent nearly thirty years making films – a career that has coexisted with Afghanistan's cycles of conflict and displacement. He claims to have made over a hundred films, tempering this number with the lukewarm disclaimer that 'some of them are documentaries'. The vast majority, however, are sagas of action, romance and drama, with plots that derive from Bollywood films of the 1980s and 90s. Shaheen's productions are like scale models of these grand enterprises, down to the inflexions and flourishes, the acting style, even the songs. 'People say I just copy Bollywood films,' he told me once with a touch of petulance. 'But if Sylvester Stallone can kill five people with one bullet, why can't I?' This is the secret to Shaheen's faith in his own genius. For him, there is no difference between Bollywood (or Hollywood) films and his work, except for the fact that he makes do with a lot less.

Or, as he often says: 'Watch. Watch how we make films in Afghanistan.' This line, that he is fond of repeating, is part testimony to the difficulties in his chosen field of work, part tribute to his own extraordinary skill.

When I met him in 2011, Shaheen was in his fifties, portly and bombastic. He talked rapidly and continuously, shooting off orders to an entourage that was always hovering nearby. In recent years, I learned, he had taken to hiding his receding hairline under an assortment of hats. And he had reluctantly

ceded the romantic lead to younger men, appearing as the
father or uncle to the heroines instead. But he was still the
centre around which the film revolved. He was still unmistakably
the star.

I had gone to his office in Qala-e-Musa with Barmak one
summer evening, to watch the 'premiere' of his latest film,
Shekast Qalbaha (*The Defeat of Hearts*). We entered through a
long, narrow passage. The wall on one side was a glass-covered
display case, with hundreds of images of Shaheen posing with
actors from Mumbai, as well as a few Afghan celebrities. In the
open courtyard, plastic chairs were laid out. Most were
occupied, all by men. Barmak pointed out some of the guests
to me – a government official, an adviser to a minister, political
figures of differing calibres. Some were accompanied by armed
bodyguards.

At one corner of the courtyard there was a statue of a large
eagle (*shaheen* in Persian) hovering over a waterfall. The water
ran over coloured lights, which also illuminated the posters for
various Shaheen Films productions on display around the
compound. We took our seats, facing a white wall. The lights
went down and the show began.

Though the dialogue was entirely in Dari, I didn't need
subtitles to follow the narrative. The story of star-crossed lovers
was told through the familiar devices of Hindi films – songs
and dances, dramatic confrontations, thrilling fight scenes. At a
riveting moment in the film, the light from the projector passed
over the faces of the audience. I saw a few of the armed guards
watching slack-jawed, leaning casually against their guns.

After the film, Shaheen stood on a platform, receiving the
congratulations of the crowd. We were ushered to a room for
dinner, a lavish meal on the *dastarkhwan* (like a tablecloth, but
spread on the floor). I was served by two young men who, I
realised, had played the villains in the film.

Afterwards, Barmak introduced me to Shaheen, who was still holding court on the platform, even as the crowd around him had thinned considerably. When he heard that I had come from Mumbai, Shaheen summoned a hovering photographer. The next time I visited his office, our picture was on the wall, along with those of Shaheen posing with celebrities.

I had arrived in the afternoon. The lights that had decorated the courtyard during the screening were switched off, the fountain silent. I was ushered into a room that was decorated with yet more photographs of Shaheen. In some he laughed in adorable abandon and danced with beautiful women, in others he brandished guns while grimacing. The remaining space was covered with trophies and framed certificates. The glitter of these items matched the opulent decor – the room had dark red wallpaper, sofas with shiny upholstery, gilt-edged display cases and a massive golden *shaheen* perched on a bookshelf.

Shaheen spoke in a rapid-fire Urdu that drew heavily from popular film dialogues and expressions, giving our conversation the emotional pitch of a Bollywood melodrama. In this suitably heightened idiom, I heard the story of his love for cinema, which is also the story of making films in the middle of war.

Shaheen grew up as the black sheep of an affluent family, he said. 'My father was a wealthy, well-known figure in Kabul, and had held a prestigious official post.' His family owned large swathes of land ('Twenty buildings!') near Shahr-e-Nau and Qala-e-Musa – where Shaheen's office was now located His uncles too were well-off entrepreneurs. 'One of my brothers,' he told me, pausing dramatically before the big reveal, 'is a mullah. He keeps trying to reform me. *I* keep trying to reform *him*.' Shaheen skipped school to watch films, and began working at a video lending library as a teenager.

In 1984, when he was fifteen, he decided to write and direct his own film. He shot the action thriller over four days, and edited it on two VCRs. Naturally, he cast himself as the hero, in a double role. 'We made a black-and-white poster for it: I was holding a gun, and had a bloodstained bandage wrapped around my head. It was called *Shikast-e-Napazeer*, or *Defeat of the Impure*. Almost immediately, people came to the video library and said, "Give us *this* film."' It was two days before the festival of Eid. Smelling an opportunity, Shaheen made ten VHS copies of the tape and charged 500 afghanis (around $5) for a three-hour rental – an astronomical amount for the time. 'After the holiday I counted my money. We had made almost two lakh (200,000 afghanis), around $2,000, in four days. I said, "This business is good. Let's make movies!"'

Shaheen's next films were also successful, and he was able to read the pulse of what his audience wanted, as well as find the kind of fame that delighted him. 'My family said, "Shaheen has gone crazy." But I embraced that madness.' The role of a lover who risks everything for cinema was one worthy of him.

The war between the Soviet-backed Communist government and the mujahideen continued through the 1980s. Shaheen spent these years making films. He kept going even after the war arrived in Kabul. In 1993, he recalled, a rocket fell on his office and killed eight crew members waiting in the courtyard. Shaheen was upstairs making breakfast for them. 'The kind of problems we faced making films during those years are impossible to explain,' he said with uncharacteristic understatement. Yet he went on to complete that film.

Making films, or more specifically making the kind of films that Shaheen makes, while living through war, seems an enterprise laden with pointless risks, even something to be condemned. ('"How can you be shooting songs during falling bullets?" people would ask me,' he said.) But for Shaheen, it was what he wanted to do, the only thing he could imagine doing. Barmak recalled listening to a radio interview when the presenter asked Shaheen, 'Why do you make cinema?' And Shaheen replied, 'Because I love it, it keeps you busy, and then you have no time for things like drugs or intoxication. If you want to be in a state of intoxication, come, let's go make a film.'

Barmak used to head the state-run Afghan Film Organisation during the Mujahideen government. One time Shaheen invited him along with a delegation of film-makers to a screening at the Qala-e-Musa office. The journey lay across difficult territory, crossing checkpoints held by different groups. The delegation had almost made it to their destination when they were stopped. The soldiers on patrol refused to swallow their story of being en route to watch a film. They were on the verge of being arrested when they were rescued by Shaheen, who was out searching for them. Incredibly, they had then gone on to his office and watched the film, spending the afternoon talking about cinema . 'The only people who were not enemies then were film-makers,' Shaheen told me. In most popular images of Kabul, it is not known as a place that nourishes creativity, or art, or culture. For me, the story was a window into a different version of this city: as a place where there was still a love for stories; where, even as rockets fell and shells exploded, there were people who took risks to be able to spend a few hours talking about cinema.

Shaheen Films remained in business until the Taliban took control of Kabul. Shaheen then moved to Rawalpindi, joining the millions of Afghan refugees across the border. There, he began making films for this large diaspora. *Shikast-e-Ishq* (*The Defeat of Love*), from this era, was one of his biggest hits. The film gave him his screen name, Qais, which sticks to him even today. In popular folklore, Qais is the name of the star-crossed lover of Laila, the equivalent of Romeo to Juliet.

He loses his mind for love for Laila, and becomes *Majnun*, one who is possessed by djinns.[3] In Shaheen's case, the beloved that possesses him is cinema.

After 2001, Shaheen Films reopened its Kabul office and began making movies in the city again. These stuck to the same formula that had served him so well in the past, but now Shaheen faced a different set of challenges. Along with the threats he claimed to receive from religious fundamentalists, he also had heightened competition from Afghan TV channels, foreign shows dubbed into Dari, and the Internet. Many Kabulis I talked to were disdainful of Shaheen's films. Young film-makers accused him of giving Afghan cinema a bad name, with his overblown and derivative work. Shaheen, in characteristic style, both embraced their derision and battled it. His real audience, he said, is in the villages and provinces of Afghanistan. 'Ask anyone there and they will know me. They will not know your big film-makers from Kabul, but everybody will know *me*.' This claim was borne out by a story I heard from another film-maker, who told me of a trip he took with Shaheen to a northern province. The event was in honour of a well-known poet from Kabul, and a huge crowd turned up at their guest house that evening. The poet was pleasantly surprised at his popularity. But the crowd had come for Qais – their home-grown movie star in a country with virtually no cinema. Their own magician with his glittering world of make-believe. His tinsel dreams may be a little less shiny, a little tattered, but they were still there; still dreams, after all.

One Friday morning, I joined Shaheen's crew for a shoot in the Shomali plains, an hour's drive to the north of Kabul. I arrived outside his office to see a dozen actors and other crew members waiting on the street. A few were clutching plastic bags containing costumes, props and food for the shoot. When

it was time to leave, the crew climbed onto a rickety bus. I rode
with Shaheen in his car.

On the highway, he sang loudly and tunefully, and shook
hands with all the policemen manning the checkpoints. On the
side of the road I saw the vineyards that the region was famous
for, which had been burned by the Taliban during their war
with the Northern Alliance. The revival that I could see had
taken place after 2001. We passed village markets and orchards
hidden behind mud walls, fed by streams sparkling with clear
water. On the roadside refreshment stalls, plastic bottles of *dogh*
(a yogurt beverage), soft drinks and fruit juices were strung up
for display. Ahead was the vista that seemed so unchanged,
despite all the transformations that had torn through the
country: the callow green of the trees, the glint of the snow on
the mountains, the baked earth on houses and walls.

Shaheen was heading for a location that lay off the main
road, and we struggled to find our way, backing into and out of
narrow tracks, churning up minor storms of dust. At a dead
end, Shaheen hopped out of the car and directed the bus using
the cowboy hat he had worn that day.

After a few more wrong turns, we found the spot – a field
surrounded by an orchard of mulberry trees, traversed by a
stream. The crew stretched out on carpets under the trees
and ate handfuls of the just ripening berries, washed down
with tea. Then they began unpacking the guns (real) and the
blood (fake, imported from Holland). Within a few minutes,
a crowd had gathered, commenting on each of the actors. As
they pressed closer, I realised there were no other women in
sight. 'Is she the heroine?' I heard a voice behind me. 'She
looks old.'

Shaheen conferred with the cameraman, a quiet man dressed
from top to toe in blue. One of the actors filled me in on the
plot of the film. *Sarzameen-e-Dilawaran*, or *Land of the Brave*,

was about a group of fighters who break out of prison to defend Afghanistan against the Soviet invasion. It was set during the years when the Communist government clashed with the resistance fighters. The central role of an ageing 'true jihadi', who sacrifices a life of ease for love of his country, was played by Shaheen.

The second lead was played by a London-based Afghan entrepreneur, who was partly financing the film. Other actors included a popular TV star, an engineer with Ariana Airlines, security guards at different embassies and an accountant. All the actors did double duty working as crew – from peeling potatoes to moving the props. I asked the engineer if he got paid for acting, and he laughed. 'It's all for joy. We do it because we love it.' 'It' being, presumably, the whole desperate magic of the enterprise: the passion for cinema, the fame, the high of being seen on-screen, the desire to let off fake bullets and get slathered in fake blood in a country that has seen decades of almost non-stop war. Or just the idea that Afghans can make movies too, and love making them, out of nothing, from thin air.

The production unfolded with practised ease. The plastic bags were emptied out and their contents disbursed. There were no lights, just men holding up reflectors, two cameras placed on tripods, a boom rod hoisted and held steadily. The crowd pressed close and was shouted back. Shaheen stood ankle-deep in mud in a shallow stream, urging on two actors who were locked in a grim clench. 'Fight, you guys, fight,' he urged, in his voice that carried further than a megaphone. The blows rained as Shaheen built up to a crescendo. 'I implore you, for the love of cinema, hit him hard. HARD! Hit him like an Afghan, man, not a sissy foreigner!' With a thumping punch to the jaw, the actor flipped his co-star into the water. The dramatic splash soaked most of the production team and nearly drenched the camera. The crew and the watching crowd broke into applause. Shaheen waded into the water. 'See how beautiful it looks, *behenji*, sister, swelling up for real,' he yelled out to me on the other side of the stream. 'Not like in Mumbai where they only pretend to hit each other. Watch! Watch how we make films in Afghanistan!'

No matter who was in the frame, Shaheen was at the heart of every scene. He instructed the actors, and choreographed the fight and dance sequences (for the latter, he played Hindi film songs on a tape recorder that was placed on a rock off-screen). He shouted in frustration at the donkeys braying in a faraway field, and broke off only to exclaim, over the script that he had written, 'How beautiful are these dialogues.'

We moved from location to location, the low-budget shoot meeting challenges with ingenuity. For one sequence, Shaheen used a firecracker to simulate gunshots. He lit it and bounded behind a boulder, hands to his ears, yelling 'ACKSHUN'. He spent a long time choreographing a complicated chase sequence across a field, only to be halted by the sound of helicopters overhead. The entire crowd gazed up. From across the field, Shaheen gave me an eloquent look, turning his palms heavenwards in a performance of exasperation.

For the last sequence of the day, we moved to some abandoned houses on top of a hill, to shoot a sequence of a village being burnt down by the villains. The crew lit a fire inside the mud rooms. One of the actors slipped on a blue chadori – and stumbled out to be 'rescued'. The veiled figure was accompanied by several screaming children, enlisted by Shaheen from the watching crowd. Time was short, with the sun dipping on the horizon, and the light fading fast.

Shaheen darted around with the camera and bellowed at the actors. His face was darkened with soot and his eyes bloodshot from the smoke. He begged and threatened the crowd, and inhaled the fumes of the fire as he directed the action. He kept going, moving the camera and exhorting the actors, until finally he was done. The crew began packing up, rushing to load the bus before dark. Shaheen sat on a rock, his face still covered with soot. He had managed to get everything, just before sunset.

'Did you see? he said. 'Watch! How we make films in Afghanistan.'

I once asked Shaheen in jest if he considered himself the 'king of Kabuliwood'. 'Not Kabuliwood, it's Besywood,' he said seriously, a pun on the Persian word *besood*, an enterprise without profit, something of no use, running on empty. 'It's an illusion, what we do, making something out of nothing.'

***

Over the next few weeks, I discovered another of Shaheen's obsessions. He was aware of and quite relished the antipathy he aroused among his fellow Afghan film-makers. But what baffled and annoyed him was being ignored by the international order – the donors, the critics, the journalists – that had come to Kabul after 2001. What's more, they chose to laud other directors, for reasons Shaheen couldn't understand. He mocked the dependence of his award-winning peers on funders, questioned their irregular output. ('Did he make another film? No? Just the one?') But he coveted what they had – the festivals they were invited to abroad, the interviews and attention from the global media. For Shaheen, his films represented Afghanistan far more clearly than the art-house films the world seemed to admire. His films were what real Afghans wanted, and he was convinced that they were what the world needed to see from Afghanistan to understand it. Not only were they as worthy as the 'festivali' films, they were better.

That's why, when I met him in his office in 2013, he was jubilant. 'A woman from Cannes Film Festival is making a film

about me,' he told me happily. He would be the envy of the
'festivali' crowd. Audiences across the world would watch him, in
the mecca of artistic cinema, as the hero of a film about making
films in Afghanistan. It didn't matter to him, at least not then, that
this honour would not be for a film that he had made himself,
but for a film made about him, by a 'festivali' director from France.

Soon after I met Shaheen for the first time, I visited the
beautiful Ariana Cinema in the heart of Kabul. The theatre is
surrounded by a mix of official buildings and hotels, and lies
close to the fountains of Pashtunistan Square. Across the square
is the entrance to the Arg, now the presidential palace, obscured
by security walls.

The theatre had been renovated in early 2002 by a group of
French film-makers. But plans to recast it as a cultural space as
well as a cinema for Kabuli families had not worked out. When
I walked in, I saw posters for Pashto films made in Pakistan,
Indian blockbusters of a thirty-year vintage, Hollywood action
thrillers, horror films and lurid creature-features. There was a
long gallery where sunlight fell in shafts through the windows.
On the ground floor were family boxes, each named after a
famous international director.

I looked inside the hall. The audience was all men. Most of
them, I was told, were either unemployed or worked as manual
labourers for low wages. There were also several young boys –
schoolchildren who were not in school.

The air was dense with cigarette smoke and the smell of
hashish. On the screen, a woman danced with abandon. The
moustachioed hero watched her impassively. The men in the
audience clapped and hooted. The glow of cigarettes, the sound
from the screen and the darkness of the hall all combined to
create a feeling of being underground. As if the cinema was a
secret city within the city, lit by a fantasy that keeps unfolding.

* * *

In an area called Ansari Watt, on a road flanked on both sides
with a mix of government offices and foreign embassies, exists
a Kabul made of old images. Since 1968, Afghan Film has
worked out of its office here, producing newsreels and
features over decades of shifting regimes. The modest two-
storey building doesn't see too many productions now, but
it is the repository of the largest film archive in Afghanistan.
These are the visual memories of Kabul from the 1950s into
the 1990s: depicting life through the monarchy, Soviet-
backed rule and the civil war. The reels are stored in rooms
that, like the Ariana Cinema, give the impression of being
subterranean: in the ways of being forgotten and buried,
and also as images of a city that lies beneath the surface of
the current one.

I had first visited Afghan Film in 2006, a few days after the
spring festival of Nauroz. I walked from the elite locality of
Wazir Akbar Khan, which lies in the shadow of Bimaru Hill.
This landmark is named after a sixteenth century figure, Bibi
Mahru. According to legend, she died of a broken heart on
hearing the news of her betrothed's death in a battle.[4] But, the
story continues, her lover had survived, and was eventually
buried beside her. A more recent landmark is the Soviet-era
open-air swimming pool, its Olympic-sized tank empty. In the
winter of 1842, one of the crucial battles of the first Anglo-
Afghan war was fought close by the hill. Not too far are the
neat perimeters of the British Cemetery.

The plain expanse below was where Amir Amanullah built
Kabul's first airstrip. During the 1970s, this plain grew into the
plush villas and walled gardens of Wazir Akbar Khan.[5] The
neighbourhood has been home to Kabul's elite – both Afghans
and foreigners – since then. After 2001, it housed embassies as
well as offices and guesthouses of international agencies. It
glowed brightly in the real estate bubble that emerged after

2003, when a home here fetched around one million dollars, and rented for an average of $30,000–$40,000 per month. In the sprawl of its flat streets, it was possible to spend Thursday night dancing to flamenco music at the opening of a Spanish restaurant. Here, you could hunt out the perfect steak or walk into a store called Republic of Yogurt.

Afghan Film is a short walk away, but far removed from this buzzy locality. It stands on a leafy road, next to the Ministry of Transport and Civil Aviation, and has high-profile neighbours including the US Embassy and the ISAF headquarters. That afternoon in 2006, the road was open, pleasant to stroll on. Walking into the building, I was once again reminded of entering Delhi's government offices. It was a place where time passed slowly. Like in the Kabul Public Library, there were kettles on the boil across the rooms. Once in a while, someone would top up the flasks of green and black tea with hot water. Then they would pump-pump-pump the tea into glass tumblers that sat on a tray, usually next to a plate of almonds and raisins, and boiled sweets. The tea was clear, lukewarm, endless.

I often returned to this institution, to watch screenings of short films and feature films of varying quality in the large auditorium on the ground floor. I watched films being shot in its grounds, and chatted with the actors, answering their many questions about Mumbai, a city they referred to musically as 'Bam-bai'. I saw the gardener tend to the roses, and sat in on long meetings between directors, sometimes conducted in Russian learned during their years together as film students in Moscow. At the back was a hangar, where Barmak once parked a Soviet-era helicopter for several months, before using it for his film recast as an American Black Hawk.

In the circles that revolve around cinema in Kabul, Afghan Film occupies a position of prominence but limited power.

The office and the studio were completed in 1968 with aid from the US government, to solve the problem of having to send film stock abroad for processing. Much of the furniture I admired for its vintage charm had come with this aid programme too. On some film cans, the original stickers had survived, showing two hands clasped firmly together under a red-and-blue flag. The features and newsreels – clips of topical information – the organisation produced were crucial for a largely illiterate country like Afghanistan.

During the Soviet-backed era, these films were viewed as important instruments to further the goals of nation-building and social change. Young film-makers and technicians were sent abroad for training to places like India, Bulgaria and the USSR. On their return, many worked with Afghan Film. Production peaked during President Najibullah's government from 1987 to 1992, when the organisation employed about 140 people. It even functioned during the civil war, when Barmak headed the organisation, making shorts and a feature film under the Mujahideen government. The arrival of the Taliban stopped production. In the years after 2001, Afghan Film didn't make movies but certified them before they were screened in cinemas.

Its most important asset is its archive, which runs into thousands of hours of film. Like with many other things in post-2001 Kabul, these had a story of being saved. But, like other such stories, this one too unfolded to reveal hidden layers.

Over my returns to Kabul, I tried repeatedly to watch these films. By the time I succeeded, in 2013, the changes that had reshaped Kabul's terrain also affected the street Afghan Film was located on. The modest building was sandwiched between too many important targets. This fraught geography meant that cycling and walking were no longer permitted on the street.

I drove there with Abdullah, who had gone back to driving a taxi. Nazira and I sat in the back of his Corolla, accompanied by the familiar voice of Ahmad Zahir, soothing our passage through the traffic-choked streets. On the increasingly built-up horizon, the encircling mountains appeared and vanished as we moved through the city. Hovering in the air was the spy balloon of Kabul. This massive white dirigible was part of the US security and surveillance efforts, which included drones and CCTV cameras, to spot suicide bombers or insurgents on the road. In most parts of Kabul, looking up meant spotting, or being spotted by, this hovering presence.[6]

As we approached the checkpoint leading to Afghan Film, our taxi was flagged down. Abdullah had already got a pass allowing us on the road, which he'd taped to the windscreen. But we were stopped anyway. Abdullah gestured towards the paper, but the soldier only looked puzzled. 'We have to go to Afghan Film,' Abdullah said. 'Where?' asked the man. It was just a few steps from where he stood, but he hadn't heard of it.

A few minutes of explanations later, we were allowed to drive down the road and through the gates. Inside, little seemed to have changed. I spotted familiar faces among the employees lounging on wooden chairs by the sheds. A rubber pipe ran like an IV line, stretching from a tap in the garden to a line of waiting pressure cookers, ready to be filled with water. I had arrived a little before lunch preparations began in earnest. The actors walked over to exchange greetings. 'So you're back,' one of them said. 'How is everyone in Bam-bai?'

I met Ibrahim Arify, who had taken over as director of Afghan Film a few months earlier. He walked us to the archive, and as we passed an open door he mentioned that it led into the room where the film reels had been hidden from the Taliban. Hungry for this story, I asked him for details. 'Everyone has saved Afghan Film,' he said drily. 'I will tell you later.'

We entered the largest storage room of the archive. Round film cans were piled into fragile towers, or scattered in small clusters. They were stacked on the shelves of rusting metal racks and cupboards, many of them covered in dust. Strips of paper were stuck on with glue or tape, handwritten in Persian, and a few in Cyrillic script. At the back of the room was a desk littered with staplers and ribbons of paper.

This visual heritage of Afghanistan had survived years of war and the zealotry of the Taliban. Twelve years after the 'liberation' of the country, it was lying under layers of dust and disregard. Still mostly unwatched, uncatalogued, unknown. In its undeniable importance, and its peculiar invisibility, the room reminded me of the stupa and statues at Tepe Naranj, vanishing in plain sight.

With a selection of newsreels and short documentaries, we made our way to an auditorium on the first floor of the building. This had a small screen and a few rows of plastic chairs. There were four square windows along the back wall, through which I could see the projectionist threading the reel. Framed in the aperture, he raised the film and examined the frames against the light, reading it for clues on which direction to place it. Arify sat directly behind me. As we watched, other staff members wandered in, interspersing the voice-overs on the reels with their own commentaries and memories – about people on the screen, or the people behind the camera. One of them saw Nazira translating for me. He asked her: 'Doesn't she know Persian yet?' Then he turned to me and said firmly, like a teacher admonishing a lazy pupil, 'You have been here many times. You should have learned by now.'

As the screen flickered to life, I watched a Kabul that was beguilingly familiar and impossibly different. I watched landmarks that seemed fundamentally transformed, streets that were in the same city where I sat now, but were divided by a rupture of memory, like a splice in the film, a jump. They existed separately from the city I walked through every day, oblivious to its past iterations, oblivious even to the fact that it had a past so different from its present. I should have learned by now, I agreed silently, watching the images unspool on the screen, that it is not enough to be in Kabul to see it.

* * *

The projectionist had arranged the films chronologically. We began with newsreels from the late 1960s when the cameras first wandered the streets. In a series of short reels, I watched ordinary Kabulis make an appearance on foot, men walking around Zarnegar Park, some wearing turbans and traditional clothes, others in suits. One film was shot atop the hill between Deh Mazang and the Bagh-e-Babur, and captured the spectacle of the noon gun being set off. This small cannon, reportedly installed by Amir Abdur Rahman Khan, was a way of timekeeping in a city that was still small enough to be regulated from a hilltop, and where most people did not own watches. I had seen the spot where the cannon used to stand from Babur's grave. I heard its sound now, on the screen, when a bearded man set it off. Image and sound fell into place; the boom of the gun completing a panorama of the city seen all those years ago, making it whole.

The documentaries made by Afghan Film were similar to the state-produced films I had watched as a child in India. In both places, they were intended to serve larger social agendas – to educate as well as motivate. So these newsreels, I recognised, were also carefully crafted fictions. In Afghanistan during the 1960s and 70s, they pushed ideas like modernisation, and women's rights. So in some reels, women dressed in trousers and skirts take the centre of the frame. Sometimes they clutch books in their arms, other times they move with the purposeful

stride of women on their way to work. In one reel some
women stroll in a leisurely way through a park, eating ice cream
and smiling as the sun bounces off their loose hair. It was only
in the background of the action that I noticed two other
women wearing chadoris. They spotted the camera and turned
away. The camera panned in the opposite direction slowly.

Another reel, shot in the late 1960s, came on screen: a report
on the new houses being built for modern Kabuli families. The
camera tours the complex. Groups of older women talk and
wander around the inner roads, between the apartment blocks.
Children splash merrily in a swimming pool. The complex
looked to me like Microrayan, but I could not place its precise
location. I asked my companions for help. Nazira and Arify
both squinted at the screen, but were unable to help. One had
left Kabul too early, and the other had returned too late, to
recognise this version of the city. This too was war, I realised –
the city slipping through the memories of those who called it
home.

The newsreels shifted to the 1970s, years of rapid and
tumultuous change. Through the early years of Afghan Film,
Arify told me, the negatives were sent to the US to be
processed. That often meant a long delay between shooting
the news and broadcasting it in theatres. These intervals must
have been especially fraught in the 1970s, when political
events unfolded rapidly.

In these short clips, Kabul slips from revolution to revolution,
all recorded with the same strikingly similar visuals. The events
they were recording were also much the same. What I saw was
what was allowed to be captured of the city, the truth the
government deemed fit to be told. The real news was kept off-
screen: the coups and the intrigues, the uprisings and the
international agendas; much of the anguish and violence that
was to shape life for Afghans for the next two generations.

We watched a film shot in 1974 that recorded the celebrations for Daoud Khan's newly established republic. It showed parades in Kabul, massive crowds on the street, people marching through Pashtunistan Square. They shouted slogans I couldn't hear, as their voices were buried behind the narrator talking about the joy of the people at this new government. The car carrying Daoud Khan raced down broad boulevards. We saw Khan standing on a podium, waving to the crowds. Then he was among the people, shaking hands, being patted on the back.

A striking montage of men on the street reading newspapers followed. The headline, bold black print on the page, was enlarged to cover the screen. '*Jamhooriyat*', it said. Republic. The calligraphy of the text seemed to snake through the streets of Kabul.

The next newsreel was shot in 1979. Only five years later, but a different era. It marked the first anniversary of the Saur Revolution, which had replaced Daoud Khan's republic with a Communist government. Daoud Khan himself was dead, killed in the coup. The central figure in the celebrations was Nur Mohammad Taraki, who headed the government. By October that year, he would be dead too, assassinated on the orders of his former associate, Hafizullah Amin. And in just over three months, Amin would also be killed, and the Soviet army would enter Afghanistan.

This bloody chronology was on my mind as I watched Taraki cheer and wave from his raised podium, as the parade filed past him. The film was in colour, and the screen was filled with red – the podium draped in red cloth, red sheets folded over the military floats that trundled past. Red armbands and uniforms and headscarves and flags.[7] I watched the tanks roll out, the soldiers saluting the smiling man at the podium. Groups of women marched by, wearing uniforms and carrying guns. People crossed the camera, arms raised in salute, shouting slogans energetically. They all looked at the camera, addressing it – addressing me –

with their eyes and bodies. They continued marching until, overwhelmed by the weight of history, I looked away. It was like watching a train wreck, a collision that I was powerless to stop. The weight of knowledge rested heavily around those images.

Who were they made for, these films that celebrated the turn of events occurring so rapidly one after the other? For the public, to convince the Afghan people of the virtue of the revolutions? Or for history, for a viewer like me, who sifted through their slogans and triumph in a dark hall long after they had ceased to matter? What did it mean to watch them now, to read their messages years after they lost relevance, or could only offer a different truth to a different era? Like the thick lines in the brochures I had seen at Rais's bookstore, they mapped a terrain of erasures, the particular ways of forgetting that defines remembering in Kabul.

Soon after the film was shot, the USSR rolled its tanks across the border. The war that began then is, in many ways, still unfolding.

On the screen, floats with missiles and aircraft continued to move past the camera, like a ghostly rehearsal. Military officers from different nations were seen in the audience. On the podium, Taraki waved a red flag. An emaciated dove sat next to him, a red ribbon gleaming around its throat.

***

In one of the newsreels showing the celebrations for Daoud Khan's republic in Pashtunistan Square, I had seen a man standing just behind the speaker. He was smiling, and looked into the camera for a brief second. Enough to register familiarity, but not recognition. Until Arify leaned forward and said, 'That was Khalid's father.' The man who had gone missing after the 1978 Saur Revolution. Whom Khalid had been searching for in different ways ever since.

The man on the screen, the man from the photo on Khalid's wall that I had seen every day for several months, had disappeared a few years after the film was shot. In the frisson of recognition I felt then, the city changed for me. The incontrovertible truth of his presence, on the same streets I frequented, and the reality of his absence, charged the air.

When the projectionist paused to change reels, I texted Khalid: 'I saw your father.' Within minutes, he had called Arify and asked him to keep the reel marked out for him. He would come and see it soon, he said. But by the time I left Kabul a few weeks later, he hadn't done so. Or perhaps, he could not bring himself to do so.

The newsreel had continued to images of President Daoud Khan inaugurating a new street. It was named 26 Saratan Road, for the date of the revolution (17 July 1973), the beginning of Afghanistan's glorious era as a republic. I searched for this street in Kabul, as well as on the Internet. I couldn't find it, or any trace of its name. Yet again, I was lost between the streets of the past and the present. Eventually I asked Khalid if he recalled it. He did, he said. It was lined with plane trees and was beautiful to walk along. He mentioned a few landmarks it crossed, and I still struggled to place it. 'What do people call it now?' I asked finally. He stared at me for a few moments before breaking into laughter. 'Who cares what they call it?' he said. 'They don't get to walk on it any more.' It was now barricaded behind the security walls and checkpoints that closed off that part of Kabul. The street and its name had vanished from the city, living only in the archive.

***

We stopped watching the films at lunchtime. Nazira and I followed Arify out of the screening room and into a newly refurbished conference room. It was a world away from

Afghan Film's vintage decor. This room gleamed with the temporary sleekness of the Chinese-made furniture I found across Kabul's offices. There were tables with pale-coloured veneers and metal legs, swivel chairs, metal filing cabinets. The light in the room was filtered through the row of trees that stood on the building's perimeter. Beyond their nodding greenery, appearing and vanishing with the breeze, was the empty street.

Arify had ordered us pizzas from an upmarket Afghan-run bakery nearby, in lieu of the rice and beans that his colleagues were probably eating at that time, warm from the row of pressure cookers I had seen. As we ate, I asked Arify to tell me the story of how the Afghan Film archive was saved.

When the Taliban had captured the capital, they had shut down the studios of the national TV channel. Radio Kabul was renamed 'Voice of Shariat Radio' and broadcast mostly religious content – a mix of *taranas, naats*, sermons and religious speeches.[8] Government officials ordered the employees of these institutions to collect their archives for destruction.

As a state-run organisation, Afghan Film came under their control too. The popular version of the story, the one I read and heard most often, was this: a few employees devised a plan to save their country's visual heritage. They went secretly into the archive and did a quick, desperate selection of which films could be sacrificed, and which reels had to be saved. The former were mostly foreign films (from India, US, Russia, France) with negatives that were safely abroad. The remaining cans of films – made by Afghans over the years – were hidden in a room. They locked the door to this room, and painted it to make it look like part of the wall. This was the door that Arify had shown me on our tour that morning.

In hiding the films from the Taliban, the employees were taking a big risk, gambling with their very lives, I had read.

The Minister for Information himself came to oversee the destruction of the films. 'If I find one reel hidden in the building, I must kill you,' he is reported to have told an employee.[9] But somehow, the ruse worked. The Taliban built a bonfire of the films they found – thousands of reels – that burned for nearly two weeks. But unknown to them, the real treasures of the archive were safe, hidden under their noses.

Arify's version agreed with the broad contours of this narrative. But while the story was true, it wasn't the whole truth, he said.

The archive had not been targeted immediately after the Taliban took power in 1996, but in early 2001, soon after the destruction of the Bamiyan Buddhas, he said. Most of the films had been burned at Pul-e-Charkhi, on the outskirts of Kabul.

Most importantly, the plan to save the film reels could not have been successful without the tacit participation of the Taliban-appointed head of the national TV channel and Afghan Film himself. 'If he had not been there, the archive could not have been saved. People get angry when I say this, that I am speaking in favour of the Taliban, but we have to tell the truth. Without him, our archives, and those of National TV, would not have survived.' In Arify's telling, this official had warned the employees of the threat, and then turned a blind eye to their ruse. The bonfire, in this version, was an elaborate pretence, a wink-and-nudge routine, optics for the movement's foot soldiers, as well as for the public.[10]

This story reminded me of a Kabuli attribute I had seen and read about in different contexts: of people keeping up appearances, going through the motions of being on different sides, while acknowledging that things may well change later. Seen in this way, the 'saving' of the archive was yet another instance of Afghans collaborating under difficult circumstances. Like a pact, that understands the transience of politics, the certitude of change, and the fact that when everyone else left, it would be just them: Afghans, facing each other. Like the two men in Khalid's garden, former foes sipping vodka, watching the choppers in the evening sky.

In Arify's account of the saving of the archive, I found a more complex narrative than the villains-and-saviours sagas that were so common in post-Taliban Kabul. Perhaps this revelation is where the power of the story lies: it shows us how important stories of Kabul being 'saved' are to listeners. And how such stories are often more complicated than they appear to be; resting on ways we choose to see, or not see, Kabul's hazy past.

We prepared to leave, and Arify walked us to the foyer. There, he perched on a marble ledge and told me about his plans to work with different international agencies and governments, of his efforts to get funds to preserve and digitise the thousands of reels that were stored in the rooms around us.

Over time, I heard of his attempts to secure funding for his proposals and pitches to various donors. I heard that he had met with mixed success.

Years later, news reached me that the archive had once again disappeared from the streets of Kabul.[11] It had left its long-time home in the leafy street near Bimaru Hill, and was now being stored in the Arg – one of the most heavily fortified parts of the city. The building that had housed Afghan Film, it was speculated, would be sold. Possibly it would vanish behind concrete walls and sandbags, like its neighbours. Possibly the entire street would vanish, like streets before it.

What would remain would be stories, of a building that had stored images of a Kabul that had existed and had not. There would remain memories of the films that had played across its screens; maps of moving images, leading to a city that was and never was.

5

WALKING WITH THE DJINNS

When roads vanish, paths lead inwards.

With each return to Kabul, I saw the city retreating into itself. By 2009, after eight years of war, the Taliban had regained ground, especially across southern Afghanistan. In response, the US announced a troop surge, sending more soldiers to push back the insurgency. The same year, Hamid Karzai secured a second term in an election marred by violence, low voter turnout and allegations of electoral fraud. A patina of disillusionment – with reports of the government's corruption and cronyism, and with the continued lack of infrastructure – lay over Kabul's streets, which were increasingly difficult to walk on.

International institutions and the Afghan government responded to rising violence and crime in the capital by withdrawing behind layers of security. Twenty-five Afghan National Police checkpoints were created around central Kabul, called the 'Ring of Steel'. These security measures added to the traffic snarls on the poorly repaired roads, especially when VIPs passing by shut down streets.

Roads were blocked off. Sometimes they simply vanished. I walked down a familiar street near the Indian consulate and found it only half there. In its place was a barrier of concrete walls, erected after a suicide bombing. These T-walls – named for the inverted 'T' they formed – took over thoroughfares, their bases jutting out onto paths. Their grey surfaces, often daubed with graffiti, seemed to me like borders. They rearranged Kabul's geography into a cruel hierarchy of vulnerability. If there was a blast in their vicinity, they protected the people within their perimeter, while turning the impact towards those on the outside.

With each return, my paths turned inwards as well. I learned to see Kabul in fragments, to move through terrains of the imagination while remaining motionless. I wandered through myths and memories, which opened like doors leading into rooms that opened in turn into inner courtyards rich with stories. Like the courtyard of my own home in Aligarh, where I had spent many evenings travelling in this way, listening to stories full of secrets and whispered details. Stories that were like the courtyards themselves – turned away from the world, intricate and deeply coded, meant to yield meaning only to those who lived within their boundaries.

My maternal grandmother had told me about how, as a young woman, she conspired to listen to the poets who would visit her father's house. In the strict segregation of her conservative family home, she was not allowed to sit in on the all-male sessions. So she would put her ear to a crack in the wall, and listen to the voices as they read their verses. I did the same with Kabul, listening to voices through cracks in the walls. These too led inwards, to stories of invisible paths seen only by those who wander them.

* * *

In Kabul, as in many other places, mental illness is considered a form of possession by djinns. In the Islamic tradition, these are creatures made of smokeless fire, who usually cannot be seen but who can affect our lives. Different djinns have different temperaments. So there are good djinns and bad djinns. In some accounts, a human gains control over a djinn, and uses it to capture immense riches and power. But the more usual stories are of humans being controlled by djinns, who take over their minds and bodies, make them behave in bizarre ways. Such possession is generally sporadic, causing havoc in the subject's life before receding again. The person is left with no memory of these events, but must live with their consequences.

I had heard dozens of such stories at home in Aligarh. During power cuts, when we sat in the courtyard by the light of flickering lanterns, conversations turned naturally to djinns. They were creatures filled with power, I was told by cousins and aunts. They were quick to anger and difficult to appease. They breathed fire and ate rocks. You found them everywhere, but most often in ruins, because they loved *sunsaan* (abandoned) places that are filled with silence. When you talk about them, they come and listen.

They were probably listening to us now.

In Kabul, where decades of war have destroyed most material things, the deepest signs of damage are often found on human beings. These are the ruins that djinns take charge of, passing into shattered bodies and minds. So the djinns of Kabul are uniquely abundant and powerful. They are metaphors for the phantoms of war and violence that haunt an entire generation of Afghans, through mental trauma and injury. In recent years, a different variety of djinns have come to inhabit the veins of Kabulis, through drug addiction.

With their unearthly powers they extend arms that can reach across space. They cross great distances in the twinkling of an eye and shape the past and the future as they please. Walking through Kabul, it is impossible not to see the djinns shadowing the steps of the living, beings of eternal, clear fire, always burning with a terrible clarity.

* * *

One of the earliest studies on mental health in Afghanistan after the Taliban's defeat was conducted in 2002.[1] This nationwide survey found around 68 per cent of respondents had symptoms of depression, and close to 72 per cent had symptoms of anxiety. The prevalence of symptoms of PTSD was around 42 per cent. 'Women had significantly poorer mental health status than men did,' the report said.

In the years that followed, a new generation of Afghans grew up with displacement and conflict. During this time, estimates of people affected by mental injury in the country varied widely. In 2010 the Afghan Ministry of Public Health was quoted in the press as estimating close to 60 per cent of the population suffered from stress disorders and mental health problems.[2] And in 2017, WHO estimated more than a million Afghans suffered from depressive disorders while over 1.2 million suffered from anxiety disorders, noting that actual figures were likely to be much higher.[3]

What all the varying statistics – and the many gaps in knowledge between them – point to is how difficult it is to measure the shades of trauma suffered by Afghans. And also, that this suffering is far from over. It continues to unfold, manifesting itself in different ways every day.

For those who seek help, the first line of treatment is often a visit to the *ziyarat*. Many people spend months, if not years, being treated by faith healers with talismans and prayers. Even if they want to see a doctor, medical facilities are limited, especially in villages. Afghanistan started a national mental health policy in 1987, which included setting up community-based initiatives. After 2001, a mental health programme envisaged setting up facilities throughout the country.[4] Since then, government efforts and support from international donors has meant that psychosocial counselling is available more readily than earlier. But most facilities for mental illnesses and trauma are concentrated in larger cities and in the capital. One of the rare free clinics for psychiatric care is located in the *marastoon* on a hill in north-western Kabul.

The *marastoon*, or 'place of assistance', is a centre for the destitute and needy. They were established in various cities in the 1930s, with support from the government as well as wealthy banks and businesses. In 1964, when the country got a new constitution, they were handed over to the Afghan Red Crescent Society (ARCS), which has been running them since. In Kabul, the *marastoon* complex includes an asylum for the mentally ill who have no families or homes.

I drove to the *marastoon* with Abdullah in his taxi, Nazira sitting at the back with me, Ahmad Zahir on the radio. We took the road from Karte Parwan towards the Kabul Polytechnic University. The institution was built with Soviet assistance in the 1960s, a time when King Zahir Shah was using the Cold War rivalry between the USSR and the US to secure advantages for Afghanistan. The broad road continued towards the weekend retreat of Qargha. The *marastoon* is located on the lower slopes of Afshar Hill. Looking towards the south, on a different hill, is Bagh-e-Bala, the erstwhile summer palace of royalty. The structure was built by Amir Abdur Rahman Khan, but there have been gardens there since the Mughal era. The spot had been popular for picnics with the Kabuli aristocracy in the nineteenth century.

Bagh-e-Bala was the 'Iron Amir's' favourite palace, and he lavished it with attention. It had fountains and reflecting pools, and the interiors were decorated with glass chandeliers. He held public durbars in this palace, wrote Nancy Dupree, and eventually died there in 1901. A narrow path down the hill led to the shrine of Pir-i-Baland, a prominent saint. The palace was originally meant to be built closer to this *ziyarat*, but work was abruptly halted by the king one day. When asked why, 'the Amir . . . readily admitted that the Pir-i-Baland had appeared

to him in a dream and smartly slapped his face. The sting of this
chastisement still tingled when the Amir awoke, convincing
him that he would be well advised to choose another site for
his palace.'[5] When I visited, I saw women in chadoris making
their way down the path, to pay their respects to the saint who
had held on to his spot on the hill.

On my first visit to Kabul, nearly everyone I met told me
about the trees that had covered the slopes of this hill. How
lush and tall they had been, how they had dominated the
skyline. There were also various stories about their disappearance.
Some said they had been cut down for fuel to help Kabul's
residents get through the frigid winters. Others said that this
was another of Kabul's abundant myths; a story told to gullible
outsiders, as the slopes had been bare since the late 1890s. But
I preferred the story I heard from Abdullah: that the mighty
trunks had withered and died after the Taliban leader Mullah
Omar got his name inscribed on them.

The gates of the *marastoon* appear on the main road that
crosses this hill, marking the complex of the ARCS. Nazira
and I passed through a security checkpoint. We crossed into a
rare terrain of silence. On both sides of the dirt road, which
lifted gently with the gradient of the hill, there were trees
laden with peaches and small apples, tended to by men wearing
Red Crescent jackets. Where there was bare land, there was
the flash of red poppies in the sun. The abundance of space
and the presence of well-tended gardens made the landscape
seem at once familiar and luxurious, like I had stumbled onto
someone's memory of Kabul, an old photograph or postcard
come to life. Further along the road rose new buildings,
flanked by a football field and playgrounds. In one such
field a group of teenaged boys were kicking a ball around.
There was an orphanage – only for boys – whose parents

were either dead or unknown. There was a hospital, and as the
road went higher, a small set of graves. Near the top of the hill
was the clinic.

Embedded in this sylvan location are memories of the years
of civil war. In the winter of 1992-93, while different factions
of the mujahideen fought each other for control over the
capital, the *marastoon's* strategic position – on a hill, surrounded
by trees – made it a valuable prize. As fighting intensified, I
read in a newspaper report, the staff of the institution had fled,
leaving around 160 residents to their fate.[6] Some of the
mentally ill inmates wandered onto the streets that were the
front lines of the war. Others stayed in the compound and
foraged for food.

I read about groups of fighters breaking into the asylum
buildings and stealing food, clothing and blankets belonging
to the sick and the destitute. Many of these men had been
fighting for years. I read of how they raped mentally ill women;
how they rounded up these victims from their hiding places.
They assaulted them in the rooms of blind men, who were
made to stand outside under the winter sky.

I thought of the doors of the asylum buildings standing
open, and the 'madmen' wandering the streets heedless of
bullets and falling rockets. It seemed likely that the men who
had been locked up were less dangerous than those who
roamed the city then.

By the end of the war, like most of Kabul, the *marastoon* had
been reduced to a shell of its former self. It was rebuilt around
2005, with assistance from foreign donors. The buildings I was
seeing were built on the skeleton of the former iteration, a
reminder of the time when Afghans had turned on one
another and torn their capital apart. As if they had been
possessed.

* * *

I had come to the *marastoon*'s mental health clinic to meet Dr Haroon Habibzada, the only psychiatrist at the facility. A dapper man in his thirties, Dr Habibzada had grown up as part of the large Afghan refugee community in neighbouring Pakistan. His family had returned to Kabul after 2001, and he had graduated from the Kabul Medical College in 2005. After a period of training in Germany, he had started working with the ARCS in 2009.

The day I met him, he had just finished his hours at the outpatient clinic. He saw anywhere between 60 and 120 patients at this clinic every day, he said. Many of them lived in Kabul, but some also found their way to him from nearby provinces. 'They tell me: "In our village, we don't have a doctor for this illness,"' he explained. Sometimes they came to him after months of being treated by faith healers. 'They come to me when those people have given up on them,' he said wryly.

Most of Dr Habibzada's patients were women, and many were in their thirties, or younger. Women were also the majority of patients under his care in the hospital on the premises. Of the eighty beds in the facility, only twenty-four were occupied by men. In part, this was due to the stigma associated with being treated for mental health problems. It was also because men faced greater social pressure not to admit to the 'weakness' of being ill, or needing help. 'Men have to be brave in our culture,' said Dr Habibzada. 'This bravery, it's the worst kind of madness.'

Sometimes Dr Habibzada recommended that patients who came to his clinic get admitted to the hospital. Other times they came referred from private clinics, where doctors were unable to provide the treatment they required, or if they were unable to pay. And sometimes they were brought by their families, or relatives who knew the symptoms, and supported the treatment.

Each of these patients got a handwritten file and a treatment plan worked out by Dr Habibzada, which was a combination of the medicines that were both available and affordable in Kabul. These were mostly generic drugs imported from India and Pakistan. I saw some stacked up in the glass-fronted cupboards in the doctor's room. Their bland colours and flimsy packaging made them appear like frail talismans, ranged against the many djinns crowding the hospital's wards. There was also a team of psychologists who offered counselling and different therapies to the patients: from sports therapy to faith-based discourses or *zikr*.

Despite the large number of patients he saw every day, Dr Habibzada knew that those who made it to the clinic on the hill were only the tip of a large, complicated iceberg. For every patient he saw, there were many others who needed help. There were few people he had met in Kabul, he said, who were not hurt in some way.

A lot of this was due to the deep damage caused by decades of war. And yet, as Dr Habibzada told me, there is more to mental illness than war. The women he treated often had nutritional deficiencies and bodies wrecked by frequent pregnancies. They faced hunger and lack of medical treatment, domestic violence and poverty. There was also the closely related issue of addiction. These were not problems unique to Afghanistan. In part they reminded me of women's lives in India. Perhaps the difference was that in Kabul they played out against a backdrop of unfolding trauma and continuing violence. To me, this made Dr Habibzada's job seem akin to a Sisyphean labour, like cleaning the dust off Kabul's streets, aware that it will be back the next day.

From the clinic, Dr Habibzada walked with me and Nazira to the asylum buildings. There was one for men, and the one we entered, for women. We walked by the boys playing football, and up a dirt path to approach the structure. We rang the tiny bell but there was no answer. Dr Habibzada banged repeatedly on the metal door until it was opened by a female guard, wearing a tunic and trousers uniform, her hair covered by a scarf. She had been tending to her vegetable patch, she explained, and the bell was not working. We walked through the entrance and saw a complex of rooms and open spaces, the whole ringed by the tall brick wall that looked as though it had been raised by a few feet recently. Barbed wire rose and fell on its summit. A transistor radio was propped by the plot where the guard had been working, playing only static.

Close to forty women lived in these quarters, I was told, spending their days and nights within the walls. I followed Dr Habibzada on a tour around the building, starting with the rooms where the women lived and slept. We were trailed by a small knot of patients, some of them asking the doctor for medicines, others trying to hold on to his hand. Dr Habibzada negotiated them expertly as he showed me the amenities with some pride. The rooms were large and clean, lined with bunk beds, dormitory-style. Each bed had several blankets piled onto it, and each room had heaters. The bathrooms, at the end of the building, were fitted with hot-water boilers, and the inmates bathed twice a week, he said. From the way he described these things, they sounded like the luxuries they were – a warm room with hot water and regular food is more than what most of the poor of Kabul can hope for.

Behind these living quarters was an inner courtyard, edged with flower beds. In one corner of this open ground, a woman with cropped hair lay stretched out in the sunshine, immune to all the movement around her. She gazed at us impassively as we passed by. There were mattresses drying in a sunny spot, and behind them a pair of swings that had been painted white, but had worn clean of their colour in patches. At the other end of the courtyard was a single-storey building. The windows were big and covered with plastic sheets, allowing the mellow sunlight to warm the room. On the window ledge were a few potted plants, their leaves a tender green. In the first room there were a few tables covered with fabric and sequins. This was where the inmates spent their days, working at different tasks. Two women were bent over a table, one of them sticking cloth flowers onto a bright pink veil. An older woman stood behind the door, her face to the wall.

The women at the table – Sadaf and Fauzia – were sisters who had been brought to the *marastoon* by their father after their mother died. He had decided to remarry and didn't want the future children from his new marriage to be 'tainted' by the same strain of 'madness' afflicting his existing children. There had been a third daughter. She had died a few years ago and was buried in the roadside cemetery we had passed on our way to the asylum. Next to the sisters sat a middle-aged woman called Breshna. She had come to the asylum as a child, Dr Habibzada told me, after her entire family was killed in her village in the Shomali plains during the war against the Communist government. Since the day she entered the premises, I was told, she had not ventured out again.

I asked one of the guards about the woman standing behind the door, her head touching the wall. She had been abandoned by her husband, I was told, when he had left for Iran with a new wife. Each time I asked about the patients, I got a medley of symptoms and life stories. Breshna for instance, was 'depressed', while the sisters had 'poor learning skills inherited from their mother'. And the woman behind the door was 'sad at being left alone. Wouldn't you be?' Many of the women in the *marastoon* had been left there by their families. A few had been found wandering the streets of Kabul, or had been sent from the provinces by the police. The pattern of loss and abandonment that emerged from these stories made their confinement even more poignant. To me, their isolation seemed like a symbol of the malaise that haunted their fraught society. A society so injured itself, it had little space for these vulnerable women. I thought of the many kinds of trauma and violence rippling through the city that lay below us. The line between 'normalcy' and 'madness' looked frighteningly arbitrary from within the walls of this asylum.

Sitting among the inmates were two social workers who were also on the staff. One of these women walked me through the rooms of the building, showing the illustrations and craftwork made by the residents that were hung on the walls. Then she sat on the carpeted floor and played a game with Fauzia, who had followed us. The game involved two sets of cards with drawings on them. One pile showed various tasks – through an image of a broom, or a toothbrush. The second pile showed rewards, like a cup of tea. When someone completed a task, she'd get a reward. Except that Fauzia wanted the tea right away, never mind the card with the broom on it. After a moment's mock hesitation, the woman relented and poured her a cup from the flask. This was what she did every day, she said – taught basic skills to the inmates who could learn, kept the women as busy as she could.

Left to their own devices, the djinns hemmed into the asylum's walls broke into violence. Sometimes the guards would get hurt trying to stop the women attacking each other. When I asked one of them if she worried about her safety, however, she just said: 'If you lock forty women up, won't you expect fights, even if they're sane?' I walked out of the room, and as I went past Fauzia, she motioned me to sit beside her. 'Stay with us,' she invited me with a smile. 'Have some tea.'

Moving between the rooms, I would sometimes hear the staccato rhythm of gunfire. Noticing my look of alarm the first time this happened, Dr Habibzada explained that it came from the police training grounds located across the hill. I tried to catch the voices of the boys I knew were playing football outside the gates. But they were sealed out by the high walls.

We walked back through the courtyard. The woman on the ground was now asleep, or pretending to be, sprawled with abandon in the mellow sunshine. Again, she didn't bat an eyelid as we passed her by, ignoring even the presence of the male doctor. Inside the walls of the asylum where she was confined, she exercised a strange kind of freedom: a woman with no ties, no 'value', no means to be controlled – except by her own particular djinn.

Even the usually urbane and self-possessed Nazira was visibly nervous in her presence. After all the stories we had heard, and all the heartbreaking displays of fragility and loss we had seen that morning, it was this woman's indifference that made Nazira clutch my hand with urgency and say, 'Enough, let's go.'

In the recent past, only one woman in the *marastoon* had been 'cured' and had left with her family. That had been two years ago. It seemed possible for several of the women to live in society again, with medication and some help. But when I asked him about this, Dr Habibzada just shrugged. The answer that lay behind his silence was one that applied to many of the women in that complex. Even if they got better, or even if there was a cure for what afflicted them, these women had nowhere else to go. This was a reality that seemed to have been accepted by the *marastoon* authorities. Like Fauzia's sister, the inmates of the asylum were expected to die there, travelling out only as far as the little cemetery on the hill opposite the high walls.

Perhaps the best the inmates could hope for was the indifference of the woman sprawled on the ground. To me, the more painful existence seemed to be of those with an incomplete partition from the world outside. Like the whispered anguish of another middle-aged woman who followed us on our way out, tapping our arms as we walked to the gate, alongside the tall walls which shut out the sounds of children at play, her voice punctuated by the bursts of gunfire persisting over the chatter of the inmates, rising over the guard's radio still relaying static by the vegetable patch, over the soothing voice of the doctor promising them all pills.

'Please,' she said repeatedly, 'please ask my family to come and get me.'

* * *

Not all the djinns of Kabul enter through the mind. Some find their way from opium fields blossoming in the countryside; through needles pricking the veins of the displaced. Behind the Kabul of the everyday is a city of crevices inhabited by this growing population of djinns, attendant to its population of drug addicts. For the government, for NGOs working in the area, as well as for faith healers, the connections between mental health disorders and substance abuse are abundant and clear. It is telling that even at *ziyarats* the same treatment is prescribed for addicts and for the mentally ill.

Many addicts inhabit a shadow city within Kabul. Boys huddle over needles in the wastelands surrounding the tombs of dead kings. Men howl and sleep and fight in the monumental ruins of the Soviet Cultural Centre, near Darulaman Road, even as Kabul's traffic builds up and dissolves around them. A park in the centre of the city, the darkness of a cinema, the narrow windowsills and crumbling rooms of abandoned homes. These are the ruins inhabited by djinns who haunt a generation of Afghans who have known only war.

These djinns are formed partly of movement, nurtured by a multitude of exiles. Perhaps for this reason, they prompt their victims to seek a stillness that is beyond the fickle shifts of politics and borders and refugee camps, beyond even the treacherous pledges of freedom and liberation. Perhaps they promise a more lasting peace than the one that came to Kabul in 2001. Or they offer relief from the ruinous tug between hope and habit. A tug that I saw mirrored between the bodies of the addicted and the city itself – veering between the hope of peace, and the habit of violence.

The presence of drug users on the hills and corners of Kabul gives these sights a sense of permanence, as if they have been a part of the landscape forever. But this isn't the case. NGO workers told me it was rare to find addicts on the streets in 2001, on the heels of the Taliban's overthrow. This changed rapidly over the next few years. In 2005, a survey by the United Nations Office on Drugs and Crime (UNODC) estimated that 3.8 per cent of the nation's total population of around 23 million used drugs.[7] In Kabul, the number of drug users had doubled from 2003 to 2005. This was around the same time when millions of Afghan refugees had returned from Pakistan and Iran, and a smaller number from other countries. 'There is a higher rate of drug use among returned refugees than among other members of Afghan society,' the survey noted.

By 2009, another UNODC survey found, the number of regular opium users had grown by 53 per cent in four years, and the number of regular heroin users had jumped more than 140 per cent across the nation. Almost one million Afghans – roughly 8 per cent of the population between fifteen and sixty-four years old – were drug users. This number was twice the global average. 'Many Afghans seem to be taking

drugs as a kind of self-medication against the hardships of life,'
said the report.[8]

Opium was the most prevalent drug, as a relatively cheap
and easily available escape from poverty, displacement, and
different shades of trauma. Afghanistan has grown the bulk of
the world's opium since the 1990s.[9] After a brief dip in 2001
due to a Taliban ban on production, poppy cultivation boomed
in the years following the US-led invasion, despite costly
efforts to contain this spread.[10] By 2007, it accounted for 93
per cent of the world's opium.[11] The swell of this illegal crop,
which grew with the insecurity and insurgency, was felt within
the country as well as the world. By 2015, Afghanistan's number
of adult drug users would rise to between 1.9 and 2.4 million
people, equivalent to 12.6 per cent of the adult population.[12]

In Kabul too, most users were addicted to opium and heroin.
By 2012, according to the Afghanistan National Urban Drug
Use Survey (ANUDUS), 5.1 per cent of the capital's estimated
3.2 million people used drugs, including 3.7 per cent of
women.[13] This rising population of drug users congregated in
the crevices of the city.

Even as the crisis grew, there were few facilities to offer
treatment or support. And then there was the intense social
stigma faced by drug users. Because drugs are *haraam*,
forbidden, in Islam, there is little sympathy with those who
succumb to their use. So users hid the habit rather than
seeking help for it.

One of the few organisations that did offer support was
Nejat – the word means sanctuary or relief. One afternoon in
2013, I sought out their centre in Kharabat, in the old city, near
the Bala Hissar. During the civil war, the locality had been
heavily shelled by warring factions, particularly by the forces of
Gulbuddin Hekmatyar, the commander who controlled the
heights of the Koh-e-Sher Darwaza. Most of the buildings I

saw as I walked that afternoon had been rebuilt or repaired only after 2001, rising over the remains of the old. For some Kabulis, these renovations were signs of the relative prosperity and security that had come with the international intervention and the new government.

Two years earlier, in 2011, I had spent an afternoon in Kucha-e-Kharabat, which is the centre of Kabul's traditional music. This quarter of singers and performers – among them families originally from India – had been settled during the reign of Amir Sher Ali Khan.[14] (The same ruler who gave his name to Sherpur, where the poppy palaces now flourished.) A short walk from the citadel, the area had provided a colourful nightlife to the court elite, and had nurtured accomplished musicians. Kharabat had a reputation in Kabul as a place of licentious behaviour. The phrase 'to have a Kharabat' meant to carouse without a care, to spend freely. But the term also had mystic connotations in Sufi poetry, one of the musicians told me, referring to the annihilation of the self that is essential for union with the divine.

I had gone to Kharabat with Siddiq Barmak, the film-maker. As we wandered through the street we bumped into Ustad Hamahang, a singer whom Barmak had admired in his youth. Now in his seventies, Hamahang – whose name means 'harmonious' – was a true *bacha-e-Kharabat* (Kharabati boy). He had learned classical music on the street – including Indian compositions – and his family had lived there for generations. The peak of his fame was in the 1970s. After one concert at the Bagh-e-Zenana (Women's Garden), the enthusiastic all-female crowd had lifted the car he was in – a Russian-made Volga – right off the ground.

During the civil war, Ustad Hamahang told me he had been trapped with his family at home. To escape the rockets, they had hidden in the basement for a week, eating only potatoes.

When they had run out of food, Hamahang had emerged to look for help. He had found the entire neighbourhood empty, he said. Everyone had fled.

He had escaped with the help of his Hindu and Sikh students who lived in adjacent areas. They'd moved his family between their homes, through secret paths of interiors, until they crossed the dangerous front line of Jada-e-Maiwand. From there the family had made their way to Pakistan. They had returned in 2005 to a transformed Kharabat. Many of Hamahang's peers had left the country for good. Other musicians had set up their homes and offices elsewhere, in the narrow lanes of Shor Bazaar, or further afield, in Taimani.

On the other side of the hill we stood on lay Shuhada-e-Saliheen, the cemetery where I had gone with Zafar Paiman and Doctor Sahab to visit Tepe Naranj. Ustad Hamahang had pointed out the route taken by people walking to the shrines there. We had wandered around the street with him that afternoon, before going to his house for tea.

In 2013, when I returned in search of Nejat, however, I stuck to the route I had been told to follow. I made my way to the landmark of Bagh-e-Qazi, one of the rare open spaces in the old city. For several years after 2001, it had housed a large bazaar of spare auto parts. In 2010 the Kabul municipality undertook an ambitious restoration as part of a larger project for greening the city. The hawkers were moved out onto a small patch adjoining the park, and the garden was once again replanted with grass and trees. The morning I saw it, it still looked bare and tentative, the saplings seeming vulnerable in the middle of the newly cleared space.

The road straight ahead led upwards, to the *ziyarat* of Asheqan-o-Arefan (the Shrine of Lovers and Mystics). It is the resting place of two brothers, who are still revered as patron saints of the city.

My destination lay before the *ziyarat*, and I entered a narrow building, climbing up to the Nejat office. The organisation had been working with Afghan drug users since 1991, first in Peshawar and then since 2003 in Kabul. The centre I was in was only for women, and provided a space for information and guidance. It was a place to remove the stigma associated with addiction, to help the women begin, if they could, the difficult and long path to recovery. Many of the women who came to the centre had returned to Kabul after 2001 from Iran or Pakistan. Most of them had been born and raised by Afghan parents in these countries. To come to Kabul, for them, was to come home to a city they had never known. There were also a few like Fatima, an older woman who had lived out the shifting wars in her small house in the old city, blotting out the conflicts through the haze of her heroin use.

'My husband died in the early years of the civil war,' she said. 'He was killed during the fighting in the neighbourhood.' Left to fend for herself and her five children, Fatima found herself unable to cope. Her body was invaded by aches and pains she could not find a cure for.

'I used to work in my neighbour's house, doing the cleaning and washing her clothes. She was also a widow. She gave me the drug and said it would make things better, that it had helped her.' For twelve days, Fatima shared injections of heroin with this woman. On the thirteenth day, the neighbour told her to find it for herself. As her addiction worsened, Fatima worked only occasionally, and retreated to her one-room home, emerging only to demand her drug from anyone who happened to be around. Usually this would be her children, who worked to feed themselves and their mother, and kept her supplied with heroin. 'They sold *bolanis* and did *spand* on the street,' she said. Like the children I had seen near the Kabul

Public Library, swirling smoke around pedestrians to protect
them from the evil eye. 'Another neighbour worked in a
restaurant, he would feed the children sometimes,' she added.
The civil war ended with the arrival of the Taliban into Kabul,
an event that barely registered in Fatima's account of her life.
How she evaded the Taliban's strictures, how her children
found her drugs and made a living during those years, she was
vague about. The one thing she kept repeating was that the
neighbour who had given her the drug had been cured of her
addiction and had moved away. 'She left, but I could not do
that,' she said. I had been told beforehand not to ask the women
how they paid for their doses, or to mention the transactions
they or their families negotiated in return for drugs.

I spoke to a woman who sat at the edge of the room. Her
name was Roya and she wore a spangled red dress that stretched
over her pregnant belly, taut with her fourth child. Her first
three children had been born addicted to the opium she had
smoked through her pregnancies, she said. One of her sons sat
on her lap, watching us with large, lined eyes. He was four years
old, but looked younger. He held an ice-cream cone tightly in
his hands but did not eat it.

Roya had grown up in a village outside Kabul after her
parents had been killed during the civil war. She was raised by
an uncle who was, she said, a famous gambler. 'When there
was money, there was lots of it,' she said, her voice touched
with quiet pride. The family moved to Iran when the Taliban
captured Kabul. There, she was married to a construction
worker. Soon after, her husband started giving her opium to
smoke to keep her quiet, 'as we were always fighting over his
using the drug'. Her husband in turn had been given drugs –
heroin powder – by his boss, an Iranian, to keep *him* quiet and
to help him work for long periods without getting tired.
When her children were born, she would 'blow some of the

opium smoke on them when they cried', to keep them quiet. The family returned in 2003 to Kabul, finding a house in the old city that they rebuilt. They shared it with several other family members and with her father-in-law, who was also addicted to opium. Poverty and constant friction at home made her even more dependent. 'All the money we made, we spent on drugs,' she said. Her husband would get a *pudia*, a small packet of opium, for 350 afghanis (around $7), that they would use for two days. On the days when the drugs would run low, there would be arguments and fights, with the neighbours getting involved. If her children started screaming or fretting in school, the teachers knew what to do. They would call Roya and ask her to take them home and give them what they needed to calm down. 'Everyone around us uses the drug,' said Roya gently. 'It's usual in this area.'

A year ago, her husband's body had reached breaking point, and he had been unable to work. The family had hovered on the edge of starvation, with the older children working to make money for the day's bread and opium. A few months ago, at the urging of the counsellors at Nejat, Roya and her husband went through a residential drug treatment programme that the organisation also runs. Since then, they had been clean, but their children were still dependent. And though Roya's husband had been fighting his habit, she worried that poverty, as well as the easy availability of drugs around them, would push him back into addiction. Roya herself was determined for her new child to grow without opium in her womb. So far, this had been giving her the strength she needed to stay off the drug. 'I want at least one of my children to be born without this curse,' she said. As she talked, her son's ice cream slowly melted away into a puddle, falling onto her chadori and then the floor. Neither of them seemed to notice or care.

Children are important in the stories of drugs in Kabul, the path the djinns take into the future. Chances are that addicted mothers will have addicted children. Even if they avoid using drugs, they are likely to be involved in some way with the traffic of *pudias* that come to their homes. Often children buy the drugs for mothers who cannot leave home, or face social stigma. The 2012 ANUDUS survey had found 2.6 per cent of children in Kabul were affected by drug use in some way, i.e. they were given the drug by an adult, or were exposed to it in their home environment.[15] Some of them, like Roya's son, were caught in the cycle before they were even born.

Fatima's children left Kabul sometime during the Taliban years. She said they cursed her for wrecking their lives. But she felt they were fortunate. She had been careful never to smoke opium around them, to make sure they didn't get addicted as well. 'I would only take injections, so they could not get it from me,' she said. She knew that her daughter had married and lived somewhere in the nearby province of Paghman, but it was unlikely that they would ever see each other. It was difficult to tell Fatima's age from her frail frame, thin bones hidden below a voluminous white shirt and skirt. Perhaps she was a little older than the oldest of Afghanistan's recent wars, just old enough to remember peace if she cared to. But her world had shrunk to a narrow pinpoint of getting her injections every day, a tiny aperture through which she extracted herself into the homes of her neighbours, to do their housework and wash their clothes and make the money she needed to pay for the heroin. She had also started coming to the Nejat centre, which had helped her cut down her intake. I asked the women around her what it felt like when they took their drugs. 'It makes the pain go away,' one said. 'It's as if you have no problems.' 'I can be peaceful.' 'I can be quiet.'

The words echoed the vague, familiar symptoms I had heard from other women in other places, in other times. Perhaps the only way for them to express what tore at their souls was to call them aches and pains. I thought in particular of my paternal grandmother. I recalled the rocking motion of her frail body as she spoke of the eldest of her ten children – the one she lost when he was still an infant, dead of dehydration after diarrhoea. The one she would remember often as she descended into depression and later dementia. It was a descent aided by doctors – often men – who prescribed medicines and surgery, who pumped tranquillisers into her body in increasing doses, all the while dismissing her complaints, 'managing' her sadness. She also spoke of aches and pains, my grandmother, little twinges of unhappiness that she could not explain. She spoke of just being tired.

I left the centre in the middle of the afternoon. On a whim, encouraged by the women I'd met, I decided to walk to the shrine of Asheqan-o-Arefan. I climbed uphill past tightly packed houses, catching glimpses of parallel streets that appeared and vanished through gaps in the buildings. As if the road was a curtain that moved with the breeze.

As I walked, I heard a boom nearby, loud enough to make my heart skip a beat, loud enough to halt my steps. I looked around. It was the sound of a mud house being demolished nearby, downhill from where I stood. It was probably making way for a new dwelling. I heard the voices of the workers, the scraping of shovels and picks, and then another boom as more walls came crashing down. The dust from the broken rooms rose and gathered into a massive outline against the sky. And then it collapsed, dancing away with the wind.

* * *

To follow the stories of djinns across Kabul is to map the path taken by war across the city and its people. But the ruins these djinns occupied were not only caused by war. They were also nourished by what came with the recent cycle of flawed, violent peace: the wealth, the poverty, the lack of accountability, the absence of belonging.

In March 2015, a young woman called Farkhunda was beaten to death by a mob near the riverside *ziyarat* of Shah-e-do-Shamshera (the Saint of Two Swords), dedicated to a martyr who kept fighting even after being beheaded.[16] Across the shrine is a small, Ottoman-style mosque, which was built by Amir Amanullah's mother. It was painted different shades of yellow over the years. Further along the riverside are graceful old buildings with painted shutters, now used as clinics, homes and shops. The crumbling charm of these facades and the sweep of the riverbed make this a pleasant part of Kabul to wander through, offering a glimpse into its past as a scenic promenade.

It was in this picturesque area that the mob assembled. Farkhunda, it turned out, had been arguing with the faith healers who worked in the courtyard of the *ziyarat*. Ironically, she had been protesting that their livelihood of selling charms and talismans was not only unethical, it was un-Islamic. It went against the Quran.

In accounts from the day, it appears that a chant went up near the shrine that Farkhunda was burning the Quran. She was beaten brutally and her body dumped into the dry river channel beside the shrine. She was set alight, and run over by a car. All this occurred under the gaze of hundreds of men, some of whom recorded the murder on their phones. The eyes of these cameras must have appeared like hundreds of djinns – watching impassively, unperturbed by the turmoil around them, unaccountable for it.

A few men were tried for Farkhunda's murder, and were subsequently spared the death penalty. At her funeral, Kabuli women defied convention by bearing her coffin on their shoulders to the graveyard. The street where Farkhunda was killed is now named after her; it is the only memorial to this murder that happened in plain sight.

To me, Farkhunda's killing seemed to have occurred in that penumbra of Kabul where the djinns dwell – a place poised between the capital's apparent modernity and its nascent violence. Between its gleaming malls and wedding halls, and its ruined palaces and blast walls. Reading about this incident reminded me of a story I had heard from Hilai, who worked as domestic help at the house I lived in at Qala-e-Fatahullah.

I heard part of this story in the winter of 2010. It was the end of the year, the week of Christmas, and Kabul was empty of its population of foreign consultants and aid workers. The streets were miraculously free of traffic, and I drove to work every day with a sense of seeing the city anew – with a beautiful bareness. Like the lines of trees that had shed their leaves. The day of the first snowfall, I had walked through the neighbourhood of Taimani to a friend's house, enjoying the cold snap in the air, the crunch and whiteness and wetness of the street. My friend had told me about the custom of *barfi* (from *barf*, or snow): if you brought the news of the first snow to a friend or relative, they owed you a meal. I remember the silence of the streets, the quiet hush over the school during vacations. Only the helicopters still passed regularly overhead. In this season of oblivion, Hilai began telling me of her brother's wife, Sameera, who was afflicted by a djinn.

The crisis she described also took place in a shadowland, between the terrain of faith healers and doctors. Hilai is a widow, in her late thirties, with three young children. She lived with her father in a locality called Deh Dana, in south-western Kabul. It lay off the broad avenue leading to the ruined Qasr-e-Darulaman. It was on the margins of the city in other ways too; part of the parallel, burgeoning city within Kabul. By 2013, close to 70 per cent of Kabul's population would be estimated to live in unplanned and illegal constructions.[17]

I knew that Hilai was trying to save enough money to build her own set of rooms, on top of her father's home. But as the crisis in her family unfolded, these hopes were replaced by the reality of things that needed to be done for Sameera, and for her brother's family. The djinn that inhabited Sameera affected Hilai too, upsetting the slow, painstaking steps she had taken towards an improved future for her children. I heard snatches of news about the illness over the years. Hilai was often on leave, forced to take care of things at home, or to take Sameera to the doctor, or to look after Sameera's six children – one still an infant – while Sameera was admitted to various hospitals. It was in the summer of 2013 that Hilai finally told me the full story.

It all began, Hilai said, when Sameera first started suffering from fainting spells, the night her husband was taken away by the police. Hilai suspected a malicious neighbour to be behind this, but she did not share the details with me. Her family made the rounds of various offices and police stations, until her brother was released a week later, unharmed but shaken. Soon after this, Sameera's young son fell ill. At the hospital, he was given an injection. As she watched this, Sameera fainted. When she came round, she was changed. Her blackouts became more frequent, and when she was revived, she would often have no memory of what had happened to her.

As Hilai described Sameera's illness to me, I was reminded of stories of other women held helpless not only by capricious djinns but also in thrall to men of authority, who managed their bodies and their lives with unquestioned (but questionable) wisdom. And there was also this – in her account, her brother being arrested was a difficult, but not unexpected, part of life in the margins of Kabul, where there are too many people fighting over too little. In Hilai's telling, the violence that racked Sameera's afflicted body seemed to be part of the spasms and savage flux that were shaping their part of Kabul.

Over the months, Sameera's condition worsened. 'She would just be sitting there, and then she would start screaming and shaking,' said Hilai. When this frenzy passed, she would not remember anything. One time this happened, her husband rushed her to a hospital near their house. The doctors told him that Sameera was in danger of choking on her tongue, but her mouth was closed so convulsively they could not get it open. To do that, they broke her teeth, six of them, until they had a big enough space to prise her jaws apart. 'We thought she was dead. We thought it was all over.' Sameera was moved to a government-run hospital, where she was admitted for ten days and then discharged. The doctors told her family that she didn't have any mental problems. It was high blood pressure and stress. 'Take her home.'

For the next few weeks, Sameera's husband and family were constantly vigilant to what she may do next. They took turns sleeping, because sometimes Sameera would wake in the middle of the night and start wandering around the house. Finally, after a family conference, it was decided that her husband would take her to Pakistan for treatment. They all procured loans to pay for the travel and the doctors. But Sameera came back worse than ever. The medicines the doctors gave her made her drowsy. 'And the baby she was breastfeeding would also sleep all day, so she stopped taking them,' said Hilai. By this time, the entire family was on edge, including Sameera's young children, who had seen their mother transform over the past year into a frightening, unpredictable being. With the failure of the doctors, Hilai took matters into her own hands. She went with Sameera to a *ziyarat* she revered, dedicated to Agha Sahib Alauddini.

I went with Hilai to the shrine, which was located near her house, one afternoon after she finished work at Qala-e-Fatahullah. Nazira was supposed to go with us, but just as we were leaving Hilai suggested Nazira swap her modern Kabuli girl attire for something more suitable for visiting a shrine. We might meet the holy man, the *mullah sahib* there, who Hilai admired greatly and hoped would pray for us. But Nazira refused to change her clothes, and declined any interest in his prayers. Eventually I ushered an incensed Hilai out the door, leaving Nazira and her Shahr-e-Nau-style outfit at home.

The *ziyarat* lay off the main avenue leading to the ruined palace at Darulaman. We turned onto a side street, which wound deeper and deeper into what seemed to be a village, enclosed by the growing sprawl of Kabul.

Walking to the shrine was partly a sign of respect, partly a necessity caused by the narrowness of the lanes that twisted and vanished away from Kabul like well-kept secrets. The dirt road grew narrower as the surrounding houses were punctuated by fields and groves of fruit trees. We passed by children on their way home from school, and an ice-cream cart stuck in a muddy puddle on a corner, playing a constant loop of 'Happy Birthday'. As we approached the gate of the shrine, Hilai instructed me to cover my face with my chador, a large white cloth that was already covering my head and obscuring most of my body. Cloaked in this pious anonymity, we slipped past a woman at the gate asking for alms, past a knot of men standing in the open courtyard, past an old-fashioned hand pump and water tank. We walked straight into the chambers of the shrine, where we could lift our veils, and echo each other's sighs of relief.

Agha Sahib Alauddini's *ziyarat* was smaller than others I had visited in Kabul, with a near rural vibe of simplicity and none of the usual crowds. (Though Hilai insisted that on Thursdays, the high day for visiting such shrines, 'You cannot walk through the road for the crowds.') 'Your heart will feel lighter,' she told me repeatedly on our way there. After a brief rest, we arranged our chadors carefully once again and approached the room where the holy man was seated on the floor. He was young, perhaps in his thirties. His long beard gave him an air of gravity, and he had the classic good looks of so many Afghans, making him seem boyish despite the beard. Hilai kissed his hand and asked him to pray for her, for Sameera. He gestured to us to sit, said a prayer and blew his blessing-infused breath over us. Then, from a small pile of paper slips lying by his side, he selected one and gave it to me. It had Arabic calligraphy on it. Hilai told me that it was a prayer, handwritten in black ink and saffron. I was to put the slip into a glass of water and drink it, he instructed. It would give me peace.

Following Hilai's directions, I tucked some money under the mattress he was seated on – it would have been inappropriate to have handed him the notes directly – then we went to pay our respects to the sarcophagi in the next chamber. I said a prayer for the dead, like I had been taught as a child, the words and the gestures returning to me instinctively. The room was quiet, heavy with the smell of burning incense, and Hilai sat in a corner in a posture of supplication. The silence was broken by a group of women who tramped in exuberantly, accompanied by a number of small children. They launched into conversations with each other as the children hung off the rails around the saint's grave, gazing in open-mouthed awe at the grand artificial flowers and crystal arrangements. These women, I found, had come from Rishkhor, a village about twenty kilometres away. They had worn their best clothes, and their best shoes – high-heeled, though they had walked a long way.

In certain *ziyarats* famous for treating mental illnesses, the afflicted are shackled, left hungry and alone in dark rooms where djinns cannot enter. Sameera was more fortunate in her treatment. When she had come to the young mullah at the shrine, he had felt her pulse and told Hilai that it was not a matter for talismans but for doctors. Hilai's other employers had then recommended a private clinic for Sameera. After eight months of treatment, she was finally getting better. What was it that had afflicted her, I asked Hilai, did you ever find out? She hadn't, being satisfied with the passing of the troubles.

Hilai and I left the shrine before sunset, walking together as far as the main road. Abdullah was waiting in his taxi to take me home, playing Ahmad Zahir, imbuing the twilight air with added melancholy. It took us nearly an hour to cross the city, battling the traffic. At one of the intersections, we narrowly missed colliding with a pickup truck that abruptly stopped by the side of the road. As I watched, a group of men clutching large guns jumped out and ran to the roadside. In some alarm, I watched them congregate around a roadside stall. My view was obscured by their heavy vests and artillery, so it took a few tense moments before I realised that all they were doing was buying fruit. Sorting through peaches and cherries with the hands that were free of weapons.

Later that night, when the house was quiet, I fished out the slip of paper – my prescribed prayer – and put it in a glass of water. The black ink swam into the liquid, swirling and writing on its surface. Words on water, flecked with saffron. A cure that was as intangible as the affliction. They hung suspended for a brief moment, and then vanished into the clear depths.

***

Across the street from the *ziyarat* I visited with Hilai, on the
other side of the broad avenue that led towards Darulaman,
was another centre run by Nejat. Its location mirrors the
shrine. To get there, I had to drive onto a side street where
large houses towered over the horizon. Many people who
lived in the neighbourhood had returned to Kabul from
abroad. They had built homes with reflective glass and
ornate tiles on the facades and columns at the entrance. I
had been told not to walk through the street but to get
dropped right by the gate. There had been kidnappings in
the area.

In this centre, as in Kharabat, Nejat ran outreach
programmes that were intended to be the first step on the
long road to recovery. There were activities for both men
and women, and also a detoxification programme for men,
where patients were admitted for fifteen days. I was shown
around by Dr Tariq Suleman, the director of the centre.
With his neat suit and dapper beard, Dr Suleman reminded
me of the public-spirited mendicants I had heard described
in childhood stories in India, who would meditate with a
quiet focus to capture the rogue djinns that wandered and
wreaked havoc in their wake. Over the past sixteen years,
Dr Suleman had seen the problem of addiction grow.
Some of the biggest obstacles to recovery was the stigma
associated with drug use, and the absence of family or
social support.

'This is new kind of landscape,' he said. 'Earlier, there were
people who consumed opium in every village. But there was
no stigma. They would continue working, people would accept
them.' With war and displacement came different kinds of
drugs as well as medicines from Pakistan, Iran and further away.
There was also the inevitable fallout from the country's own
massive production of opium, which was sent out to the world.

'Now our young generation is also using the drug,' he said. 'There is no such thing as rich or poor addict, it is everywhere. It is used by the mullah and the politician.'

On his desktop computer, Dr Suleman had hundreds of photographs taken on the streets of Kabul, in every season. He clicked through them, watching my reactions carefully. 'This is the situation,' he said, showing me images of drug users in crumbling houses, sitting under blankets and huddled around a fire. Finally, he closed the images and said with great deliberation, 'Drug is a part of our lives.' This was a phrase he repeated often, his accent making the English words something of a litany, imbuing it with an agenda. As if by repeating the words often enough, he could sweep away the layers of stigma and denial that surrounded this bald fact, and everything else it implied. 'Drug is a part of our lives in Afghanistan.'

I asked him why the problem had grown in Kabul, and as a reply he gave me a few pamphlets that his team used for public outreach. On their pages I saw a series of illustrations – simple drawings of people witnessing a bomb blast, amputees, women weeping over a child's grave, a man grown thin and scared from being near a blast. Different people have different reasons, he said. During the civil war, he often met a commander who was addicted to opium. 'I asked him why he did the holy jihad but took drugs,' said Dr Suleman. 'He told me, "If I am taking it, I have no fear. The aeroplanes seem like butterflies."'

In the courtyard outside Dr Suleman's office, there were around thirty men sitting on benches – drug users who had come to the centre for the day. They had a meal, a shave and a bath, and if they wished, they could spend the night at the centre. As I walked past, I saw a Nejat worker standing on a small platform at the head of the crowd, leading them through exercises and games that were punctuated by outbursts of clapping. Some of the men in that group were in wheelchairs, and others had their prosthetic limbs leaning against the benches.

We went past the courtyard into a small building. On the first floor was the detoxification centre. We walked the long corridor that had three wards for patients in different stages of withdrawal. Only one room was barred – it was for patients who had been admitted most recently. The second room was open, with patients lying or dozing on their beds, most with IV lines running into their arms. From the third room came a babble of voices, some raspy and slurred, others argumentative, used to commanding and getting their way. This was for patients who had almost finished their treatment, and were close to being discharged. On one of the beds was sixty-year-old Rashid Ali, who had taught chemistry in a nearby school for seventeen years, while secretly nurturing a drug habit. As he saw Dr Suleman, he launched into a lengthy petition. 'Fifteen days is too short for the body to recover from an addiction of thirty years,' he argued. 'You should keep us here at least a month.' Soon, the discussion turned into a very Kabuli exchange, with blessings and compliments being traded liberally. 'This is your house, I am just your servant,' said Dr Suleman. 'This doctor is an angel,' declared Rashid Ali to me. 'My beard has turned white with age, but I have never seen an angel like him.' 'Why are you calling yourself old?' protested Dr Suleman, as courtesy demanded. 'You are a young man!'

Behind the rhetorical flourishes and polite phrases, both doctor and patient were aware of the grim odds stacked against the men on the beds. Chances of relapse for recovered addicts in Afghanistan could be as high as 85 per cent, especially in the absence of community support, Dr Suleman told me. It was as Rashid Ali said: even when wiped clean of drug use, the body retained its stigma, as well as the memory of drugged serenity. And when the person changed only to find that nothing else had changed, or was likely to change – was it then a kind of betrayal, one met by a return to the blessed habit of oblivion? For many of the men in the clinic, the brief flirtation with ideas like freedom and happiness was to prove a mirage. 'They end up back on the street,' said Dr Suleman, back with the djinns that wander there.

Dr Suleman also introduced me to Wali, who had come to the centre as a patient. He had successfully rid himself of an addiction to heroin and crack, and now worked as a cook at Nejat. Even after two years of being off drugs, however, Wali avoided venturing out of the premises, except to buy groceries and vegetables. In the story he recounted for me appeared the now familiar signposts of a childhood spent in Iran and the return to a post-2001 Afghanistan, with hope and habit fighting in his body, as in his country.

After succumbing to drug use, Wali was disowned by his family. He left his village in the province of Daikundi and came to Kabul, destitute and entirely on his own. For a few weeks, he wandered the streets, unearthing the secret city known only to addicts. In the small, busy kitchen he now ran, he mapped that place for me with a mixture of thrall and fascination, as something that was receding but was still not far enough away.

'In the mornings I went to the Sar-e-Chowk,' he said, referring to the roundabout at the centre of Jada-e-Maiwand, with the black and blue monument I had seen. Dozens of labourers waited there with whatever tools they had, hoping to be hired for a day's work. Wali had no tools, but he sometimes got work as a construction labourer, making 300 afghanis (about $6) for the day. In the evening, he would go to Pul-e-Sokhta, a bridge that had become a hub for drug dealers and addicts. 'I would buy the drugs and fall asleep right there, under the bridge,' he said. Why there, why not anywhere else? I asked. Because he would want to simply eat, get his fix and fall asleep wherever he was, he said. But how did he know where to find the drugs? 'I knew. The way anyone else would know where to find bread.'

Following the advice of his companions under the bridge, Wali learned to navigate the city. He found ways to make a living, places to sleep, places to get a cheap meal that would leave more for the next pouch he bought. Until one day he returned from work to find the entire settlement under the bridge gone. The police had rounded them up and taken them to a detox centre, he was told. 'For a day, I wandered in a daze, unsure of where to go, unable to find my usual fix of the drug.' Finally he went to the police station and asked them to take him to the same place they had taken the others. He wanted to shake off his djinn.

In the Nejat centre, he found some of his companions from Pul-e-Sokhta. But while most of them left, he stayed, completing the treatment programme and then getting work in the same compound. A few of his companions still visited him, he said, but he avoided going out with them, as down that road lay his past. 'If I have to cross that bridge, my heart beats like crazy,' he said. If he remembers the high, it will claim him again. He blocks off its memory with the sting of onions in the kitchen, the demands of forty recovering drug users who want their lunch on time, and the satisfaction of being a role model, a talisman of success for those in the wards.

He also had his phone calls to his family in Daikundi, asking them to accept him again. For the first time in years, he was hopeful. 'I am trying to save enough money to get married,' he said. On his arm was a *taveez*, a charm. It was a wad of parchment inscribed with prayers, wrapped in a cloth, to protect him from the habit that stalked him – the djinn that lurked dormant in his veins, like the taste of blood on his tongue.

★ ★ ★

At one point during the day I spent with him, Dr Suleman told me what it was like to work with addicts, and how he dealt with the stigma that also rubbed off on him and his colleagues for associating with 'bad people'. 'These are not normal times we live in,' he said. Every morning, he would arrive in his office and make a few phone calls to find out if his children had got to school, if his wife had made it to work safely. 'People are not ready to trust anyone else, or to care for someone else.' The city had become possessed with a constant anxiety about survival that refused to let people help those who had fallen along the way. 'It is as if they fear that by helping them, they will become like them.'

Or, to put it another way: they are afraid to look at them too closely, because they may recognise themselves in their faces. Like the women abandoned in the *marastoon*, cast out by a damaged society for being imperfect.

I thought of his words as I walked through the narrow lanes of Muradkhane, the locality that adjoins the old city across the river and has a shrine at its heart. But unlike previous times, I did not linger in their buzzing rhythm, or admire the skill of the ironmongers whose shops lined the streets. I walked past the shrine's small door and kept going. Past walls protecting embassies and offices. Past a graceful house with shuttered windows. Past scrawled graffiti and looming billboards advertising mobile phones and airline tickets. And past a wall with watchtowers, displaying signs forbidding photography. It was topped with barbed wire, and soldiers with guns scanned the street from their posts, perched high above the earth. On this wall were also pictures made by children about the horrors of drug addiction. 'Drugs turn life into hell for those you love,' said one panel. Along the way, *spandi* children skipped past me, swinging tin cans of fragrant smoke above their tiny heads, offering to perform the incantation that would protect me from the evil eye and from evil djinns for just a dollar. I complied. I asked them to make me *nazarband*, sealed off from harm.

I thought of the man who had walked past me near the shrine, smiling amiably and vacantly as he made his way through the crowded streets of the neighbourhood. The only man in Kabul with no fear, as he turned aeroplanes into beautiful butterflies.

6

VEILED CITY

Love is a secret language that runs through the streets of Kabul.

In the summer of 2011, I spent my afternoons walking through the broad, tree-lined paths of Kabul University. These strolls occurred in my imagination, through a story borne to me every day by a young man in love.

Saleem, the lover, worked at the same TV channel where I was based. In the morning, he attended classes on the campus, where he was an undergraduate student. In the afternoon, he helped make shows for the channel. He would appear every day after lunch with the cups of green tea that washed down the meal. Joining our small group crowding into an office, he would tell us what had happened that morning in the latest episode of his love affair. Listening to him was like listening to the erstwhile storytellers of the bazaars of Delhi or Lucknow, who drew out threads of a saga day after day to a faithful audience. It was our version of an afternoon soap opera.

The girl Saleem liked also studied at the university. He had first spotted her in front of their faculty building. But they had no classes together. Saleem had no way to exchange greetings with her, not even an excuse to introduce himself. Telling her the truth – that he really liked her – was impossible. It would make her think he was a creep, he feared. That he didn't understand the codes with which love could proceed between them. He never so much as saw her alone, as she was always surrounded by her female friends. All he could do was, and what he made sure he did, was for their paths to cross on campus. He appeared in front of her and hoped to be seen; and for his presence to mean something.

The university that was the setting for these daily encounters was just a few minutes' walk from where we sat. I had walked through these relatively quiet, secluded roads numerous times. Over the years, as the rest of Kabul had changed, they had managed to stay constant and welcoming, like a loved one – familiar and known. War was transforming the city yet again, impacting it more often and more directly than before. It had grown physically, climbing onto and over the slopes of its hills, and the population was estimated to be between 4 and 5 million.[1] In 2011 there were several bloody attacks, including on a supermarket close to the heavily guarded Western embassies in Wazir Akbar Khan. The same year, Osama bin Laden was killed by US forces in Pakistan, and former Afghan president Burhanuddin Rabbani was assassinated at his home in Kabul. The US began pulling out its 'surge' troops that had arrived two years earlier.[2] Saleem had been about ten when the Taliban had been defeated. This was his only experience of peace. This was his first love.

As Saleem spoke, I could see the paths he described – mud tracks leading off from the wider road lined with trees and neat hedges. The leaves of these trees dappling the sun on its paved surface. The Soviet-style buildings on the campus, some with stone seats in front. Benches edged with rose bushes. Dust and light mingling in the open spaces. The perimeter walls in the distance, and as you approached the gates, the hum of the traffic and the city outside. In Saleem's telling, this familiar terrain was overlaid with his romantic journey.

Each step was full of possibilities, each move imbued with potential heartbreak and rejection, or elation. One day, he reported, she had looked at him a little longer than she had to. One day she had lingered at a turn. One day her friends had laughed when he had appeared. Did it mean something?

This romance would have seemed peculiar to many people, but to all of us in the room, it was normal. The fact that the couple had never spoken to each other, the intense scrutiny to nuanced signs – we were accustomed to this. That was how love played out, in Kabul as in Aligarh. Like an elaborate ritual, where this everyday exchange of glances could be an end in itself.

One afternoon, Saleem came to work thrilled. His beloved had sent him a message, through a mutual friend. She had told this friend that Saleem should style his hair in spikes more often. 'It suits him', she'd said. A code he took to mean that she'd noticed him too. Unlike all the other men on Kabul's streets, who she was trained to ignore, to deliberately not see, to behave as if they weren't there. By seeing Saleem, she had marked him out. From that day on, Saleem's hair was impeccably spiked. His romance had entered its next phase.

When I told this story about blind love in Kabul to Baba, he told me another story in return, that raised the stakes even higher. It was about a couple who fell in love without even seeing each other. We were talking in his study in Aligarh, and by the time we had this conversation, Baba's eyesight was starting to fail. He saw the world in a hazy way, he said, like we were all behind a veil. His biggest fear was that he would no longer be able to read. He was preparing for the day when his eyes failed him completely by mapping his movements through the house, using a series of tactile cues. Slowly, he tapped and felt his way from his bedroom to the dining table, from the table to his reading desk, from his desk to my grandmother's side. Frailer than Baba, she spent most of her days in bed. So each morning and each evening Baba would make his way to her bedside, where they would converse in short sentences, in raised voices. The effort would exhaust them both. They listened to the radio, or summoned their favourite classical compositions on their tape recorder. Sometimes they held hands.

The evening we talked about Kabul, Baba's ailing eyesight meant he could no longer refer to his copy of the *Shahnama*. So he recited the story from memory. It was a monsoon evening, and his voice was interspersed by the lash of falling rain, the calls to prayer from all the neighbourhood mosques, and the discordant thunder of generators powering his housing colony through the inevitable power cut that followed the cloudburst. His words lit up the room.

Baba's story was about Rudaba, a princess of Kabul. Like all princesses, she was beautiful and accomplished. She was also feisty and willing to take risks for her happiness. She fell in love with Zal, a handsome prince visiting her city, without ever seeing him, based only on tales of his prowess. It was an unlikely match. Rudaba was 'fairy-faced' and beloved. Zal had been born with white hair, and had consequently been abandoned by his father. The magical bird Simurgh had raised him in a nest in the mountains. Grown up, he had reconciled with his family. This was the man Rudaba pledged her heart to with such sudden abandon. Rudaba's ladies-in-waiting protested. This outsider was no fit mate for her. But Rudaba refused to listen.

> She shrieked at them,
> With frowns that shut her eyes exclaiming: 'Bah!
> Ye strive in vain: it booteth not to hear.
> If to some star I lost my heart, could I
> Find any satisfaction in the moon?
> ... Zal, son of Sam, is tall enough for me

> . . . To me he giveth peace of soul and mind.
> Talk not of other men, be his my heart,
> Bit as it is by love of one whom I
> Have never seen!'[3]

Baba recited parts of the poetry to me in its original Persian, calling up the verses from memory in his room in Aligarh. I read the rest of the story in an English translation, in my room in Kabul.

The chastened ladies hastened to Zal's camp by the river to inform him of Rudaba's plight. The prince was already smitten, having heard tales of the princess too. That night he stood under Rudaba's bower and begged for a glimpse of her moon-like countenance. Rudaba immediately plaited her long and beautiful hair and flung it down for him to use as a rope. They spent the night together under the Kabuli sky. As the horizon grew lighter, they addressed the rising sun with the tearful reproach of lovers the world over.

> 'O glory of the world! One moment more!
> Thou needst not rise so soon.'[4]

But so much for the happy beginning. The story soon took a tragic turn. There was a seemingly unsurmountable obstacle to the union. Rudaba was descended from the dragon Zohak, a deadly enemy not only of Zal's family but also of the great King Minoucher. Zal's father was ordered by the king to destroy Kabul. Faced with such opposition, what were the love-struck couple to do?

* * *

I grew up on such stories and such dilemmas. In the books I read and the films I watched, there was a predominance of

romance and passion. Love and its accompanying emotions –
heartbreak, betrayal, pride and regret – were everywhere. It was
also taboo, invisible, off-limits, a scandal. This was a contradiction
of the kind that made perfect sense in the structure of our lives,
and was impossible to explain to others.

So love was all around us in Aligarh, and it was nowhere.
The idea of romance was mostly tolerated so long as it
culminated in the legitimate ending of a wedding. But the idea
of *being* in love, of engaging in an affair – even with 'suitable'
boys – was a mire of complicated rules and sanctions. Naturally,
these rules were often broken or at least subverted.

The first such entanglement I encountered came from a
love letter addressed to my teenaged cousin by an anonymous
admirer. He followed her to college every day, he wrote, and
she was the most beautiful girl he had ever seen. If she loved
him back, all she had to do was clutch the leaves on the mango
tree outside our house, then he would know she felt the same
way too. The letter ended up in the hands of her adolescent
brother, who fumed and threatened to beat up the (unknown)
writer. My cousin, meanwhile, wept in shame at what she had
done, not quite sure how she had done it. I, still a child, was
horrified and thrilled by the drama. At the time, the only
reaction I found jarring was my father's, who tried to calm
them both down while fighting back his laughter. Everything
else was as it should be. Love without sanction of this kind was
a tragedy, a freakish emotion, shameful.

I recognised these thoughts in Kabul, years later, by which
time I had also learned other things about love. That it was
mendacious and comic, sneaky and resilient. That it was a
risk. And that it usually found a voice. Spiky hair. Mango
leaves. It revealed itself in such innocuous sights on the streets
of Kabul and Aligarh, to signal romance to those who could
read the signs.

Seen this way, love is a secret language that hides behind the everyday city. It winks from messages scrawled on the backs of cars and trucks, painted in verses about joy and heartbreak and betrayal. '*Mohabbat gunah nest*' – 'Love is not a sin' – these vehicles declare as they trundle their way towards the snow-capped mountains. Cyclists pedal past humming a refrain from a love song. Posters show couples in embrace. Glances dart across streets, smiles appear and are returned. As in every other city in the world, in Kabul too lovers find places to meet, ways to talk, endings to aspire to. And oblivious to such endings and emotions, the opaque surface of the city continues to tap out the code printed on it by those who live there. All the age-old promises of love, speaking to those who can read them, those they are in fact intended for.

Looking for love in Kabul is something like looking at a mirror under a veil – it reveals and conceals the secret face of the beloved.

***

Love transforms. It changes the interior and exterior landscapes of our lives. The street on which the beloved lives, or is met, or is glimpsed, is different from every other. It is the path that transforms the terrain. In Urdu and Persian poetry, love is referred to as *nasha*, intoxication. It turns the banal into the extraordinary. Nothing is as it used to be. For lovers, the city appears anew.

Mentioning love transformed the atmosphere in the house at Qala-e-Fatahullah too. It brought sheepish smiles on the faces of the men gathered around Khalid. Their voices became nostalgic, dipping in and out of the decades, teasing each other, spilling secrets mercilessly. The awkward wooings of their teenaged ghosts formed a map of Kabul when it was a small, mostly peaceful city through the 1970s. I heard the snatches of a Hindi film song, played by Khalid's cousin through each of his heartbreaks. Khalid's friends recalled evenings spent on rooftops, waiting for the girls they admired to walk through the street. Khalid himself talked of a glimpse he had caught of a woman when he was around ten years old, which had etched itself into his memory. He had seen her one afternoon through the open door of a trendy night spot called Club 99, on his way home from tutoring classes in the long winter vacations. The woman was sitting at the empty bar, her hair was loose, and she was smoking a cigarette. In Khalid's description, she remained the most beautiful woman he had seen. That winter was the first after the Soviet invasion. The city was on the verge of transforming when Khalid walked past that club, its door standing open during the day. These memories spilled out, fresh and vivid, touched with emotion, as though these things had happened yesterday. As though I could still walk to Shahr-e-Nau and find her – that woman, at that bar.

These conversations led me to a famous story about a pair of lovers in Kabul's old city, called 'Real Men Keep Their Word'. The short text reveals the way love blossoms like quickfire in Kabul – behind the walls of its homes, on its streets and in the sky. It was written by Akram Osman, who became famous in the 1960s for reading out stories on the radio. A collection of his work, titled *Mardara Qawl As*, was published in Dari in 1988, with the English translation appearing in 2005.[5] Osman's stories are set in the 1950s, and describe the lives of people in Kabul's old city. For English readers like me, the translation provided a rare glimpse into the alleys and forgotten customs of this quarter; the everyday courtesies between kinsmen, vignettes from the lives of *pahlawans* (wrestlers), singers, street hawkers, kite sellers and courtiers. It is dense with the carnivals of Kabul, and its silences; with its rhythms and its seasons.

There are several ways to read Osman's text – as a story about lovers in Kabul's old city, as well as a love letter to a version of Kabul that was already gone. Soon after his book was published, Kabul was overtaken by war, and the city that Osman himself knew was destroyed. He escaped in 1992, shortly before the internecine fighting breached the capital, and lived in Sweden until his death in 2016.

Like many such stories, it is a tale of love and separation.

The story begins on a winter afternoon like any other, with teenaged Sher and his cousin Tahira in the same room. Sher was by the window, Tahira by the stove. Something moved between them that day, and just like that, everything else changed as well. But before Sher could confess his feelings to Tahira, a malicious neighbour whispered to her father about Sher's attentions. The angry patriarch banned Tahira's visits to her cousin's home. Weeks passed by. Finally, the night before the festival of Eid, Sher devised a way to reach out to her. An expert kite-maker, he created a kite with 'Happy Eid' emblazoned on it. The next morning, he climbed on his roof and flew it around Tahira's house, swooping and turning it above her courtyard. Tahira read the words on the fragile paper and bamboo fluttering in the air. She went on the roof and saw Sher holding the string. Distracted, he sent the kite crashing into her yard. That's how the Kabuli duo began their romance.

In 1984, Afghan Film produced a movie based on the story. It was partly shot in the old city, and in one scene the camera captures Eid celebrations across the city as a song plays in the background. 'Eid Mubarak to lovers (everywhere),' say the lyrics. We see images of festivities: a fairground, a richly decorated marketplace, children hugging. We see the rooftops, connected like a city within the city, and the sky with several kites dancing on the horizon.

In the story, the sky turns into a secret billet, a tender scrawl in a familiar hand that can be read by just one pair of eyes, through a kite pirouetting on the horizon. Like the hidden mirror, reflecting its message only to the beloved.

In Aligarh, as in Kabul, such currents of love are a form of subterfuge against the world, both a fraught conspiracy and a triumph of willpower over circumstance. The city has changed, but Kabuli lovers are still skilled in sending forth and reading signs that colour the air. Once I knew to look for them, I found them everywhere. 'Don't cry girls, I'll be back,' declared the backs of large Land Cruisers that hurtled down the streets, unheeding of pedestrians and other traffic, as brazen as a wolf whistle. The misspelled legend 'No girls no tention' played it cool and hard to get, with the tinted windows of the cars adding to the exclusivity of its inhabitants. Some added a line in a smaller font, 'Just kidding'.

Romance hummed through the ether, apparent only in the postures of men and women hunched over phones, or gazing with tenderness at their laptops. The most hectic forms of flirting occurred virtually: through texts, online messaging, or phone calls. In Internet cafes and offices around the city, keyboards busily clicked on Facebook accounts. Many of them used fake names and pictures, or had multiple accounts, to shield their profiles from their families. Like the kite flying over Tahira's house, these online lives were proxies for signs and emotions. And sometimes they too crashed. A young man recounted to me how his cousins living abroad had spilled the beans to his parents about his Facebook flirtation. 'I had to open another secret account and make sure my family didn't know about it,' he said bitterly. 'They live in Canada,' he added, 'but they don't want me to have a life in Kabul.'

Meeting in person was a luxury, to be planned carefully and sparingly. A young woman I worked with asked me if it was possible to go out with young men in public in India. 'Can you just be there, a boy and a girl, together?' she asked, with wonder in her voice. 'Depends on where you are in India,' I replied, thinking of mango leaves in Aligarh, and Delhi malls full of couples holding hands.

One afternoon in 2013, I walked with Nazira seeking out the places where lovers met, through the lanes of Karte Seh, a hotspot for couples looking to spend some time together.

The locality had developed during the 1940s as an extension to Shahr-e-Nau. Its houses had large gardens and had been built to accommodate university professors and civil servants. During my time in Kabul I had seen it transform from a tranquil area with wide roads to a denser mix of villas and multi-storey apartments, with large steel gates and armed guards at the entrances. According to Khalid, the area had been one of the chic localities of Kabul during the 1980s, thanks to the presence of several elite girls' schools, a French bakery and a billiards hall. The Barikot cinema, which I had seen only as a ruin, was then new and popular. It had a rooftop restaurant where a live band performed in the evenings.

On the route we walked that afternoon, the streets were dotted with restaurants, bakeries and grocery stores. We walked past small cafes that occupied the ground floors of commercial buildings, with hand-drawn images of coffee cups and French fries displayed on their facades. Some of them had tightly drawn curtains blotting out their windows, the cloth dark blue and impermeable. Other cafes looked like American diners (or how these diners look in the movies), with images of burgers and pizzas illustrating the menu boards, and glittering chrome counters. 'They call these places "cappuccinos",' Nazira told

me. 'As in "Let's meet at the cappuccino this evening".' 'There's
a cappuccino near our house,' she added. 'Everyone goes there
to have sheesha and to do flirting.'

These 'lenient' cafes offered at least a notional anonymity,
providing a rare space for young Afghans where nobody knew
them, or would report them back to their families. This was a
tough proposition in Kabul. Even when you were in a public
space, you could just as well be in the sights of your family. I
had seen this invisible watchfulness in action when my friend
Karim had lit up a cigarette in the courtyard of a theatre.
Within minutes he had got a phone call from his father in
Switzerland, telling him off for smoking. And I had seen it in
Aligarh as a teenager. In the years before mobile phones and
easy long-distance calling, the owners of public call booths
would tip off parents if their daughters were seen making
frequent phone calls alone. 'Mariam is speaking to Delhi a lot
these days,' they would say casually, the words like a grenade
being thrown into a room.

We had gone inside one of the restaurants on the main
road that Nazira said was popular among young couples. It
seemed unremarkable from the outside; on my own, I may
well have walked past it. The interior too seemed dusty and
uninviting, with empty tables lined up against the walls of a
large room. Nazira led me past this musty room, and out into
an inner courtyard. We walked onto a lawn, which also had
some chairs and tables arranged under umbrellas, also empty.
We kept walking, to another part of the garden separated by a
thin woven mat hanging like a curtain. Beyond this were
takhts (seating platforms) scattered with bolster pillows – the
kind of relaxed seating arrangement found across gardens and
picnic areas in Kabul. On these *takhts* were groups of young
men and women, talking and laughing, smoking hookahs and
sipping tea.

Nazira and I had a coffee under one of the lonely umbrellas, and talked of the romances we had witnessed in Kabul. For Nazira's generation in particular – young, educated Afghans who had spent time abroad – offices provided a good setting to pair off with each other. Over the years, in different places, women had described the mechanics of these relationships to me. Noora had started flirting with a guy on the phone, but had stopped when he told her she looked beautiful in a chador, in her *sada husn*, or plain beauty. She liked to wear jeans, she said. And she loved make-up. Rabia was in love with her cousin in Germany. They talked every day on Skype, and were going to get married soon. Sana was into a colleague who took the same shuttle as her to work. They flirted on the commute. He was the second guy she liked, and she hoped he would turn out to be nicer than the first one. 'Everyone is doing it,' Nazira said, talking about her female friends chasing romance. 'But they don't tell anyone about it.' Unlike Saleem, who recounted his romance to us each afternoon. Men told their love stories, women tried to find ways to hide them.

I asked Nazira if she was interested in any of the young men in her office. She was not, she said firmly. Love was a *museebat*, a problem. For instance, if she used her phone to text any male friend, and her family found out about it, she would have to stop working. She had seen girls betrayed by their boyfriends, forced to leave college, or their jobs. Sometimes, as we both knew, the consequences were far worse.

Even if the romance worked out, and a girl got married to someone she loved, Nazira continued, sooner or later her husband would object to her being out, or talking to other men. Like Rabia, who moved to Germany after getting married, a few months after my conversation with Nazira. When a male colleague called her, she had contacted Nazira and said, 'Tell him not to call me again. My husband doesn't like it.'

What Nazira knew, like I had learned in Aligarh, was that the cost of romance was almost always paid by the women involved. And in Nazira's personal reckoning of her life, it was too high. Under the Taliban government in Kabul, she would not have gone to university, or held a job. Sitting under the umbrella, Nazira counted off everything she loved about her life in Kabul – all the things that would have been impossible a few years ago. She enjoyed her job. She went where she pleased and wore what she liked. She could talk to anyone, any time, she said. She was not going to give all this up for a man.

We left the restaurant and walked towards the university, crossing the many stalls and small businesses that gave the street a constant frisson of activity: the *bolani* stalls hissing out vapours of frying dough, the fragile frame of a puncture-repair shop, several carts piled with fruit. And the ubiquitous figures of children whirling cans of *spand*.

We slipped through the metal gates into the campus and walked on a wide road lined with trees. Kabul University had opened to women in the 1960s, and they had formed a significant number of its student body through the 1970s and 80s, as I had seen in the newsreels at Afghan Film. In 2012, there were around 4,000 female students enrolled, out of a total of nearly 17,000.[6] This too was a rebuilding of the city, and of women's lives, after 2001.

We walked through the paths that Saleem had restlessly paced during his summer romance. When Nazira was a student here in 2004, she said, the police used to round up young couples if they sat and talked on a bench under the trees, or outside their faculties. 'They would ask what we were doing there. "Do your parents know you're here?"' Friends would have to come and rescue them, and convince the cops that they merely studied together. 'Now it's not such a big deal if you're just sitting with a boy and talking.' But only, she added, if *all* you intended to do was talk. And even then, if you were in a secluded corner or under too many trees? That was not allowed.

That is why in Kabul, the key to finding love depended as much on time as on place. Nazira explained this to me as we walked out of the campus, which was emptying as the day approached its end.

'All *ishq-wishq*, love and romance, has to happen within office or college hours,' she said. 'In the evening, everyone has to go home.'

***

If love is a secret language, a code tapped out beneath the surface of the city, Kabuli weddings are the opposite. They are declarations of love and manifestations of romance on a monumental scale, etched into the very architecture of the city. Both aspiration and extravagant declaration, they are impossible to ignore. In the duality of Persian poetry, they represent the *zahir*, the overt, and the apparent manifestation of all that the *batin*, covert, codes of love conceal.

If the secret city of love ends with sunset, Kabuli weddings light up the night.

Weddings have always been a big part of life in Kabul. On one of my evenings at home, I read some interviews with residents of Kharabat about their memories of love and marriage in Kabul's old city during the 1970s. This was the area I had walked through with Ustad Hamahang, and where Sher and Tahira lived in Osman's story. To read these accounts was to encounter a city fraught with desire, and its culmination – marriage. They were also rich with details on the rituals that had bound communities, the celebrations enmeshed with networks of families and neighbourhood spaces.

Women described the proper way to observe engagements, and the etiquette of gift giving. 'Some families took presents for the first night of winter or the longest night of the year, when they would eat watermelon at midnight . . . On the night of *barat* [15 Sha'ban], the groom's family would also take fireworks, fruit and clothes, and light candles and sit with the bride until dawn. On this night, when there is a full moon, the family fills a bowl with water and watches the reflection of the moon, and wish that their lives should be as beautiful as the moon. The bride and groom did not see each other before the night of the wedding'.[7] They talked of the soup that was cooked overnight by neighbours, and how families visited nearby shrines to seek blessings for the union.

The invitations to the nuptials would be handed out in the shape of *nuqls*, or sugared almonds. 'If you received two *nuqls*, this meant that two members of your family were invited, while if you received a handful of *nuqls*, the entire family was invited . . . In those days, if you were to invite someone with a card, he wouldn't come to the party, because you had used a piece of paper.'

Before the *nikah*, the formal wedding ceremony, women would apply henna to the bride's hands. After the *nikah*, the bride and groom would be brought together for a ceremony called *aina mashaf*. It was a ritual I had seen performed often, and knew to be a moment of stylised auspiciousness, originally intended to provide a first glimpse to the married couple of each other. In a mirror held under a veil, the bride and groom gaze first at the pages of the Quran, and then at each other.

Things were already changing by this time, however, as the elite and those who could afford it were getting married in hotels or clubs. Several friends showed me videos or photos of their parents or their siblings at the upmarket Kabul Intercontinental Hotel. '*Everyone* got married there,' one of them told me in the tone of the privileged describing their small world. 'There was nowhere else to go.' In these images the brides wore the white gowns so popular with Kabuli women, since Queen Soraya's dashing sister Khayria Tarzi wore one for her wedding in 1909.[8] There were other pictures of women in elegant dresses and high heels, couples dancing around the room, singers with long sideburns and dashing suits.

The disruption of the civil war tamped down the celebrations, and the strict social control of the Taliban government brought silence to the ceremonies. So after 2001, among the first things to boom in Kabul were weddings. Magnificent wedding halls mushroomed across the city. Accompanying the boom in these venues was a network of associated enterprises – of clothes and decorations, food and music. It was like an explosion after a long period of tension – unrestrained, and with unforeseen consequences spilling to unexpected places.

In areas like Shahr-e-Nau, entire streets were taken over by businesses devoted to weddings. Next to the dress shops were rows of beauty parlours, with images of brides bedecked in finery. There were cake shops with elaborate, cream-festooned confections in several tiers. And there were decoration centres for cars, where plastic and foam and flowers transformed the sleek vehicles that carried the bride and groom into their new lives. I had seen these threads converge during my first spring in Kabul. As the weather turned warmer, it became routine to get caught in traffic alongside a bridal party. The couple would be in a car trailing flowers and tinsel hearts, gamely waving at a camera crew that leaned out of an adjacent car, recording every move. In their outburst of merriment as well as their ferocity, such festivities contained something of the rattle of war, something of the madness of love.

Over the years, these 'hall weddings', as they are called, became increasingly expensive, pushing tens of thousands of dollars into the industry. The total cost of a wedding in 2013 could range from anywhere between 5 and 25 lakh afghanis (around $9,000 to $ 45,000 at the time). While the groom's family paid most of the bills, traditionally the bride's family made the decisions about decorations, catering and music. Even those who could not afford it took on debts to fund these lavish occasions.

These wedding halls mushroomed across Kabul – from just four in 2001 to over eighty in 2008.[9] They were particularly congregated around a strip of road near Taimani in the north of the city. I had seen this locality first with a few houses rising from behind ruined mud walls. Then the modest road had been widened and was soon lined with massive structures built of glass and steel. They had water features and decorations and gates that towered above passers-by. Some had imposing drives sweeping up from the main road, others had plastic trees strung with glowing lights. Somewhere in the midst of this always escalating opulence was the first wedding hall I had seen in Kabul, the Shaam-e-Paris ('An Evening in Paris'). With its plastic replica of the Eiffel Tower on its lawns, it had seemed ludicrously overblown then, out of place in the city. Within three years, it had been eclipsed into shabby obscurity by its flamboyant neighbours.

Imposing as this 'wedding quarter' was during the day, it truly came alive after sunset, when the entire area glittered with fountains, fireworks and colours. Cars waited in long queues to enter the different venues. Seeing this road at night was like encountering a misplaced fragment of Las Vegas. If you flew into Kabul after dark, you could see the lights from the sky.

Hall weddings were essential symbols of their era. They reflected the shifts that had recast Kabul after 2001, when some people became very rich, very quickly. The large aid budgets and the presence of NATO bases created high rates of economic growth till 2012.[10] This was an economic boom fuelled by war; it enriched a certain section of Afghan society, and provided a degree of material security to another. The uneven growth of the era was to prove ephemeral, like the uneven, brittle peace it came with. But until then, Kabul was alight with the energy of this bubble. In their fevered embrace of excess and ever increasing demonstrations of wealth and prestige, wedding halls represented this new reality of the city.

As a result, these halls were often where generations and social values also clashed. A colleague had taken her aged father-in-law on a rare outing to a cousin's wedding that had been held in one of the biggest halls in town. The old gentleman had been traumatised by the entire event, she told me, horrified by the brazen display of both wealth and limbs. But wasn't it a segregated event? I asked. 'Yes, but the women came to pay their respects to him,' she explained. And that had almost been his undoing. 'The poor man nearly collapsed right there. All that money, all those naked legs.'

* * *

Within the parameters of these modern hall weddings, the norms of everyday life were reversed. Entering these spaces was like falling through the looking glass – what was taboo was permitted, what was hidden was not only revealed but flaunted. This was especially true for women. Within the strict boundaries of the wedding celebrations, they appeared adorned and unveiled.

I had my first glimpse of this licence in the shopfronts displaying the white wedding gowns worn by Afghan women after their *nikah*. Walking from Kolola Pushta to Shahr-e-Nau, I passed small dressmaker and tailor shops, as well as marble-floored shopping plazas in the main bazaar. On that short walk alone I encountered a wide range of wedding dresses – skin-tight mermaid styles, meringue-shaped creations, sleeveless and low-backed gowns. Not only the dresses themselves, but the images of brides on the wall boldly staked their space.

Alongside these were traditional Afghan outfits for other nuptial ceremonies, as well as Indian ensembles inspired by TV shows. Then there was what seemed to be a sartorial underground of glittery party dresses – costumes embellished with leather and metal, silken cocktail dresses and short frocks. These would have been bold wardrobe choices in most places in India. In Kabul, in the midst of women wearing staid ankle-length skirts and scarves, they seemed outrageous, an impossible whim of shopkeepers. In fact, I learned, these were the clothes women wore to hall weddings. 'Only within the hall,' explained the colleague I was with, seeing the disbelief on my face. 'Only with our families.' I was fascinated. These clothes were my first inkling of the glamour of Kabuli weddings. They lit up the streets with their celebratory sparkle.

I began keeping a wish list of dresses, an inventory of desire that I maintained as a way of inhabiting this imagined celebration. There was a purple floor-length silk gown (in my mind, all rustle) with swirls of fabric gathered at the front. A backless dress in electric blue that came with a matching hat, trimmed with plastic feathers and flowers. There were gold lamé dresses, and dresses that seemed to be made of sequins and beads. I dreamed of sashaying into a wedding in Aligarh wearing one of these outfits. In fact, I lacked the nerve to wear them even in Kabul.

From the dresses, I moved to the beauty salons, where the bride and her close female relatives went to prepare for the different ceremonies – the henna celebrations, the *nikah* or formal wedding ceremony, and the post-wedding reception. The salon visit is an essential part of modern Kabuli weddings, and was paid for by the groom. Men often complained about this, and women fiercely defended it. A colleague told me how his cousin's fiancée had sent all her female relatives to the salon, 'just to make the groom suffer. Everyone went. Even the old women, even the hopeless cases,' he bemoaned. 'Why wouldn't they?' a female colleague argued in return. 'That is how things are done'. A sentiment I had often heard in India, usually to justify the curtailing of some kind of pleasure or liberty to women. These salons were where women transformed into the magnificent creatures I had met at weddings, their make-up and stiff hairdos making familiar faces hard to recognise. It was as if they had donned a different skin, setting them free to act in ways that they chose, and that were briefly permitted. Like a veil, or an armour, over their everyday selves.

I had frequented Kabul's salons for years, enjoying the conviviality and conversations there. But it was only in 2013 that I watched a bridal party being prepared, at a parlour in the northern suburb of Khair Khana. The area used to be so far removed from the city that an agricultural fair was held there. And the journey there felt so long, Khalid had said with a laugh, that his mother used to boil eggs to take along on the drive. Now it was a burgeoning locality, with orderly crossroads and a perennial water shortage. I had been there a few weeks previously to offer my condolences to a friend, whose son had been murdered on the street in front of his house. He had been shot by a neighbour during an argument and died on his own doorstep at the age of twenty-five.

The parlour was in a different part of the locality, on a street lined with several salons and other wedding-related businesses. The shops stretched away in parallel lines of white gowns and ribbons, giving it an air of perennial celebration. Inside, gauzy curtains blocked off the glass storefront, and no men were allowed beyond the threshold. The owner and six attendants were working on the wedding party, though by Kabul standards, this was a small establishment. Three women were sunk deep inside various pieces of equipment for blow-drying, dyeing or bleaching. The others sat waiting on the sofa. Behind them, some young children were asleep, bolstered by cushions. One wall had floor-length mirrors, flanked by shelves filled with bright bottles and jars of cosmetics and hair products.

The women had scattered their plastic bags on the floor, with their everyday clothes peeking out of the top. They were already wearing their embroidered outfits for the evening. There was leftover food nestled inside tinfoil containers and newspaper packing on a glass-topped table – kebabs, naan and rice. An electric kettle was plugged in and glass cups smudged with lipstick traces sat on a tray. The air was heavy with the smell of oranges, grilled meat and hairspray. The bridal party had been there for a large part of the day.

It takes at least six hours to complete a bride's make-up, Sediqa, the owner of the salon, told me. Most of her business came from bridal groups, like the one I was watching. Her charges varied according to the demands of the clients, and the financial status of the groom. People who married for love spent more, she told me, 20,000 afghanis (around $400) or upwards. For those who couldn't afford her rates, she gave a reduction, charging only 5,000 afghanis (around $100), because it was a work of *khair*, goodness, to help women look beautiful, to make them happy on their wedding day. There was rarely a question of a Kabuli bride not going to a salon, even if it was a small one, even if it was hard to afford. 'We have this one day to fulfil all our dreams,' she said, echoing what I had heard in many places. 'I have to make sure it is perfect, and that the bride will have beautiful memories for her whole life.' The ephemerality of this beauty was what added to the zeal behind its construction. It was like a dream; it would soon vanish.

Each time I had walked into a salon in Kabul, it had felt like entering a community, or a conspiracy, of desire and pleasure. As a place where women adorned themselves, and appeared as they wished to be seen, it was both something of a sanctuary and something of a minefield. That was why one of the women protested when she saw my camera. 'Don't take my photo,' she said, sitting bolt upright in the salon chair. Even as Sediqa reassured her, she kept repeating in a dazed voice, 'If my husband thought I was being photographed here, he would divorce me.' 'God forbid,' we all murmured piously, as I put the camera away.

Perhaps for the same reason, the women who worked at the parlour were touched with the same moral complexity. Sediqa negotiated a delicate balance every day, and the success of her business depended not only on how good her make-up and haircuts were, but also on the spotlessness of her personal reputation. Sediqa was in her forties, and spoke Urdu fluently from her years as a refugee in Pakistan. Her dyed burgundy hair was cut into stylish waves, she wore a smart black tunic and trousers, and had carefully applied her subtle make-up. She was the image of a modern Kabuli woman.

She told me about parlours where 'families wouldn't send their women because the owner had a bad reputation' and about parlours where 'a rough crowd harassed the owners'. By 'rough', she meant 'people who had moved to Kabul from the provinces'. Who were not sophisticated city dwellers, who haggled over money, whose menfolk were likely to burst into the salon carrying weapons. For this reason, salons could be dangerous places, reflecting the state of flux in Kabul in 2013. A week ago, she said, the owner of a large salon in Shahr-e-Nau had reportedly paid a ransom for her nine-year old son, who had been kidnapped from outside his school. 'Who will take responsibility for anyone here?' she asked. And then she answered her own question. 'Nobody is taking responsibility for anyone here.' So she was thinking of leaving Kabul once again. Maybe for India, where she could continue running a parlour.

Working in a salon was risky for women in another way too. None of her assistants, Sediqa said, had told their extended families that they worked at all, let alone in a beauty parlour. Helping brides prepare for their wedding day was not a good path to getting married yourself.

I remembered my friend Meena, who ran a salon and was a fan of Bollywood films. Whenever I visited her home, she served me a lavish meal, and kept her siblings on their toes through her efficient orders. She was beautiful and vivacious, and almost thirty – an advanced age to be a single woman in Kabul. Each time she was close to being engaged, the question of her work would cause the groom's family to object. Recently, she had got engaged to her cousin, who worked as a driver. The match had been arranged by her family. I asked Meena if she was happy with their choice; she replied that her fiancé had agreed to her continuing with the salon.

As I watched, Sediqa's assistants prepared the bride's relatives, applying foundation that turned their faces an even shade of almost white. They threaded and painted on eyebrows. Curled hair and sprayed it, adding false ringlets and pinning spangly veils that bobbed impertinently on the towering bouffants.

The last and most important job was the bride's make-up. Sediqa took charge once her assistant had laid the foundation.

She applied layers of cosmetics and then tiny beads of glitter – in the hair, carefully over the eyelids, on the cheekbones. It glimmered like ice on the thickened lashes. On the woman's hair she built a mighty edifice where the bridal veil would be placed. At every step the bride became stiffer, her expressions more mask-like, each step another layer between her and the onlookers, like veils that concealed even as they revealed. This was the face that would live in her memories and her wedding photographs.

It was nearly dusk when Sediqa finished. The women were late, but it didn't matter. Slowly, very slowly, they began leaving the salon, with many thanks and handshakes and kisses to Sediqa and her assistants. The men waited at the door, collecting the pieces of their family emerging from behind the curtains. They deposited the children, then the plastic bags and the leftover food containers – all the debris of the everyday that the women could no longer carry in their fairy-tale avatars, stiff with mousse and waterproof mascara. The ladies covered up their faces, their hair and their clothes, before getting into the cars. They would unveil at the wedding hall.

The last to leave was the bride. She came out of the parlour with her clothes completely covered with a white chador and an umbrella shielding her so that no one saw her in all her splendour. The bride took the few steps down the street in her high-heeled shoes before ducking into the car, her red mouth a perfect O on her chalk-white face, framed by the posters behind her, of dozens of brides posing on the street.

* * *

A few days earlier, I had visited a wedding hall with Sardar, a wedding videographer. Sardar represented the end of the process I had followed on the streets, taking the images that form the record of the wedding. It was a lucrative job, but a dangerous one. He had to ensure that the beautiful images he captured were visible only to those they were intended for.

Sardar picked me up from my house. I had asked if we could walk to the hall, and he had demurred, saying it wasn't safe. On the way, he joked about how long it had been since a suicide bomber had attacked Kabul. 'They'll get out of practice,' he quipped, with the dark humour so common in Kabul. 'As it is they can barely ever hit their targets.'

Sardar had started working at Afghan weddings in the refugee community of Peshawar, apprenticed with an older cameraman. After 2001, he returned to Kabul with his family. He was in his twenties then, and started his business with his younger siblings, who helped at night after school, and later while holding moderately well-paid day jobs. I had met Sardar through his younger brother, who worked as a director in a video production house, much to Sardar's pride.

The journey of this family-built business paralleled the growth of Kabuli weddings. When they began, the brothers would rent a camera and edit on borrowed machines. Over the years, they had ploughed back the profits from their work into hardware and invested in equipment, to be able to keep up with the competitive market. 'People want the latest things for their weddings and their wedding videos,' Sardar told me. 'They want their films to be no less than Bollywood films.'

We drove on the wide road that led to the neighbourhood of Karte Parwan. I saw apartment blocks, supermarkets, carpet sellers and mansions along the street. In the gaps left by these bigger buildings I also saw smaller mud homes and roadside shops, often little more than sheds. Many of the people who lived in the area had moved to Kabul from the provinces, or had returned from Iran and Pakistan or other places to create a home for themselves. By a roundabout was a large building where the hall was located.

It was the first time I had seen one of these venues during the day. The reflective glass covering its exterior glinted malevolently in the sun, like the glares of the men lounging around the car park. We entered the hall and walked through the different rooms, which were lit by chandeliers. The hall had several rooms, or 'salons', for all the different ceremonies and the hundreds of guests that are routine at Afghan weddings. The smallest of these could hold a minimum of three hundred people. The bigger salons had capacities of a few thousand. The hall also provided security services to its guests, including a weapons check-in facility and armed guards to intervene if the situation required. (If the guests became too violent and inclined to reach for their weapons, for instance. If anyone ogled, or was thought to ogle, the women. Or if the men sneaking drinks in the car park began exchanging insults that were too robust.)

All the salons had arrangements for segregation between the sexes, and most of the seats were on the women's side. Depending on their budgets and desires, the couple could sit under crescent moons or silk tents, and walk to the stage over a small wooden bridge, flanked by rocks and green ferns. In between these diverse backdrops were images of Bollywood actors dressed in bridal finery, laughing in marital rapture at the couple and their guests. Even the elevator had their faces painted on it. It was the iconography of a fairy-tale wedding. And like the best fairy tales, they were spun from thin air. From the columns to the furniture, from the outfits to the chandeliers – nearly everything I saw in the massive hall was imported into Kabul. The fairy-tale halls were built piece by piece with material untouched by the dust of the city.

I stood on the stage of one of the halls, looking at the rows
of beribboned chairs solemnly facing me. At the far end of
the room, the heavy pink curtains had shifted a few inches.
Beyond the bright yellow light of the chandeliers, behind the
pink-hued chairs, the rocks and running water, I could see
Kabul peeping through the window. The buildings were still
growing, new constructions spreading out further into the
mountains. I walked to the window and saw a dog tied in a
yard nearby, a girl fetching water in a plastic canister. The
tinted glass covered the city with a sepia film.

* * *

Weddings are closely linked to both honour and status in
Afghanistan, much like in India. In Kabul, it is a matter of
prestige for the groom's family to invite a large number of
guests, and host lavish celebrations. Each wedding in the hall
I was in could be customised to fit various budgets and scale,
as well as accommodate different kinds of taste. In 2013, for
instance, a family would have started off spending three to
four lakh afghanis (around $5,500 to $7,000) just for hiring
the rooms here. Then there were the pre-wedding parties,
clothes and jewellery for the bride, visits to the beauty salon
for her and her female relatives, a live band, plus paying for
photographs and a wedding video. I had a colleague whose
brother worked in Iran but had come to Kabul to be married.
The entire family pitched in for the event, for which the hall
rental alone was $6,000. My colleague's monthly income was
less than $300. I asked why his family didn't have a simple
wedding elsewhere. 'It's not a wedding if it's not a hall
wedding,' he said, in imitation of the bride's family. If he
couldn't afford it, his brother was told, he should come back
when he could. I also asked Sardar why so many people

wanted hall weddings now given how expensive they were. 'Kabul is a modern city,' he said. 'People here want to get married in a modern way.'

Sardar led me out of the large salon to his office, through a door that opened onto a stairwell. At the bottom was a dark corridor lined with rooms on one side. Sardar knocked on one of the doors and we heard the lock turn. Sardar's young assistant let us in, and then locked the door again. The office was two windowless rooms, the first with three chairs arranged around a desktop computer, and the back room with another computer and several hard drives on the desk. It was a world away from the chandelier-lit glamour we had wandered through earlier.

Sardar inhabited this terrain between erasures and appearances, between what had to be exaggerated and what had to be hidden away. He spent most of his evenings working in the salons, adding even more light to the brightly lit stage and ceremonies. I had seen teams like his at work: sharply dressed young men in suits, clutching video cameras, directing the relatives and the couple with fierce concentration. During the day he retreated to his dingy office, from where he made beautiful images appear. Like the mirror that also conceals as it reveals.

As he entered, Sardar whispered instructions to his assistant, who left the office and soon reappeared carrying plastic bags with bottles of sweet mango juice, which Sardar offered to me. I sipped the thick, chilled drink and watched the dazzle of Kabuli weddings play out on his screen.

The video was of a reception from a few nights ago. It followed the standard format for such films, I was told, as a redolent voice proclaimed, 'In the name of Allah, the Beneficent, the Merciful' – the invocation that Muslims begin tasks with. Then came a song from an Indian film, over which credits rolled for around two minutes. These included the name of the couple, their wedding venue and the names and telephone numbers of the beauty salon, the videographer, the decorator and the musicians. 'In some of these we cannot use the bride's real name,' Sardar told me. 'Some grooms don't want their wives' names to be on the lips of every man in the bazaar.' The video cut to a photo montage of the couple in various romantic poses – leaning on each other, eating cake, driving away in their decorated car. All these poses were arranged and choreographed by the videographer. 'This is the part that takes the longest to do because of all the effects it needs,' he said, as the couple's faces dissolved in a burst of fireworks.

The movie then showed the wedding hall from the outside, its fountains and lights in full flood, before moving the narrative to scenic locales. The bride and groom appeared juxtaposed in front of the Taj Mahal, then the Eiffel Tower, then the lakes of Bamiyan. Pictures of the couple, with their arms wrapped around each other, in a studio. It was a montage heavy with romance, with the couple sometimes gazing at the camera, sometimes at each other.

The family came on-screen, dancing to traditional Afghan songs, and then gyrating to pop songs, their moves as choreographed as those on music videos. I asked Sardar who the intended audience for these wedding films were. Only the family themselves, he said. Nobody other than the people in the videos would get to watch these recorded images, so layered with seduction, so heavy with love.

Sardar's job as the video producer was to package this day into an epic romance, fitting the scale of the couple's love. He was to provide an extra layer to the already flamboyant event, and move the audience from the ruined streets of Kabul, to a place where they were the stars of their own reality.

None of this is unique to Kabul. Wedding videos the world over are replete with kitschy imagery and grand romances, which may or may not have any basis in reality. In Kabul, however, the wedding videographer must achieve this effect within a confined conceptual and physical space. If even a few of these frames were to find their way out from his hard drive to the outside world, Sardar said, it was unlikely he would ever work as a wedding videographer again. 'It's a very dangerous job,' he said. 'People have even been killed after this.' That's why when he finished with a video, he deleted the footage from his computer in front of a family member, like the groom or his brother.

If the images he took were so dangerous, I asked, why did they have to be shot at all? 'If they didn't, the couple's relatives would regard them badly,' Sardar explained. 'If a groom didn't arrange for such a video and such a ceremony the girl would cry and say that he did not love her.' The whirlwind romances produced by Sardar for the camera were one more essential frill of modern Kabuli weddings.

Within the space of the wedding hall, Sardar stood in the delicate position of being the only non-family member in rooms filled with women dancing and celebrating uninhibitedly. This meant that, like Sediqa, he had to maintain a reputation for absolute integrity, and make his persona harmless, turn himself into a mere extension of the lens. There were several people, he said, who only called him for their events. He was like a member of their family now. Recently some clients had started asking for women videographers. In such cases he would politely turn down the job. There were not enough qualified camerawomen in Kabul, and he could not risk dissatisfied clients later. For now, he had to be treated as at least a temporary relative to the ladies on the dance floor, and be permitted to arrange the bridal couple in embraces for photographs.

Despite all his precautions, Sardar had seen his share of
trouble at weddings. 'People are often drunk or emotional
there, or just want to show they are "heavier" than the
others.' By 'heavier', Sardar was referring to the power games
that happen at weddings everywhere, but in Kabul may end
up having more dire consequences. At one wedding, he
recalled, the bride's family had taken exception to his
shooting the women's section and had sent him away. 'Then
the groom's brother had seen me and said: "What are you
doing here? Go back in and shoot."' A fight had ensued,
which had escalated and moved out onto the street. 'The
groom's uncle went to the salon and rubbed dirt on the
bride's face. Then her brothers went round and beat up the
groom's brother and uncles.' Incredibly, the reception went
ahead the next day. 'The groom married her and kept her at
home while he took another wife,' he said, and was silent for
a while in contemplation of this cold revenge. 'It's all become
about power and one-upmanship. It's as if it's not a wedding
but war.'

He had seen strange things, tragic things, silly things in
the twilight zone of the wedding halls, where so-called
Afghan values were both paramount and suspended, he said.
'Anything can happen here, it's all about honour. It's like we
are in a place where there are no laws, you can do whatever
you like,' he said, and I listened, unsure whether he was
talking of Kabul, or the world, or just the halls he spent his
days and nights in.

I asked Sardar how many weddings had taken place in this
particular hall that year. He laughed, unable to even venture a
number. He did tell me that during the wedding season of
spring and summer, the hall was booked for at least two parties
every day, one from 9.30 a.m. to 3.30 p.m., and the second
from 4 p.m. to midnight. The former time slot, he said, was

preferred by wedding parties that came from the provinces, where it's a sign of prestige to get married in a Kabul wedding hall. I asked how much profit the hall made over a month but he refused to answer. All he said was that there were new halls being built all over the city. It was one of the few growth industries in the country, something he was sure would not go away. Even with the looming economic uncertainty, and the political flux, Kabul's wedding halls would endure.

Sardar discussed weddings in terms of costs and transactions. For every video he made, he charged $600. This was a profit of about $300 for every video. There were few weddings through the long winter, but during the spring and summer months he worked double shifts and shot an average of two weddings a day. Often he ended up seeing three or four weddings a night, if his crew took up work in a different hall. Sometimes he didn't go home for long spells, but spent his days in his office, and nights in a shiny suit at the hall. He had seen thousands of weddings, he estimated, over the course of his career. All of which had given him a pragmatic attitude towards love and marriage.

Sardar was the eldest brother, which meant he was first in line for marriage. I asked if he had plans for a wedding soon. He answered my question with another list of figures and accounting. Two years ago he had paid for his younger brother's wedding in an upmarket hall. 'We got the best of everything. Every possible frill and feature.' He was still repaying the loans he had taken out for that celebration. For now, however, he couldn't afford the expense of another wedding. But what if he fell in love? I asked. Wouldn't he want to get married then? He shrugged, a man proposing an impossibility. 'Only if I find a woman who is ready to get married for a hundred dollars,' he said.

***

As Afghan weddings have gone from being merely ostentatious to extravagant, there have been various attempts over time to contain them. In the 1920s, Amir Amanullah's government enacted a law that limited expenditure at weddings. In 1978, after the Saur Revolution, the PDPA government attempted to set a ceiling on the 'bride price', the amount paid by the groom to the bride's family.[11] These were followed by backlashes – from the indignant clergy in the 1920s to anti-government propagandists in the late 1970s. In 2011, once again the state attempted to regulate the extravagance around weddings by drafting a law, which also faced protests.

The provisions of this law sought to reduce the expenditure on hospitality, by limiting the number of guests and the amount that could be spent on each invitee. It also sought to impose cultural controls, including stipulations that the bride and the guests not wear garments that were too revealing or too tight.[12]

The proposed law was welcomed by some young men and women who wanted to begin married life unencumbered with debts. But it also sparked anger from Afghans who resented the government interfering in how they got married or entertained their guests. (Ironically, legislators and high-ranking government officials were among the biggest spenders at wedding halls.) Protesters included a mix of wedding-hall owners, human rights groups and women's lobbies.

These proposed measures, along with the rising clout of the insurgents and increased insecurity, made it seem that the festivities were up against a ticking clock. Perhaps that was why Kabul's trippy wedding quarter was animated by such furious urgency.

Maybe the revellers were moved by a spirit of defiance, an urge to thumb their noses at the diktats of government and Taliban alike. Maybe they just wanted to grab happiness and have fun while they could. Like the girls taking risks to watch Bollywood films in darkened rooms, they wanted to stake a claim to existing, even briefly, even through the most trivial of acts, outside the suffering that often seemed to define their city.

For some, perhaps the frenzied celebrations of life and love that took place in Kabul's wedding halls were a way to navigate their tenuous present. A way to obliterate the uncertainty, a way to live before life changed once again.

I had attended a wedding reception in Kabul with a friend and his family when the law on weddings was being discussed at every gathering. We had arrived in Taimani after dark, and had driven slowly down the street, soaking in the glory of the different halls. Our party was in one of the newest, biggest venues. There were decorated cars parked near the entrance and patterned lights cascading down the glass front of the building. As we walked into the foyer, the walls almost hummed with energy. We crossed a security check and a gun deposit. My invitation had included a request to leave my camera behind, and my bag was searched for this before I entered. In the foyer I saw constellations of young men and women form and disappear. They sat for a bit on the sofas, talking and admiring their joint reflections in the mirrors. And then they dispersed, acting on some internal calculation, vanishing before they became too conspicuous.

I walked into the women's section and plunged into a crowd of around five hundred ladies, who had removed their outer garments to display their festive outfits. Here was the sartorial city I had first spotted in the shop windows, packed into the hall. I saw women wearing long gowns with deliciously high slits, and plenty in dresses with irregular slashes around the midriff. I had accompanied my friends on visits to their tailor, and knew that some of these styles had been copied from the pile of glossy fashion magazines like *Vogue* and *Vanity Fair* that the best *khayatis* kept in their shops. My friends had picked their dress patterns from photographs of Hollywood actresses at red-carpet events. In my unembellished outfit, I was the most conspicuous guest there, so much so that my appearance had to be explained. ('She isn't from here.')

Relatives and friends and neighbours stopped to say hello, planting kisses carefully on each other's scented and powdered cheeks. I was introduced to a few elderly aunts and grand-mothers: silver-haired ladies dressed in white tunics and wide, embroidered trousers. Some watched the glittering throng around them with bemused tolerance, others with disapproval. The room was separated by shimmery curtains, and over the chatter of eight hundred voices I had heard the singer on the men's side of the room. He was singing mostly Afghan pop and Bollywood songs, accompanied by musicians on keyboard and drums.

The talk among the guests had been of the war, the poppy boom, the magnificence of the hall we were in and the latest government scandal, and inevitably also of the Taliban, back in the lives and conversations of Kabulis. As the singer picked up the tempo, the camera passed over the male guests in the hall, projecting their images on a screen in the women's side of the room. Most of them were sitting around chatting morosely in their incandescent suits. On the women's side, there was dancing. Some of the men who were close relatives of the bride had slipped in from behind the dividing curtain and joined in. Others stood clinking spoons on glasses, making a beat of encouragement and applause. Eventually the bride, wearing a white dress, walked in with her husband. Behind them came a trail of bridesmaids, wearing matching green sheath dresses and throwing flower petals over the couple, pirouetting gracefully over the carpeted floor.

The singer performed the traditional Dari song that heralds the bride's arrival. '*Ahista boro, mah-e-man*' – 'Walk slowly, my moon'. The couple moved slowly, perforce, trailed as they were by the girls, a camera and several lights. An elaborate three-tiered cake was brought to the stage and cut by the couple. There was a long round of photographs with relatives. Gradually other rituals unfolded, all captured on camera. I watched as the crowd around the couple prepared for the *aina mashaf*.

In the centre of the hall, the bride and groom disappeared under a red veil, concealed in full view. The girls around them angled the glass, giggling. In Kabul, as in Aligarh, this simple ritual was a moment of pause, a beat of intimacy in a crowded spot. It was not the first time they were seeing each other, but it was the first time they appeared to each other as a couple, bound together.

The mirror reflected the veil, its glass surface moving constantly, revealing images in glimpses, beautiful and disordered. The girls lifted the veil to adjust the mirror once again. It caught the dazzle of the lights overhead.

* * *

Weddings provide endings to stories. Like the marriage of Zal and Rudaba. The couple were able to overcome opposition from their families with the help of a prediction from royal astrologers. Their offspring would be Rustom, the mighty ruler, and one of the heroes of Persian literature. Their wedding was celebrated in Kabul, and the festivities lasted for many days, making them fitting ancestors for the city's revellers.

Weddings also provide beginnings to new stories. With my friend's family, I watched the rituals and joined the queue for photographs on the stage. The couple left once again to change for the next round of festivities. Food appeared, wheeled out on trolleys by young men who served us with harassed expressions and practised movements. The quantity of delicacies that appeared on each table was the kind that bred disregard for waste. Pulao was shovelled around in heaps, dishes of kebabs were picked at and abandoned, bottles of yogurt slurped by children and discarded.

After dinner the dancing started again, this time in earnest. The bride and groom appeared in their new outfits and took a twirl around the room. Then they vanished again, their exit barely noticed in the merriment that was unfolding. The dancing reached a crescendo, with male relatives joining their arms in a circle, and the women pairing off to execute complicated moves. Slowly, the hall began to thin out.

In a now empty corner, I watched a woman whirling round and round merrily, her tightly knotted hair coming loose, shaking free of its confining clips. She had been dancing most of the evening. But now her young daughter had woken up, and was chasing her, crying and trying to cling to her legs, which were visible through the slits of her tight green dress. The party was almost over, but the woman was not done dancing.

Despite the confining embrace of her child, despite the stares of the elderly guests, despite the lateness of the hour and her own dishevelled state, she danced on. Much like Kabul itself, at that moment, admiring itself as it swirled and exuberantly breathed in the aroma of transient, expensive abundance, relishing the music and the lights, the cameras and the attention. Like Kabul at that moment, aware that soon there would be departures, and forgetting, and the cameras would leave as they had done before, and there would be only darkness and silence. In her twirling form, in her defiant celebration of the present, there was something of the spirit I had felt in the explosion of wedding festivities. As we started to take our leave, I saw a woman approach the whirling form, trying to get her to hold her daughter. 'She is crying, poor thing,' I heard the reprimand. The dancer in green stooped and picked up the child, only to thrust her into the relative's reluctant arms. 'Let her cry,' she said. 'For such a small nuisance, should I waste my life?'

7

RETURNS

The legend of Kabul begins with a bridge, a road appearing on the water. In the story of the city as an isle on a magical lake, the king built a bridge leading to it from the shore. The same bridge is the path to depart the island. Returning to Kabul and leaving it are not endings but states of movement, of travel.

On the flight I took from Delhi to Kabul in 2013, my fellow passengers were mostly Afghans returning home, after medical treatment or a holiday. It seemed like a reversal of the journey I had made in 2006, when the flight was full of international workers and consultants. I was travelling at the end of the narrative arc that had started in 2001, with the US-led invasion.

Within a few months, by the end of 2014, ISAF would formally end combat operations in Afghanistan, after thirteen years of war. Foreign troops were pulling out, and the reduced number that would remain would focus on providing training and advice to the Afghan security forces, who were now responsible for keeping the peace. The international reconstruction effort was also scaling down, with a negative economic impact on the entire country. The changes these departures implied cast a long shadow of uncertainty over Kabul. The fragile and partial gains made over the years faced the possibility of being eroded once the international establishment left. Elections scheduled for 2014 faced threats of violence from the insurgents. Questions and fears hung over the city that spring like the haze, clouding the future.

It was a very different season from the one I had first arrived in, seven years before. I did not know it then, but this would be my last return to Kabul.

I drove from the airport with Abdullah to a different home, shared with Doctor Sahab and Khalid, in Taimani. It was just a few minutes' walk from our previous place at Qala-e-Fatahullah, but it marked another shift in the tenor of our lives. The house was a smaller version of the mansions of Sherpur. It had marble floors and a terrace none of us ever ventured onto, that overlooked the street. My friends had ended up living in a place that represented much of what they had disparaged about new Kabuli homes.

Since he was spending less time in the city now, he said, Khalid had picked a place that needed less looking after. There was no garden here for him to turn his erratic attention to. Instead, there was a covered garage and a small porch at the front of the house. Here, Doctor Sahab had built a cage where he kept two white doves. The birds were beautiful and almost completely silent. He was attached to these fragile creatures in a way I had never seen before. Each morning, he fed them before he left for work, walking down the still-potholed street to his office. Each evening, on his return, he would go and check on them before entering the house. They were the quietest birds in Kabul. I never even saw them flutter around their cage.

Some things remained the same. In the evenings, Khalid's friends came round and took over the living room, propping their guns by the sofas, topping story with story, filling the house with their voices and laughter.

I drove through the streets in Abdullah's yellow-and-white taxi. The colours were a legacy of Hafizullah Amin, who had headed the Communist PDPA government for around three months in 1979. Amin had studied at Columbia University in New York.[1] I learned he had ordered the Kabuli taxis to be changed from black and white to yellow to echo the cabs he had seen as a student.[2]

My walks were fewer, taken with direction and purpose. There had been a kidnapping not far from our street, I heard. I walked down the road that led past our first guest house in Kolola Pushta, and between the sandbags and the security barriers, and the new apartment blocks on the street, I was lost in minutes. The once familiar road had disappeared.

Wandering in this city that had turned unfamiliar called up a memory from my childhood, of how home changes, and roads vanish.

On a foggy morning towards the end of 1989, I had set out to school at an earlier hour than usual. Aligarh was under a curfew, but I was lost to the implications of this fact, chasing some extra-curricular activity that I assumed would still be on. The entire region of northern India was torn by communal riots that winter. It was a time of bloodshed and fear.

Despite all this, somehow on that morning, all I cared about was getting to school.

I had walked out into the winter chill. The house was asleep. School was just a five-minute walk away. I remember fog and morning mist obscuring the view; my route appearing and vanishing. Perhaps that is why I was more than halfway down the street before I registered how empty it was. As a breeze lifted the curtain of mist, I saw a police van parked by the gate of my school. I remember a spasm of fear, the realisation of my folly in being out. I turned and walked rapidly away. Nothing had happened. But the road back was not the road I had walked on minutes earlier. Somewhere in between the two journeys, I had lost the feeling that home would always be a sanctuary.

That it would always be a place where I belonged. That I could always find it, at the familiar bend of the road.

I had forgotten all about that walk until it was called forth by stories of Kabulis leaving home, seeking refuge in different ways. In all their departures, I found an echo of that misty morning.

You turn round, and the road to home has disappeared.

* * *

I took stock of the changes. Shahr-e-Nau market was crowded with malls and restaurants. Places that had been glamorous in 2006 now seemed old and dated. The cafes where expats met were more tightly sealed, now accessed through two sets of steel doors and a weapons check. These were less popular than earlier too, after a number of attacks. There were fewer cybercafes, and more supermarkets. The real estate slump had added half-constructed buildings to the city's ruins. And the sprawl of homes and offices, private universities and massive mosques reached all the way to Darulaman. Only the skeleton of the ruined palace remained the same, silhouetted in the perennial dust.

This was the city, shifting shape. And then there were my own landmarks, also changing. I went to visit Nazira, who had moved from Microrayan to Shahrak-e-Aria, an upmarket gated community near the airport. Its apartment blocks, topped with eye-catching red roofs, offered modern, secure accommodation for affluent Afghans (much like Microrayan had in an earlier era). There was a security check at the gate, and lawns and parking areas, a mosque and a shopping centre, all connected by neat pathways. The *shahrak* ('small city') was like an island, separated from the city by the broad road leading to the international airport. Cars zipped past at high speed, making it difficult to cross on foot. It was this very distance from the city that made the colony attractive for many of its residents. As we walked around the grounds, Nazira said her family was happier here than in their old neighbourhood. Her mother and sister could go outdoors freely. They felt safe within these walls.

I also planned to visit Ismail Sahab at his home, but a mutual friend told me that his family too had moved to an apartment on the edge of the city. The house in Kolola Pushta had been sold. I thought about his garden that had survived the cycle from peace to war, back to peace again. The rows of *nastaran* that had lined the hedges, the empty rocket shells filled with earth and leaves. I asked my friend how Ismail Sahab had taken the loss of his realm. He couldn't really look after his garden any longer, he said, which was one reason why they had moved.

These empty spots on my personal map of Kabul corresponded with the vanishings I saw across the city. With the NATO troops, many of the trappings that had accompanied their presence were also retreating. This meant the restaurants and the guest houses, the contracts and the constructions, the aid budgets and profits. According to the World Bank's World Development Indicators, annual GDP growth in Afghanistan fell from 14.4 per cent in 2012 to 2 per cent in 2013 – indicating the dependence of the economy on the international military presence and aid.[3] The foreign armies were on their way out, along with the bubble of aid and reconstruction. But the war remained, multiplying and shifting shape.[4]

Since 2001, the Taliban had gained strength, partly by waiting out the international forces. By 2013, they were part of a larger, more complex security problem that included powerful regional commanders and local militias (some armed by the US as a bulwark against the insurgency), corruption among Afghan security forces and 'green on blue' attacks, the term referring to ISAF soldiers killed by Afghan allies. According to a UN report, close to 3,000 civilians were killed and over 5,000 injured in the country in 2013.[5] This included a higher proportion of women and children than earlier. These numbers were imprinted with the scale and the omnipresent spread of the war – the conflict reaching ordinary Afghans while they went about their everyday lives.

In this backdrop, if the international withdrawal was not quite an exit, it was certainly a scaling back. The reduced number of expatriates who remained found ways of removing themselves from the city. The spike in suicide bombings and attacks on Kabul meant that most of the city was practically off-limits for those who came to work there from abroad. In the security measures implemented for aid workers and consultants in 2013, I found the progression of the same advice I was given seven years ago, when I was told not to walk.

One afternoon I drove with Abdullah to visit a friend in the compound of an aid organisation. We went along a highway that had been surrounded by an empty, arid landscape in 2006. It was now flanked by long stretches of concrete walls, and large tankers stood by the roadside. The compound itself was fortified, sealed off with multiple checkpoints. My taxi was not allowed inside. The men at the sentry post checked my papers, and conferred first with each other and then on their radio sets. I stood by the boom barrier for several minutes, watching other vehicles make their way in and out. These were mostly armoured cars, large SUVs with tinted windows and emblazoned logos. After a few minutes, the guards waved me in.

In a few steps, the sky shrank and the city vanished completely behind the blast walls – the kind that had taken over Kabul's streets. These were topped with razor wires. With my friend I walked through the roads of this fortressed township, with living quarters made out of large shipping containers, between which were neat flower beds, or pocket-sized greenery. Dinner was in a restaurant also fashioned out of a container, with a small sit-out at the back. I recalled reading somewhere about how NATO's war in Afghanistan is also called the 'container war'. With the luxury of distance, some Afghans grouse that the Soviets had at least built infrastructure for their country. The Americans, they quip, just left behind containers.

Despite my friend's hospitality, I was eager to leave the feverish conviviality of that uneasy village. It was only when I was back in Abdullah's taxi, on the street leading home, that I breathed freely again. I felt protected by the anonymity of his vehicle, and comforted by what I saw as the 'equal opportunity risk' of being part of Kabul's commuter traffic.

But I knew that this feeling was not based in fact. Had there been an attack, those behind the walls would have been protected, and the impact turned outwards, towards the street. As we approached the city centre, I thought of the bubbles of armoured cars and blast walls that foreign workers moved through, and the *shahraks* that provided walled enclosures to wealthier Afghans.

And I thought about the plans to develop Kabul New City, a massive new urban settlement to the north of the capital, beyond its encircling mountains. This expansion was to be privately funded, including by international backers. And like the other 'new' Kabuls I had read about, it was proposed as the solution to the problems of overcrowding, sanitation and poor infrastructure that existed in the current city; by moving further and further away, leaving the chaotic streets behind. That spring, Kabul was riddled with invisible channels and subtle escapes.

* * *

Across roads, in offices, in homes, in most settings, the talk was of the jagged, uncertain shape of the future. The end of ISAF's combat mission was the topic of discussion on social media, and on TV sets playing in room after room. It hung over the city like the spy balloon. In the years to come, the military withdrawal would unfold far more slowly than planned. But at the time, the imminent departures of 2014 seemed to portend a new era.

In all the talk and the noise was the unsettling fear that Kabul was once again entering an era of silence. The departure of the foreign troops would be paralleled by Afghanistan vanishing from the gaze of the world, like in the years of the civil war. In a video shot in 1993, a man speaks with desperate urgency to the camera, as though it is vital for him to say these words as soon as possible.[6] 'In Kabul there is no peace. We ask the United Nations, please if you can take our voices to the UN, tell them to help the Afghan people because they are also human.'

The silence that met his words then seemed to haunt Kabul now.

And yet there were those who were putting down roots into this uncertain earth. A former colleague invited me to his newly completed house near Taimani's many wedding halls. He had left for Pakistan during the civil war and had returned in 2009, to escape the worsening security conditions there. After years of living in rented houses, he had saved enough money to build his own place. He told me it was a matter of great pride for him to be able to host me under his own roof.

I had read somewhere that among the first things refugees returning home did was plant a tree. To provide shade, but mostly as a symbol of stability, to mark their homecoming. It seemed to be an act of equivalent faith for this colleague to create a home on Kabul's shifting terrain. To build windows and doors, and furnish rooms and buy complete sets of dinner plates, while surrounded by conversations about the uncertain future. In its audacious hopefulness, it seemed akin to falling in love. Or maybe it was simply what he could do then.

For some of my friends, however, to live in Kabul that spring of 2013 was to think of leaving it. The city was mediated by its potential absence, its vistas obscured by the looming possibility that they may soon be left behind.

The talk with them was a catalogue of possible cities where they could seek sanctuary. The streets of Kabul for them were dappled with the shapes of these other cities, their names resonant with placidity and peace, moulding themselves into the shape of a home. They turned the names of these sanctuaries over and over, like prayer beads. That spring, they talked of roads leading away from Kabul. Some traversed land, some led to the sea.

In this planning of future exits, I found, were echoes of previous displacements. Many of those discussing leaving Kabul were people who had come home to the city after 2001, after living as refugees abroad.

Like my friend Murad, who had already witnessed several cycles of departures and arrivals in his young life. I had first met him in 2006, when he had been in his early twenties, working in a friend's office as a manager. Over time I learned that his family had roots in Kabul that went back generations. Murad himself seemed like a poster child for the youth who had come of age after the Taliban. Shy and soft-spoken, he had impeccably good manners. Two of his brothers held jobs in international aid agencies. They were young, English-speaking Afghans, familiar with laptops and Facebook and malls, amenable to the kind of modernity that came with the NATO forces.

Over the years, Murad and his brothers' careers progressed impressively. He received assignments abroad, and always turned up to work in sharp suits. His elder brother celebrated his wedding in a hall, and promptly started a family. It was a success story of the kind particular to post-2001 Kabul.

I visited his home one afternoon in 2009. The family lived in Karte Seh, not far from my workplace. The single-storey house was separated from the road by a long drive. It had several carpeted rooms and a large garden. Murad told me they rented it from his aunt, who lived abroad. The garden was carefully tended by his father, who had planted pomegranate trees and rose bushes. His mother showed me several photo albums, leafing through the laminated pages slowly. She lingered on the pictures of her eldest daughter, who was married and lived abroad, and the grandchildren she rarely saw – playing on manicured parks, being pushed around in their large prams, strapped securely into their seats. Her youngest daughter had also left to study on a scholarship abroad. She would return in another year. Murad's mother looked forward to her children being together; her sons and their growing clans, her family under her roof.

A few months later, I heard that Murad's father had moved to a European country. It was the family's response to the growing insecurity in Kabul. The future that they had hoped for in the city had disappeared again. And Murad's life had moved to the state of half-presence that was both telling and common. He was there and not there, even as he went to work, went shopping, watched TV with his nephew and helped his mother in the house. I wondered what it meant to see the familiar city this way, as something flickering in its reality. Or perhaps he was the one who appeared and vanished, as he walked through its thoroughfares.

I saw Murad's family again in 2011 at the same house. The trees his father had looked after had grown under the diligent care of his sons. Murad's mother had patiently endured the long separation from her husband. I heard news about Murad's father: that he was fine, but tired of being away from his family, alone. 'Life in Europe is not easy,' he'd told them. 'It's not like we hear.'

I went with Khalid to visit the family again on my last visit. The father had returned to Kabul earlier that year, swimming against the current of departures. After years of living in limbo, he had been granted permission to stay in Europe, but on his own. And he was tired of waiting for his family, tired of the uncertainty. He had chosen to come home instead. Murad's youngest sister was also back, having finished her degree. But after university life on a modern campus, she chafed at her restricted horizon in Kabul. She talked of moving to India, of her brothers settling with her there until the rest of the family could join them. Or until they found another place where they could all be together again.

We ate lunch in a room with the *dastarkhwan* crowded with the hospitality of home-cooked food. Murad's sister and his brother's wife first ensured the guests had eaten, then joined the group with the children. We took photographs, arranging ourselves in different combinations. ('Now the girls.' 'Now the mothers with the kids.' 'No, please, I will take it, you get in the picture.' Directions so familiar to me from similar afternoons in Aligarh.) There was a foreshadowing of future journeys in that gathering, hovering in the air around us, like dust in the sunbeams. The uncertain future of Murad's family was made even more poignant by the fact that it was the second time they would leave home as refugees.

The family had fled Kabul during the civil war, in 1993. Murad and his siblings had grown up in Islamabad and Rawalpindi, as part of the large community of Afghan refugees across the border. The brothers had worked at a tailoring shop

his father opened, taking a loan from a relative. Their story was
a familiar one among Kabulis, of a family fallen on difficult
times, away from their own city. But the boys had also gained
the education and the skills that had proved so useful to them
later. In 2005, the family had moved back home. The life I saw
had been hard won. Murad had worked and attended evening
classes for over two years to get a degree that would help his
career. His younger brother had lived in India as a student,
with the same aim. And now, the family was planning their
second departure. Preparing once more to don the skin of
refugees. Only this time the journeys were being undertaken
piecemeal – each member striking out alone.

The talk that afternoon was of a more immediate departure.
Murad's aunt was thinking of selling her house before the real
estate prices in Kabul crashed even further. The family had
been looking for a new place where they could live together,
but had not found anything suitable so far. From where we
were sitting, I could look out of the large windows and see
how the trees in the garden had grown.

I drove back with Khalid after lunch, and we had only just
left the house when Murad called. There had been an attack on
the guest house of an international NGO, not far from Taimani.
He suggested we turn back and wait out the trouble. But
Khalid decided to keep going. Soon, we were stuck in a traffic
jam, minutes away from home. Smoke rose into the sky, a single
plume that grew darker. In the cars ahead of us, news of the
attack spread, as drivers and passengers alike answered their
phones, and craned their heads out to watch the dark cloud
growing. My own phone buzzed with messages, including
from someone I was to meet that afternoon. 'Please don't come
out,' he said. 'The fighting seems to be close.' When we talked
later, he told me he'd been entertaining guests from abroad
when the attack began. They had been horrified at hearing

gunfire so close, and kept asking him what they should do. 'Wait,' he'd said. That was all they could do.

Once home, I listened to the sounds of the gun battle and explosions with rising trepidation. I was frightened and unsure how to react. It seemed strange – to do nothing but wait. My friends were both amused to see my fear and touched. 'It's good,' Doctor Sahab said with his characteristic dry chuckle. 'It shows you're still normal.'

They turned on the TV, which was showing music videos, and sat around as the gunshots rang out in bursts. 'That one sounded close,' someone would say occasionally.

I went upstairs and looked out from my window. Dusk was falling on the deserted streets. Lights began appearing in the homes on the hills, illuminating the horizon. Behind these homes, in the fragment visible through the curtain I carefully lifted, were Kabul's encircling mountains, hazy and uncertain through the smoke and dust.

I thought of a morning in May 2006, when, during the early rush-hour traffic, a US military vehicle caused an accident near Khair Khana. The incident grew into a full-blown riot that affected large parts of the capital and left at least fourteen people dead. Crowds moved through the city, attacking and burning restaurants and offices. They raised slogans against Karzai and the US.[7] The outburst of violence was a portent of the changes ahead, and the first time there was such palpable anger against the Afghan government, and the international establishment, in the capital.

I was in Bamiyan when the riots occurred, and read about them in a small cybercafe after spending the day at the empty niches of the Buddha statues. I had returned to a city on edge – quiet, but tense. A friend told me later that soon after the incident, he had attended a party in an expat guest house. The revelries had started before sunset, and ended at dawn, to coincide with the night-time curfew that had been imposed. I thought of that long-ago dawn as I watched the city darken from my window, the smoke from the afternoon's attack still thickening the air.

A few months after this attack, Murad's elder brother moved to a different country, taking his family with him. And soon after that, Murad also departed for a snowy town in Canada. His parents stayed on in Kabul.

* * *

In the imagination of the world, Kabul is a place that people flee from.

By 2013, as another paroxysm of departures racked the city, Baba told me stories that showed it in a different light, from a time when Kabul had offered sanctuary to those caught in the currents of war and conflict. In these tales it stood for safety; the city at the end of the journey rather than the beginning.

I read, for instance, that during the First World War, German, Austrian and Hungarian prisoners of war who had been captured by the Russian Empire managed to escape into Afghanistan. Amir Habibullah, who had resisted British pressure to join the Allied forces, offered them sanctuary. They ended up living in Kabul until the war ended. From the heart of the old city, they moved to Aliabad, in the middle of the Chardeh plains, overlooking fields and fruit orchards. 'Recruited to various duties according to their skills, they served in the Afghan army as instructors but most notably in building construction,' I read.[8] These refugees helped create the then nascent modernity of Kabul, building a hospital and residences, including a house for the future Amir Amanullah. It is likely that they turned for inspiration to the structures they knew well, creating in Kabul an echo of their faraway homes.

Baba's stories, though, were more concerned with the paths between Afghanistan and India. Specifically, for Indians struggling against British colonial rule. As early as 1915, an Indian government-in-exile was formed in Kabul. Raja Mahendra Pratap, an Indian freedom fighter who hailed from Aligarh, attempted to persuade Amir Habibullah to declare war against the British, with German support. Spies, revolutionaries, students on their way to join anti-Raj struggles in other locations and secret missions – Kabul provided sanctuary to these varied agendas. The path to the freedom they all dreamed of led through this city.

The most dramatic story Baba told me was of the *hijrat*, migration, of 1920. This was the name given to the exodus of Muslims from the northern provinces of British-ruled India to Afghanistan.[9] Reading historical accounts of the migration, I found the story of a massive, voluntary dislocation that has all but vanished from popular memory in India.

The roots of the *hijrat* lay, I found, in the swell of nationalist sentiment that swept my country after the First World War. A large section of the population was angered at being denied greater self-rule despite Indian participation in the war effort alongside Britain. Muslim leaders and the community had an additional, powerful grievance. Britain, as part of the Allied powers, was instrumental in stripping the Ottoman Empire of its territories. This effectively reduced the caliph, the notional leader of Muslims worldwide, to a mere figurehead. Indian Muslims were shamed and angered by their role in assisting this disintegration. There were also fears that their customary laws would be replaced by British rules. Among several responses to this outburst of anti-British feeling was the idea of *hijrat*.

The argument in its favour was this: under the rule of the British, India was no longer safe for Islam. So it was the spiritual duty of Muslims to leave and seek sanctuary elsewhere. There, they must also strive to free their homeland of British rule so they could return. The idea did not get wide support from the nationalist currents of the time, nor did it animate much of the Muslim clergy. But certain leaders backed it.[10]

The movement may well have stayed marginal but for its endorsement from an unexpected quarter. In February 1920, Amir Amanullah 'undertook to welcome all those Muslims and Hindus who intended to migrate. He even offered to sacrifice his own life for the Faith and for the defence of the Khilafat [Caliphate]'.[11]

Amanullah had declared Afghanistan independent of British suzerainty in 1919. It is possible he was seizing this fresh opportunity to establish the upper hand in the impending negotiations with the British government. It is also possible that the speech was mere propaganda, not intended to be taken seriously. But the offer was reiterated by his foreign minister Mahmud Tarzi when he arrived in India for negotiations with the British, and it received publicity in the Indian press. As one official noted, 'Whatever may be the fate of the emigration movement, the *hijrat* of men's mind towards Kabul has commenced.'[12]

The migration began in May, just as the blistering north Indian summer set in. Initially, the majority of those leaving were impoverished peasants hoping for better prospects in Afghanistan, and the pace was slow. But it soon picked up speed, and there was excitement along the way. The travellers were welcomed by villagers on their path; the Afridis of the border region even served them with iced sherbet.[13] The greatest response to the campaign was in the North West Frontier Province, with smaller numbers departing from Punjab and Sindh. These included migrants from better-off communities.

The British response to this exodus was measured, and the administration did not attempt to interfere or stem the flow of

migrants, hoping instead that the excitement would wear itself
out. Nevertheless, as the fervour for *hijrat* began to spread to
the army, police and bureaucracy, it caused rising unease in
official circles.

From historical accounts, the picture that emerges is of a
moment of emotional upheaval. Unlike refugees fleeing war
or disaster, the *hijrat* was at least notionally a voluntary
departure. Yet at its heart was the perceived compulsion of a
transformed homeland. Among the *muhajirin* – migrants –
were fiery freedom fighters who brought their *kafans*, or
shrouds, with them. There were also peasants who had sold
their lands and livestock at a fraction of their value. Entire
villages undertook the migration, and even the reluctant were
forced to leave with their community. This was an era when
home was settled for generations, and travel was both costly
and difficult. Many of these villagers may never have left their
own province before joining the caravans for Afghanistan.
Reading the accounts of people on the verge of being
uprooted, I wondered at the depth of feeling that lay behind
their move. The *hijrat* was a heartfelt gesture of protest, by
those who saw their absence from their homeland as the most
potent tool at their disposal.

Despite its scale and the fervour of the travellers, the
movement remained non-violent. The *muhajirin* sang songs
along the way, pledging their destiny to the city that had
offered them sanctuary. To me, these verses offered an unusual
view of Kabul, as it appeared in that historical moment – as a
city of hope, a refuge.

> For destruction, we do not care.
> For unhappiness, we do not care.
> O Friends, come what may,
> Proceed to Kabul! Proceed to Kabul![14]

By August 1920, official estimates put the number of *muhajirin* who had crossed the borders – most through the Khyber Pass – at around 40,000. Unofficial estimates go as high as 60,000.[15]

The scale of this migration quickly overwhelmed the Afghans. Land allotted by Amir Amanullah for a *muhajirin* colony soon ran out. As resources dwindled, the initial welcomes wore thin. The Afghan government began trying to turn the tide.

New regulations stipulated that each *muhajir* must possess at least 50 rupees in cash when entering Afghanistan. The government also detained and interrogated refugees travelling without their families. Caravans were looted along the road. Amir Amanullah was forced to raise funds to cater for the newcomers, which added to the resentment from the local population.

Within three months, the movement collapsed. Amir Amanullah issued a *farman* stopping any further immigration, and Afghanistan closed its borders to the caravans. A large party arriving a few days later was faced with armed border guards. The indignant migrants threatened to break the barrier. A compromise was eventually worked out, but it was an unceremonious end to the journey.

Slowly, the direction of the caravans turned, with the assistance of the secretly relieved British government. But many travellers died of exhaustion and disease on the road back, and others were looted and harassed. 'The road from the Frontier to Kabul was dotted with *muhajirin* graves,' I read.[16] It is estimated that about 75 per cent of the migrants returned home, with a few going further to Turkey or Russia.

In the path taken by these forgotten caravans, I found echoes of displacements and migrations closer to my own time. From the initial welcomes to the suspicion; from the offering of shelter to the nebulous fear – the emotions seemed to speak across the decades. From my friends in Kabul, I had already learned that seeking refuge was a difficult road to travel. From these obscured voices of the past, I learned that it is also a fraught gift to offer.

It is possible to read the story of the *hijrat* as an insight into how home can change overnight, from a place where you belong, to a place you are compelled to leave. It was a reminder that we live on invisible fault lines, and arbitrary borders can appear anywhere.

You turn round one day and find the road to home has disappeared.

***

On my departure from Kabul in 2013, Abdullah drove me to the airport, and Radio Ahmad Zahir delivered an apt melancholic tune in farewell.

The taxi was stopped fairly far from the airport building. I said goodbye to Abdullah and walked towards a security checkpoint. This was a small shed with a curtained enclosure, where three women in brown tunics and trousers were eating *kulcha* and sipping tea. The rims of the glass cups were smeared with lipstick, and one of them kept eating as she patted me down with disconcerting thoroughness. The shed was overheated from the warm day; it smelled of sweat and the wood it was made of, and the succession of meals eaten there. The guard's hands seemed to have an edge of anger in their probing. One of the other women opened my bag, then my wallet, and extracted the afghani notes. 'Will you need these where you are going?' she asked. 'Why don't you leave them with us?' When I hesitated, she said aggressively, 'Are you coming back?' I had not thought about it till then. But I left the money with her.

On one of my last afternoons in Kabul, I had attended a farewell party held for a departing diplomat. The event was deep in the secure zone of embassies that had gradually been sealed off from the city, from 2009 onwards. Like at the airport, I had left Abdullah's taxi at the very first checkpoint and walked past the guards. I crossed a school, whose students were among the select few allowed into the zone. I crossed several security checks before being allowed into the beautiful house that was the venue for the event.

The party was outdoors, in the large garden that adjoined the residence. There was going to be music in the evening, and I saw a group of Afghan musicians waiting in a gazebo at the side of the lawn, tuning their instruments. That afternoon, Kabul was buffeted by strong winds that swirled clouds of brown dust in the air, casting it with a haze, and making the coiffures of the attendees whirl. There were speeches made by diplomats and aid workers. Then we dispersed to have tea and snacks. As we ate, a helicopter positioned itself above the garden, its noise thundering out conversations. I made my way to say goodbye to the host. He was standing by the flower beds, and pointed to the roses that had emerged into the mild sunshine. Raising his voice above the noise of the chopper, he talked about how beautiful they looked. 'They came out in just a few days,' he shouted. 'This doesn't happen anywhere but Kabul.'

I learned then that to leave Kabul was to take it with you.

In all my years of travelling to Afghanistan, a road to Kabul had appeared from Aligarh too. The city had carved a path to my grandparents' house, in small habits and objects, building on what had existed earlier. It was a piece of Kabul outside Kabul.

The city shimmered in the tea Baba drank each morning, using the fragrant leaves I got for him from Mandayi. Until his eyesight failed him, he prepared it himself, to ensure it came out right. It was in the dry apricots and almonds that my grandmother relished from the shops at Qala-e-Fatahullah. It lay within the pages of the books on Baba's shelves, which now included volumes I had brought for him. It grew with each conversation we shared about the city.

Two years after my last visit to Kabul, my grandmother passed away at home. Baba seemed unmoored in the few weeks he lingered after her. Two months later, he did not wake up from his sleep.

The silence that fell over their rooms extended to my life. Without Baba, I lost my bearings. It was as if I had been describing Kabul for him, and he had been dictating the city to me. Now, I had lost my maps and my stories, my audience and my guide. I had lost the place we had created together.

Each time I had left their house after dark, I had stopped on the small porch outside their living room and watched them through the window. I had gazed at them in the small square of light, seated at the dining table that was older than me, listening to the radio or just sitting in silence together. I had fixed the image in my memory each time, like a talisman. 'This is what they are like without me,' I told myself. 'This is how I will find them when I return.'

I had never gone on to think what I was like without them.

Or what it would be like to walk down that familiar road turned dark and strange, with no light. With even the window gone.

* * *

In the years after 2014, and as Afghanistan vanished from the eyes of the world, Afghans appeared everywhere. Refugees dominated the headlines, and the world's media watched as millions of displaced people sought asylum in Europe. In 2015, Syrians fleeing the war were the largest refugee community in the world. But Afghans still formed the largest protracted refugee population under UNHCR care, and that year there were still 2.7 million Afghan refugees worldwide.[17] This community formed a country without borders, built over generations of conflict. Among the new arrivals to this diaspora, I knew, were friends from Kabul.

Watching the news of this migration, I remembered a story Baba often told me, about a freedom fighter who spent most of his life struggling for the cause of liberating his homeland. He left India as a young man to join a movement abroad. He had been captured and given a lengthy prison sentence. When he was released, the old man had made his way back to his village. There, he had stood at the crossroads for a long time until someone spotted him. He had forgotten his way home.

Baba always told me this story with an upward lift to his voice at the end. 'He had forgotten the road to his home.' Imagine, his tone said, such a thing happening.

Stretched like an invisible thread between these stories of those who left were the verses Baba had recited for me years ago, when I had returned from Kabul for the first time.

> *Ghurbat mein hon agar hum*
> *Rehta hai dil watan mein*
> *Samjho wahin humein bhi*
> *Dil ho jahan hamara*

> Even in exile
> Our hearts dwell at home
> Think of us as being there
> The home where our hearts live

The word *jahan* can also be translated as 'the world'. So the
line written by Iqbal can be reimagined to declare 'Our hearts
contain the world'. Or, we carry home wherever we go.

***

Home is the city that travels with us. It is the known that we
cast into the unknown, the delicate web of knowledge and
emotions through which we decipher other cities and other
places. Like Baba, casting poetry into Kabul for me. Like
Babur, creating channels of running water wherever he went.
Like Doctor Sahab, resurrecting the city of his childhood
night after night.

As I told stories of Kabul, I too was telling stories of all the
places I consider home. In the portraits of this city that felt so
familiar were sketches of all the worlds my grandfather
contained, which he opened up for me. When I left Kabul, it
became part of the shadow city I saw dappled onto other cities,
the place that lay behind the places I now inhabit.

As I began recording my walks in this book, I realised I was
describing my paths in reverse. Each road, each landmark, each
sight appearing on the page as neatly opposing reality as if seen
in a mirror. As if by writing Kabul, I was learning to see it
from afar.

In the space between what I saw and what I wrote, Kabul
twisted its shape and changed. It has changed again, even as
you read it. *Bood, nabood.* It appears and vanishes with the shift
of the kaleidoscope, with the way of seeing.

Not long ago a friend sent me a picture of Kabul taken from
the top of a hill. It was a vantage point familiar to us both. It
used to be his home. From that height, Kabul was spread before
me. But in the image, I could not find the city I knew. I was
lost among the tall, glimmering buildings, in the clusters of
houses, in the tightly packed complexity of the streets. My

friend had left Kabul years ago, he now lived as a refugee abroad. We were both absent; the city had continued.

Last night I dreamed I was walking up that hill. I felt the earth soft and yielding beneath my feet, the air crisp and cold. There was snow on the ground. The road twisted; from behind the trees I could see the panorama in glimpses. At the top of the road, though, was the city from the photograph. A Kabul I did not recognise. I searched for a clue to the vistas I knew, but they seemed to keep slipping away. Finally, I saw a flash of earth towards the east: a hillside, its slopes glistening and wet with mud, with the silhouette of a fort on top. A fragment that caused the pieces to fall into shape. There it is, there it is not. In my dream, Kabul appeared.

ACKNOWLEDGEMENTS

This book started taking shape in 2006, growing gradually with each journey I made to Kabul. Most of these returns were for assignments to work with Afghan media professionals. The people I met through such work became my friends, who showed me paths into the city. In their company, and with their friends and families, I found the stories that eventually became a part of this book. Their presence shaped the direction taken by these walks – they were my lens to seeing the city with intimacy, through the everyday. Thanks to them, I returned on each trip to transformations, but also to a welcoming continuity. Some of these relationships have endured and remain a part of my life. For this, and so much more, I am grateful.

My deepest gratitude is to everyone in the book, for sharing their stories with me and for letting me into their lives. The names and identifying details of some of these people have been changed to protect their privacy. Heartfelt *tashakor* to Syed Habibullah, Karim Amin and each of the friends and colleagues in Kabul who guided my steps, and watched my back.

Over the years, my wanderings took various shapes on paper. For keeping faith over this drifting, and offering comfort when the words seemed to still, thank you Alice Albinia, C. Rajeev, Giuseppe Caruso, Avanti Bhati, Snigdha Poonam,

Anjum Hasan, Shuddhabrata Sengupta, Jonathan Page. Laura Lampton Scott and Rakhi Basu, thank you for getting into the trenches with me, and for pulling me out when it was time. Thank you Rahul Soni, for always having the answers. Jolyon Leslie gave his expert comments on my draft, and generously shared his deep knowledge of the city. Thanks also to the readers in Kabul and Canada who offered feedback and information with unflagging good humour. Naveena Naqvi turned a historian's eye to these wanderings, as did Syed Ali Kazim. My thanks to Shiva Sanjari and Siddiq Barmak for their help with the translations of Persian phrases and poetry; and to Professor Azarmi Dukht Safavi, who also provided valuable insights into the intricacies of Persian verse.

Enmeshed in the city I wrote is the virtual city that nourishes my work. For writing solace and practical wisdom, thank you Anuradha Sengupta, Naresh Fernandes, M. T. Connolly, Adrian Nicole LeBlanc, Rafil Kroll-Zaidi, Azmat Khan, Anastasia Taylor-Lind, Michael Scott Moore, Jonathan Meiburg, Tom Jennings, Kristen Cosby, Jane Park, Marjorie G. Sa'adah, Michelle Memran, Karen Jennings, Aunohita Mojumdar, Anshika Misra, Urmi Juvekar, G. Sampath, Sanchita Ain. Special thanks to Shakyla Husain, Julie Billaud, Prashant Sharma and Sonia Muller-Rappard, for warmth and open doors. And to my friends and family in Mumbai, for providing both solitude and community. Sadia Saeed and Toni Stevens, thank you for helping me through the rough bits; Farah Batool and Desmond Roberts, for being my sanctuary.

My gratitude to the team at Chatto & Windus, who gave these words a home, especially Clara Farmer and Greg Clowes. Thanks also to Katherine Fry, who provided order to wayward passages; and to Juliet Brooke for her early guidance. At Penguin Random House India, my editor Swati Chopra sought out this book before it even existed; Aslesha Kadian watched over what emerged with care. I am indebted to Julia Connolly, Harshad Marathe and Gunjan Ahlawat for the beautiful cover art. Emma Paterson, agent and sage advisor, I am fortunate to have you as my champion, and my voice.

I wrote parts of these walks at Sangam House International Writers' Residency, the MacDowell Colony, the Logan Nonfiction Fellowship at the Carey Institute for Global Good, and the Jan Michalski Foundation for Writing and Literature. A Swiss Arts Council Pro Helvetia studio residency supported my time at the ICRC Film Archives in Geneva. Thank you also to the friends who offered beautiful shelter: Deepa Pathak and Ashish Arora, for the gift of Sonapani; Jaya Peter, for many days on the blue bench; Lalitha Suhasini and Nandan Nadkarni, for tough love and tiffins. Thank you, Saumya Roy, for your friendship; the Roy family for opening your home to me.

My writing from Kabul has appeared in various newspapers and magazines since 2006. I am grateful to the following publications and their editors for publishing essays and articles that went on to form chapters, or parts of chapters, in this book: *The Caravan*, 'Reading Kabul' and 'Dhishum Dhishum Hero' (2011); *Berfrois*, 'Images in an Archive; or, How to see Kabul from a Distance' (2014); *Himal Southasian*, 'Shootings in Kabul' (2015); *Guernica*, 'The Buddha of Kabul' (2016); *Cityscapes* #8, 'Street of Kabul: Roadscapes and Stories' (2017).

Lastly, my gratitude to my wonderful family everywhere – in Aligarh, Rampur, Kanpur, Lucknow, Mustafabad, Delhi and beyond. Thank you for teaching me the value of listening, and for always caring about what I had been up to – a writer could ask for no greater gift. Thanks also to the Kumhrauli clan for their unstinting support and love over the years. Above all, my mother, the pole star of my life, for giving me the freedom to wander. And my father, most beloved traveller, never forgotten.

My grandmother, Zehra Mehdi, does not appear in these pages too often, but nevertheless she is present throughout. She told me my first stories, and showed me the beauty of creation spun from the everyday. These stories are a tribute to her memory; I think my Baba, S. M. Mehdi, would have liked it this way too.

Finally, thank you, Asad, for always walking by my side.

NOTES

FOREWORD

1 Daniel Balland, 'Preface to the French Edition', in May Schinasi, *Kabul: A History 1773–1948*, translated by R. D. McChesney, Leiden and Boston: Brill, 2017, p. vii

2 Darran Anderson, *Imaginary Cities*, London: Influx Press, 2015, pp. 236–7

1: RETURNS

1 May Schinasi, *Kabul: A History 1773–1948*, translated by R. D. McChesney, Leiden and Boston: Brill, 2017, p. 1

2 Jos J. L. Gommans, *The Rise of the Indo-Afghan Empire, c.1710–1780*, Delhi: Oxford University Press, 1999, p. 9

3 Iqbal Husain, *The Rise and Decline of the Ruhela Chieftaincies in Eighteenth Century India*, Delhi: Oxford University Press, 1994, p. 175

4 Thomas Barfield, *Afghanistan: A Cultural and Political History*, Princeton: Princeton University Press, 2010, p. 275

5 See 'Country Dashboard', Fragile States Index, https://fragilestatesindex. org/country-data. In 2014, the ranking was renamed 'Fragile States Index'.

6 Transparency International's 2007 Corruption Perception Index ranked the country 172nd out of 180 countries: see https://www.transparency. org/research/cpi/cpi_2007/0 (accessed 19 June 2019)

7 This 'walk' draws from Nancy Hatch Dupree, in collaboration with Ahmad Ali Kohzad, *An Historical Guide to Kabul*, Kabul: The Afghan Tourist Organization, 1972; Schinasi, *Kabul*; Xavier de Planhol, 'Kabul ii. Historical Geography', *Encyclopædia Iranica* XV/3, 2011, pp. 282–303, available online at http://www.iranicaonline.org/articles/ kabul-ii-historical-geography (accessed 19 June 2019)

8 Planhol, 'Kabul ii'

9   L. B. Poullada, 'Amānallāh', *Encyclopædia Iranica* I/9, 1985, pp. 921–3,
     available online at http://www.iranicaonline.org/articles/amanallah-
     1892–1961-ruler-of-afghanistan-1919–29-first-with-the-title-of-amir-
     and-from-1926-on-with-that-of-shah (accessed 19 June 2019)

10   Nancy Hatch Dupree, *The Women of Afghanistan*, Islamabad: Office of
     the UN Coordinator for Afghanistan, 1998, p. 2

11   Dupree, *An Historical Guide to Kabul*, p. 58

12   Schinasi, *Kabul*, p. 147

13   Nancy Dupree, 'A Building Boom in the Hindukush: Afghanistan
     1921–1928', *Lotus International* 26, 1980, p. 2

14   Schinasi, *Kabul*, p. 147

15   Tanya Goudsouzian, 'Afghan first lady in shadow of 1920s queen?', Al
     Jazeera website, 1 October 2014, https://www.aljazeera.com/news/asia/
     2014/09/afghan-first-lady-shadow-1920s-queen-2014930142515254965.
     html (accessed 19 June 2019)

16   D. Balland, 'Bačča-ye Saqqā', *Encyclopædia Iranica* III/3–4, 1989, pp. 336–
     9, available online at http://www.iranicaonline.org/articles/bacca-ye-
     saqqa (accessed 19 June 2019)

17   Barfield, *Afghanistan*, p. 281. Also for the background to the Soviet
     invasion and civil war in Kabul, see pp. 210–254

18   Marcus Schadl, 'Kabul – A City That Never Was: Reflections on the
     Revitalization of the Old City', *Trialog* 88, 2006, pp. 10–15

19   'Timeline: the fall of Kabul', *The Guardian*, 13 November 2001, https://
     www.theguardian.com/world/2001/nov/13/afghanistan.terrorism18
     (accessed 19 June 2019)

20   Jolyon Leslie, 'Kabul', *Encyclopædia Britannica*, 7 February 2019, https://
     www.britannica.com/place/Kabul (accessed 19 June 2019)

21   Estimate cited in 'Kabul: Urban Land in Crisis – a Policy Note', 13
     September 2005, available at http://documents.worldbank.org/curated/
     en/417221467994630457/pdf/704180ESW0P0830al0KabuloLandoRepo
     rt.pdf (accessed 19 June 2019)

22   *Babur Nama: Journal of Emperor Babur*, translated by Annette Susannah
     Beveridge, New Delhi: Penguin, 2006, p. 125

23   Nancy Hatch Dupree, in collaboration with Ahmad Ali Kohzad,
     An Historical Guide to Kabul, The Afghan Tourist Organization, Kabul
     1972

24   Barfield, *Afghanistan*, p. 281

25   World Bank Data, https://data.worldbank.org/indicator/NY.GDP.
     PCAP.CD?locations=AF&page=1 (accessed 19 June 2019)

26   *Afghanistan Development Update*, World Bank, August 2018, p. 2, available at
     http://documents.worldbank.org/curated/en/985851533222840038/
     pdf/129163-REVISED-AFG-Development-Update-Aug-2018-
     FINAL.pdf (accessed 19 June 2019)

27 For a discussion on this, see Jonathan Goodhand, *Contested Transitions: International Drawdown and the Future State in Afghanistan*, NOREF, November 2012, p. 9

28 All videos from the 1990s referred to throughout this book were viewed in the Film Archives of the International Committee of the Red Cross (ICRC) Geneva. This video titled *Afghanistan: Tools of Peace*, 1996. Reference V-F-CR-F-00347

29 My translation, verses from Muhammad Iqbal, *Tarana e Hindi*, 1904 https://www.rekhta.org/nazms/taraana-e-hindii-saare-jahaan-se-achchhaa-hindostaan-hamaaraa-allama-iqbal-nazms (accessed 19 June 2019)

2: WRITTEN ON THE CITY

1 Rabindranath Tagore, *Kabuliwala*, 1892, various reprints. See, for instance, *Selected Short Stories: Rabrindranath Tagore*, (ed.) Sukanta Chaudhuri, New Delhi: Oxford University Press. 2002

2 D. Balland, 'Bačča-ye Saqqā', *Encyclopædia Iranica* III/3–4, 1989, pp. 336–9, available online at http://www.iranicaonline.org/articles/bacca-ye-saqqa (accessed 19 June 2019)

3 Nancy Hatch Dupree, in collaboration with Ahmad Ali Kohzad, *An Historical Guide to Kabul*, Kabul: The Afghan Tourist Organization, 1972, p. 134

4 Steve Coll, *Ghost Wars: The Secret History of the CIA, Afghanistan, and Bin Laden, from the Soviet Invasion to September 10, 2001*, London: Penguin Books, 2005

5 Khaled Hosseini, *The Kite Runner*, London: Bloomsbury, 2003

6 All references to Babur's memoirs here are from *Babur Nama: Journal of Emperor Babur*. Translated by Annette Susannah Beveridge, New Delhi: Penguin, 2006

7 Ibid., p. 126

8 Ibid., p. 215

9 Ibid., p. 300

10 Translated by S. M. Mehdi

11 Åsne Seierstad, *The Bookseller of Kabul*, translated by Ingrid Christophersen, Boston: Little, Brown, 2003

12 In 2011, an appeal court in Norway cleared Seierstad of invading the privacy of Rais's family. See Alexandra Topping, '*The Bookseller of Kabul* author cleared of invading Afghan family's privacy', *The Guardian*, 13 December 2011, https://www.theguardian.com/world/2011/dec/13/bookseller-of-kabul-author-cleared (accessed 20 June 2019). Shah Muhammad Rais, *Once upon a Time there was a Bookseller in Kabul*, Kabul: Shah M Book Co, 2007

13 Abul Qasim Firdausi's *Shahnama* (The Book of Kings), was completed in the early eleventh century. See English translation by Arthur George

Warner and Edmond Warner, *The Sháhnáma of Firdausí*, 9 vols, London: Kegan Paul, Trench, Trübner, 1905–25

14   Dupree, *An Historical Guide to Kabul*, pp. 71–72

15   Maryam Papi, 'Why is Persian dying out in India, despite its deep roots? An Iranian finds the answer in Kolkata', *Scroll*, 7 September 2017, https://scroll.in/magazine/848675/why-is-persian-dying-out-in-india-despite-its-deep-roots-an-iranian-finds-the-answer-in-kolkata (accessed 20 June 2019)

16   May Schinasi, *Kabul: A History 1773–1948*, translated by R. D. McChesney, Leiden and Boston: Brill, 2017, p. 58

17   Franklin Lewis, 'Golestān e Saʻdi', *Encyclopædia Iranica* XI/1, 2003, pp. 79–86, available online at http://www.iranicaonline.org/articles/golestan e sadi (accessed 20 June 2019)

18   All translations from Persian unless noted otherwise are by Shiva Sanjari and Siddiq Barmak

19   Afghanistan has one of the lowest literacy rates in the world, estimated by the UN to be around 31 per cent of the adult population, i.e. over 15 years of age. See 'Enhancement of Literacy in Afghanistan (ELA) Programme', UNESCO Office in Kabul website, www.unesco.org/new/en/kabul/education/youth-and-adult-education/enhancement-of-literacy-in-afghanistan-iii (accessed 20 June 2019)

20   Dupree, *An Historical Guide to Kabul*, pp. 94–5; also Schinasi, *Kabul*, p. 35

21   Dupree, *An Historical Guide to Kabul*, p. 68

22   Nile Green, 'Introduction', in Nile Green and Nushin Arbabazadah (eds), *Afghanistan in Ink: Literature between Diaspora and Nation*, London: Hurst, 2013, pp. 10–11

23   Ibid., pp. 12, 76

24   'Qahar Asi', habibpune/YouTube, 15 April 2012, https://youtu.be/P4ZEmfTvwZw (accessed 20 June 2019)

25   James Rattray, *Scenery, Inhabitants, & Costumes of Afghaunistan*, London: Hering & Remington, 1847.

26   Annemarie Schimmel, 'Iqbal, Muhammad', *Encyclopædia Iranica* XIII/2, 2006, pp. 197–200, available online at http://www.iranicaonline.org/articles/iqbal-muhammad (accessed 20 June 2019)

27   For an account of Iqbal's journey see Nile Green, 'The Trans-Border Traffic of Afghan Modernism: Afghanistan and the Indian "Urdusphere"', *Comparative Studies in Society and History* 53(3), 2011, pp. 479–508

28   Translated by Professor Azarmi Dukht Safavi. The poem *Musafir* by Muhammad Iqbal was originally published in Lahore in 1936. See https://www.rekhta.org/ebooks/masnawi-musafir-allama-iqbal-ebooks (accessed 20 June 2019)

29   Muhammad Iqbal, *Javed Nama*, 1932, https://rekhta.org/ebooks/javed-nama-allama-iqbal-ebooks; 'Afghanistan, the Heart of Asia', Hashia blog, 15 May 2011, https://hashia.wordpress.com/2011/05/15/'afghanistan-the-heart-of-asia/more-40 (both accessed 20 June 2019)

30   Qayoom Suroush, 'Reading in Kabul: the state of Afghan libraries', Afghanistan Analysts Network, 9 April 2015, https://www.afghanistan-analysts.org/reading-in-kabul-the-state-of-afghan-libraries (accessed 20 June 2019)

31   Dupree, *An Historical Guide to Kabul*, p. vii, quoting an anonymous translator

32   'Kabul' (2013), unpublished poem by Ramazan Ali Mahmoodi. Translated by Shiva Sanjari and Siddiq Barmak

3: ABSENCES

1   May Schinasi, *Kabul: A History 1773–1948*, translated by R.D. McChesney, Leiden and Boston: Brill, 2017, pp. 52–53

2   Ibid., p. 140

3   There are various media reports on this, including Ron Synovitz, 'Afghanistan: land grab scandal in Kabul rocks the government', Radio Free Europe/Radio Liberty website, 16 September 2003, https://www.rferl.org/a/1104367.html (accessed 20 June 2019). Also see Joanna Nathan, 'Land grab in Sherpur: monuments to powerlessness, impunity, and inaction', Middle East Institute, December 2009, https://www.mei.edu/publications/land-grab-sherpur-monuments-powerlessness-impunity-and-inaction (accessed 20 June 2019)

4   For an overview of the Anglo-Afghan hostilities, see J. A. Norris, L. W. Adamec, 'Anglo–Afghan Wars,' *Encyclopædia Iranica*, II/1, pp. 37–41, available online at http://www.iranicaonline.org/articles/anglo-afghan-wars (accessed 20 June 2019)

5   Nancy Hatch Dupree, in collaboration with Ahmad Ali Kohzad, *An Historical Guide to Kabul*, Kabul: The Afghan Tourist Organization, 1972, p. 51

6   Ibid., p. 54

7   '#001: Who is the Cemetery Keeper?', Kabul at Work/YouTube, 4 July 2011, https://youtu.be/yjjLDm_C4tA (accessed 20 June 2019)

8   Mark Fineman, 'A rogues' gallery of foreigners: for expatriates in Kabul, hard times on war's edge', *Los Angeles Times*, 10 May 1989, https://www.latimes.com/archives/la-xpm-1989-05-10-mn-2773-story.html (accessed 20 June 2019)

9   Svetlana Alexievich, *Zinky Boys: Soviet Voices from the Afghanistan War*, translated by Julia and Robin Whitby, New York: W.W. Norton, 1992, p. 126

10   Thomas Barfield, *Afghanistan: A Cultural and Political History*, Princeton: Princeton University Press, 2010, p. 238

11   Rod Nordland, 'In Kabul, a service for slain aid workers', *New York Times*, 12 August 2010, https://atwar.blogs.nytimes.com/2010/08/12/scenes-from-a-memorial-service-for-slain-aid-workers (accessed 20 June 2019)

12   Dexter Filkins, 'A nation challenged: in memoriam; at a Kabul cemetery, British soldiers honor the victims of wars past', *New York Times*, 23 February 2002, https://www.nytimes.com/2002/02/23/world/nation-challenged-memoriam-kabul-cemetery-british-soldiers-honor-victims-wars.html (accessed 20 June 2019)

13   Schinasi, *Kabul*, p. 192

14   On this history of the Soviet invasion, mujahideen resistance and the civil war in Kabul, see Barfield, *Afghanistan*, pp. 233–254

15   Ibid., p. 234

16   Sayd Bahodine Majrouh (ed.), *Songs of Love and War: Afghan Women's Poetry*, translated by Marjolijn de Jager, New York: Other Press, 2010, p. 40

17   Barfield, *Afghanistan*, p. 281

18   *ICRC News* 44, November 1996, cited in Chris Johnson and Jolyon Leslie, *Afghanistan: The Mirage of Peace*, London and New York: Zed, 2004, p. 6

19   Ibid., p. 6

20   'Blood-Stained Hands: Past Atrocities in Kabul and Afghanistan's Legacy of Impunity', Human Rights Watch, 6 July 2005, https://www.hrw.org/report/2005/07/06/blood-stained-hands/past-atrocities-kabul-and-afghanistans-legacy-impunity (accessed 20 June 2019)

21   ICRC Film Archives, Geneva. *Afghanistan, February 1993*, Reference V-F-CR-F-00430

22   *Casting Shadows: War Crimes and Crimes against Humanity 1978–2001*, Afghanistan Justice Project, 2005, p. 5. Available at https://www.opensocietyfoundations.org/sites/default/files/ajpreport_20050718.pdf (accessed 20 June 2019)

23   The introduction to 'Blood-Stained Hands' parses this phrase in detail

24   Majrouh, *Songs of Love and War*, p. 39

25   See *Babur Nama*, p. 227 on the tomb of Qabil. Babur on Khizr's spring is referred to in Dupree, *An Historical Guide to Kabul*, pp. 114–15. Also see Schinasi, *Kabul*, p. 42 on this spring and shrine

26   ICRC Film Archives, Geneva. *Reportage Afghanistan, Février 1992*, Reference V-F-CR-F-00242

27   The history of the archaeological site draws from Zafar Paiman and Michael Alram, 'Tepe Narenj: A Royal Monastery on the High Ground of Kabul, with a Commentary on the Coinage', *Journal of Inner Asian Art and Archaeology* 5, 2010, pp. 33–58. I also refer to N. H. Dupree, 'Afghanistan viii. Archaeology', *Encyclopædia Iranica* I/5, 1985, available online at http://www.iranicaonline.org/articles/afghanistan-viii-archeo; Carla

Grissmann, 'Kabul Museum', *Encyclopædia Iranica* XV/3, 2011, available online at http://www.iranicaonline.org/articles/kabul-museum (both accessed 20 June 2019)

28   Grissmann, 'Kabul Museum'

29   Schinasi, *Kabul*, p. 174

30   Dupree, *An Historical Guide to Kabul*, p. 117

4: MAP OF MOVING IMAGES

1   May Schinasi, *Kabul: A History 1773–1948*, translated by R. D. McChesney, Leiden and Boston: Brill, 2017, p. 141

2   Helena Malikyar, 'When Clint Eastwood came to Afghanistan', Al Jazeera website, 29 February 2016, https://www.aljazeera.com/indepth/opinion/2016/02/clint-eastwood-afghanistan-cinema-oscars-160225090238611.html (accessed 20 June 2019)

3   See Arley Loewen and Josette McMichael (eds), *Images of Afghanistan: Exploring Afghan Culture through Art and Literature*, Oxford: Oxford University Press, 2010, p. 199

4   Nancy Hatch Dupree, in collaboration with Ahmad Ali Kohzad, *An Historical Guide to Kabul*, Kabul: The Afghan Tourist Organization, 1972, p. 148

5   Named for Dost Mohammad Khan's son Akbar Khan, who played a prominent role during the first Anglo-Afghan War

6   Graham Bowley, 'Spy balloons become part of the Afghanistan landscape, stirring unease', *New York Times*, 12 May 2012, https://www.nytimes.com/2012/05/13/world/asia/in-afghanistan-spy-balloons-now-part-of-landscape.html (accessed 20 June 2019)

7   The Afghan flag under the Communist government was also a red standard, with a sprig of wheat and a mechanical gear. Robert D. Crews, *Afghan Modern: The History of a Global Nation,* Cambridge, MA: Belknap Press, 2015, p. 243

8   John Baily, *War, Exile and the Music of Afghanistan: The Ethnographer's Tale*, Abingdon: Routledge, 2017, pp. 153–4

9   Erlend Clouston, '"If I find one reel, I must kill you"', *The Guardian*, 20 February 2008, https://www.theguardian.com/film/2008/feb/20/features.afghanistan (accessed 20 June 2019)

10   See also Loewen and McMichael, *Images of Afghanistan*, p. 288

11   Various media reports including Khwaja Baseer Ahmad, 'MPs oppose moving film archive to Presidential Palace', Pahjwok Afghan News, 8 July 2018, https://www.pajhwok.com/en/2018/07/08/mps-oppose-moving-film-archive-presidential-palace; '"Arg archive would only be run by MoIC," President Ghani', Ministry of Information and Culture, 21 July 2018, http://moic.gov.af/en/news/arg-archive-would-only-be-run-by-moic-president-ghani (both accessed 20 June 2019)

5: WALKING WITH THE DJINNS

1   Barbara Lopes Cardozo et al., 'Mental Health, Social Functioning, and Disability in Postwar Afghanistan', *JAMA* 292(5), 2004, pp. 575–84

2   Quoted in 'Mental health problems in Afghans', *Dawn*, 11 October 2010 (original source cited as AFP), https://www.dawn.com/news/570706 (accessed 20 June 2019). See also Ron Moreau, 'Do the Taliban get PTSD?', *Newsweek*, 6 December 2010, https://www.newsweek.com/do-taliban-get-ptsd-68973 (accessed 20 June 2019)

3   'Depression a leading cause of ill health and disability among Afghans – fighting stigma is key to recovery', World Health Organization Regional Office for the Eastern Mediterranean, 9 April 2017, http://www.emro.who.int/afg/afghanistan-news/world-health-day-2017.html (accessed 20 June 2019)

4   *WHO–AIMS Report on Mental Health System in Afghanistan*, Kabul: World Health Organization Afghanistan, 2006, available at https://www.who.int/mental_health/evidence/Afghanistan_WHO_AIMS_Report.pdf (accessed 20 June 2019). Also see Ghulam Dastagir Sayed. 2011. 'Mental Health in Afghanistan: Burden, Challenges and the Way Forward', *Health, Nutrition and Population (HNP)*, Washington, DC: World Bank. http://documents.worldbank.org/curated/en/692201467992810759/Mental-health-in-Afghanistan-burden-challenges-and-the-way-forward (accessed 20 June 2019)

5   Nancy Hatch Dupree, in collaboration with Ahmad Ali Kohzad, *An Historical Guide to Kabul*, Kabul: The Afghan Tourist Organization, 1972, pp. 133–4

6   Tim McGirk, 'Asylum inmates left to suffer and die: one man is trying to save patients at a Kabul mental hospital from starvation and marauding guerrilla bands', *The Independent*, 15 May 1993, https://www.independent.co.uk/news/world/asylum-inmates-left-to-suffer-and-die-one-man-is-trying-to-save-patients-at-a-kabul-mental-hospital-2322937.html (accessed 20 June 2019)

7   *Afghanistan: Drug Use Survey 2005*, UN Office on Drugs and Crime (UNODC), available at https://www.unodc.org/documents/afghanistan/Opium_Surveys/Price_Monitoring/2005/Afghan_Drug_Use_Report_2005.pdf (accessed 20 June 2019)

8   *Drug Use in Afghanistan: 2009 Survey – Executive Summary*, UNODC, available at https://www.unodc.org/documents/data-and-analysis/Studies/Afghan-Drug-Survey-2009-Executive-Summary-web.pdf (accessed 20 June 2019)

9   For an insight into Afghanistan's history of opium production and its connection with cycles of conflict starting in 1978, and for the Taliban's ban of 2000, see *Global Illicit Drug Trends 2001*, United Nations Office

for Drug Control and Crime Prevention, 2001, pp. 30–41, available at https://www.unodc.org/pdf/report_2001–06–26_1/report_2001–06–26_1.pdf (accessed 20 June 2019)

10   For an overview of these policies see *Counternarcotics: Lessons from the US Experience in Afghanistan*, Special Inspector General for Afghanistan Reconstruction, June 2018, https://www.sigar.mil/interactive-reports/counternarcotics/index.html (accessed 20 June 2019)

11   In 2007, Afghanistan produced 193,000 hectares of opium poppies. This was surpassed in 2013 with over 200,000 hectares. See *Afghanistan: Opium Survey 2007*, UNODC, October 2007, available at https://www.unodc.org/documents/crop-monitoring/Afghanistan-Opium-Survey-2007.pdf; *Afghanistan: Opium Survey 2013 – Summary Findings*, UNODC, November 2013, available at https://www.unodc.org/documents/crop-monitoring/Afghanistan/Afghan_report_Summary_Findings_2013.pdf (both accessed 20 June 2019)

12   *2015 Afghanistan Drug Report*, Ministry of Counter Narcotics, Afghanistan, 9 December 2015, available at https://www.unodc.org/documents/afghanistan/UNODC-DRUG-REPORT15-ONLINE-270116_1.pdf (accessed 20 June 2019)

13   'Afghanistan National Urban Drug Use Survey (ANUDUS)', INL Demand Reduction Program Research Brief, December 2012, p. 4, available at https://2009–2017.state.gov/documents/organization/212957.pdf (accessed 20 June 2019)

14   Schinasi, *Kabul*, pp. 52, n. 178

15   'ANUDUS', p. 4

16   Schinasi, *Kabul*, p. 44

17   Matthieu Aikins, 'Kabubble: counting down to economic collapse in the Afghan capital', *Harper's Magazine*, February 2013, https://harpers.org/archive/2013/02/kabubble (accessed 19 June 2019)

6 VEILED CITY

1   'Afghanistan: Kabul vs New Kabul City', *The Telegraph*, 1 April 2011, https://www.telegraph.co.uk/news/worldnews/asia/afghanistan/8420583/Afghanistan-Kabul-vs-New-Kabul-City.html (accessed 20 June 2019)

2   Ewen MacAskill and Patrick Wintour, 'Afghanistan withdrawal: Barack Obama says 33,000 troops will leave next year', *The Guardian*, 23 June 2011, https://www.theguardian.com/world/2011/jun/23/afghanistan-withdrawal-barack-obama-troops (accessed 20 June 2019)

3   Arthur George Warner and Edmond Warner, *The Sháhnáma of Firdausí*, 9 vols, London: Kegan Paul, Trench, Trübner, 1905–25, vol. 1, p. 261–262

4   Ibid., p. 273

5   Akram Osman, *Real Men Keep Their Word: Tales from Kabul, Afghanistan – A Selection of Akram Osman's Dari Short Stories,* translated by Arley Loewen, Oxford: Oxford University Press, 2005, pp. 1–23

6   Ministry of Higher Education, Government of Afghanistan, Higher Education Statistics, cited in *Higher Education in Afghanistan: An Emerging Mountainscape,* World Bank, August 2013, available at http://documents. worldbank.org/curated/en/307221468180889060/pdf/809150WP0Afg ha0Box0379822B00PUBLIC0.pdf (accessed 20 June 2019)

7   Unpublished draft of oral testimony about marriage practices in the old city of Kabul, Aga Khan Trust for Culture, 2009

8   Nancy Hatch Dupree, *The Women of Afghanistan,* Islamabad: Office of the UN Coordinator for Afghanistan, 1998, p. 2

9   Kirk Semple, 'Big Afghan weddings, banned under Taliban, are back', *New York Times,* 14 January 2008, https://www.nytimes.com/ 2008/01/14/world/asia/14iht-wedding.1.9190667.html (accessed 20 June 2019)

10 Charles Recknagel and Mustafa Sarwar, 'The changing face of Kabul: after years of foreign-fueled growth, an uncertain future', Radio Free Europe/Radio Liberty website, 13 June 2016, https://www.rferl.org/a/ changing-face-of-kabul-uncertain-fututure-foreign-troops-leaving/27795414.html (accessed 20 June 2019)

11 In 'The bride price: the Afghan tradition of paying for wives', Afghanistan Analysts Network, 25 October 2016, https://www. afghanistan-analysts.org/the-bride-price-the-afghan-tradition-of-paying-for-wives (accessed 20 June 2019), Fazal Muzhary explains the difference between 'mahr' and bride price, and also the historical context of the law on the festivities

12 Discussed in Bente Scheller, 'Import ban on bridal dresses: a draft law of the Ministry for Women's Affairs asks for moral guards to control private celebrations', Heinrich Böll Stiftung website, 1 May 2011, https://www.boell.de/en/2011/05/01/import-ban-bridal-dresses-draft-law-ministry-womens-affairs-asks-moral-guards-control (accessed 20 June 2019)

7 RETURNS

1   Robert D. Crews, *Afghan Modern: The History of a Global Nation,* Cambridge, MA: Belknap Press, 2015, p. 235

2   Sandra Schäfer, 'Every Change Engendered Its Own Specific Films', interview with Siddiq Barmak and Engineer Latif Ahmadi, 2004, available at http://mazefilm.de/publications/essays-by-sandra-schaefer (accessed 20 June 2019). This interview is a revised version of a text that was first published in Sandra Schäfer, Jochen Becker and Madeleine

Bernstorff (eds), *Kabul / Tehran 1979ff: Filmlandschaften, Städte unter Stress und Migration*, Berlin: b_books, 2006

3   'The economic disaster behind Afghanistan's mounting human crisis', International Crisis Group, 3 October 2016, https://www.crisisgroup.org/asia/south-asia/afghanistan/economic-disaster-behind-afghanistan-s-mounting-human-crisis (accessed 20 June 2019)

4   There was also the illicit economy of the drug trade. See, for instance, Alice Speri, 'Afghanistan's opium economy is doing better than ever', *Vice News*, 21 May 2014, https://news.vice.com/en_us/article/ev7kzw/afghanistans-opium-economy-is-doing-better-than-ever (accessed 20 June 2019)

5   *Afghanistan: Annual Report 2013 – Protection of Civilians in Armed Conflict*, United Nations Assistance Mission in Afghanistan (UNAMA), February 2014, available at https://unama.unmissions.org/sites/default/files/feb_8_2014_poc-report_2013-full-report-eng.pdf (accessed 20 June 2019). See also 'Afghan civilian casualties similar to record levels of 2011 – UNAMA report', UNAMA, 8 February 2014, https://unama.unmissions.org/afghan-civilian-casualties-similar-record-levels-2011-unama-report (accessed 20 June 2019)

6   ICRC Film Archives, Geneva, *Afghanistan, February 1993,* Reference V-F-CR-F-00430

7   Carlotta Gall, 'Afghans riot after deadly crash by US military truck', *New York Times*, 29 May 2006, https://www.nytimes.com/2006/05/29/world/asia/29cnd-afghan.html (accessed 20 June 2019)

8   May Schinasi, *Kabul: A History 1773–1948,* translated by R. D. McChesney, Leiden and Boston: Brill, 2017, pp. 9, 102

9   For the history of this era, I referred to the following texts, which use a number of sources and analysis: Dietrich Reetz, *Hijrat: The Flight of the Faithful – A British File on the Exodus of Muslim Peasants from North India to Afghanistan in 1920,* Berlin: Verlag das Arabische Buch, 1995; M. Naeem Qureshi, 'The "Ulamā" of British India and the Hijrat of 1920', *Modern Asian Studies* 13(1), 1979, pp. 41–59; Lal Baha, 'The Hijrat Movement and the North West Frontier Province', *Islamic Studies* 18(3), 1979, pp. 231–42

10 For the wider context of the Khilafat and Non-Cooperation movement in India at the time, see Reetz, *Hijrat*, pp. 13–22

11 Qureshi, 'The "Ulamā" of British India', p. 45

12 Quoted ibid., p. 55

13 Reetz, *Hijrat*, p. 47

14 Quoted in Baha, 'The Hijrat Movement', p. 236

15 Qureshi, 'The "Ulamā" of British India', p. 57

16 Reetz, *Hijrat*, p. 69

17 *UNHCR Mid-Year Trends 2014*, UNHCR, January 2015, p. 4, https://www.unhcr.org/uk/statistics/unhcrstats/ 54aa91d89/mid-year-trends-june-2014.html (accessed 20 June 2019)

BIBLIOGRAPHY

The writings of May Schinasi and Nancy Hatch Dupree form an enduring path into Kabul's past for later travellers like myself. I am grateful for their committed scholarship, and their enthusiasm for the city. See May Schinasi, *Kabul: A History 1773–1948* (Leiden and Boston: Brill, 2017) and Nancy Hatch Dupree, *An Historical Guide to Kabul* (Kabul: The Afghan Tourist Organization, 1972). The late Nancy Dupree was the force behind the establishment of the Afghanistan Center at Kabul University (ACKU), which has documents and resources on the country available online at http://acku.edu.af.

I also referred to the online version of the *Encyclopædia Iranica*, http://www.iranicaonline.org.

FOREWORD

Rebecca Solnit's *A Field Guide to Getting Lost* (Edinburgh: Canongate, 2006) comprises essays that interrogate the very idea of being without direction. On the challenges and pleasures of wandering in India, see Shilpa Phadke, Sameera Khan and Shilpa Ranade, *Why Loiter? Women and Risk on Mumbai Streets* (New Delhi: Viking, 2011), also Subuhi Jiwani (ed.), *Day's End Stories: Life after Sundown in Small-Town India* (Chennai: Tranquebar Press, 2014).

1: RETURNS

Population figures for Afghanistan tend to be estimates, and shift across sources. The first nationwide census was conducted in 1979, among political tumult, and found a total of nearly 14 million people. The continuing ambiguity about this basic demographic data indicates how little we actually know about the country. See Daniel Balland, 'Census ii. In Afghanistan', *Encyclopædia Iranica*, http://www.iranicaonline.org/articles/census-ii.

On the use of the term 'Dari' for Persian in Afghanistan, see p. 131 of *Images of Afghanistan: Exploring Afghan Culture through Art and Literature*, ed. by Arley Loewen and Josette McMichael (Oxford: Oxford University Press, 2010).

On Queen Soraya, and on the influence of Flapper-era fashion on Afghan politics, see Nancy Dupree, *The Women of Afghanistan* (Islamabad: Office of the UN Coordinator for Afghanistan, 1998).

Anne Feenstra discusses Kabul's kitschy wedding cake architecture in an article of that title on Afghanistan Analysts Network, 27 August 2010, https://www.afghanistan-analysts. org/kabuls-kitschy-wedding-cake-architecture.

The introduction to *Shahr Ashob*, ed. by Dr Na'im Ahmad, Delhi: Maktabah Jami'ah, Ltd. 1968, has been translated from the Urdu by Frances W. Pritchett http://www.columbia.edu/ itc/mealac/pritchett/00urduhindilinks/workshop2009/txt_ naim_ahmad_1968.html.

Rana Safvi discusses Delhi and Shahr Ashob in 'Shahjahanabad, Shahr Ashob Poetry and the Revolt of 1857', Sahapedia, https://www.sahapedia.org/shahjahanabad-shahr-ashob-poetry-and-the-revolt-of-1857.

Additionally, Robert D. Crews' *Afghan Modern: The History of a Global Nation* (Cambridge, MA: Belknap Press, 2015) reframes the perceived isolation of Afghanistan by tracing its centuries-old cosmopolitanism to more contemporary currents of exchange. For an even wider lens on this traffic of ideas and people, see Pankaj Mishra, *From the Ruins of Empire: The Revolt against the West and the Remaking of Asia* (London: Allen Lane, 2012). Dževad Karahasan writes about a beloved city lost to war in *Sarajevo, Exodus of a City*, translated by Slobodan Drakulić (New York: Kodansha International, 1994).

2: WRITTEN ON THE CITY

The story of the Kabuliwala by Rabindranath Tagore has been translated into many languages. It has also been adapted into several films. Most of the Kabuliwalas or traders who visited (then) Calcutta were actually from the southern Afghan provinces like Paktika and Paktia. A photo project by Nazes Afroz and Moska Najib documents this diaspora at https://www.kabultokolkata.com.

Brief sketches of Haideri Wojodi and Qahar Asi are in *Images of Afghanistan*, p. 80 and p. 85.

For a discussion on travelogues and the Afghan quest for modernity see Nile Green, 'The Afghan Afterlife of Phileas Fogg: Space and Time in the Literature of Afghan Travel', in Nile Green and Nushin Arbabzadah, *Afghanistan in Ink: Literature between Diaspora and Nation* (London: Hurst, 2013), pp. 67–90. The European travelogues I read included Annemarie Schwarzenbach's *All the Roads are Open: An Afghan Journey 1939–1940*, translated by Isabel Fargo Cole (London: Seagull Books, 2011) and Ella K. Maillart's *The Cruel Way: Switzerland to Afghanistan in a Ford, 1939* (Chicago: University of Chicago Press, 2013). Both women had driven together from Geneva.

On early Afghan literary production, and the figure of Mahmud Tarzi, see May Schinasi's *Afghanistan at the Beginning of the Twentieth Century: Nationalism and Journalism in Afghanistan:*

A Study of Seraj Ul-Akhbar (1911–1918) (Naples: Istituto Universitario Orientale, 1979).

The character of Mulla Nasruddin is referred to variously as Khwaja, Khoja and Hodja, across Central Asia, Turkey and beyond. He is often accompanied on his wanderings by his faithful donkey.

Nazes Afroz also translated the memoir of Syed Mujtaba Ali, who went from India to teach in Kabul in 1927. *In a Land Far from Home: A Bengali in Afghanistan* (New Delhi: Speaking Tiger, 2015) is an insightful and often very funny account of the crucial period of Amir Amanullah's modernisation measures, seen through Indian eyes. Ali was caught up in the tumult of the 1929 rebellion and was eventually evacuated in an airlift from the Sherpur airfield.

3: ABSENCES

Thomas Barfield's *Afghanistan: A Cultural and Political History* (Princeton: Princeton University Press, 2010) provides valuable context for the conflicts from the Soviet invasion to the Najibullah government, and subsequent internecine battles in Kabul; see pp. 211–54. For an overview of the period of Anglo-Afghan tensions see Dupree, *An Historical Guide to Kabul*, pp. 49–55.

Najibullah tried to flee to India after the fall of Kabul to the mujahideen factions, but was forced to seek refuge in the UN compound. He survived the civil war but was brutally executed by the Taliban in 1996 when they gained control of the capital.

The Afghanistan Justice Project is an independent, non-partisan organisation. Its 2005 report, *Casting Shadows: War Crimes and Crimes against Humanity 1978–2001*, is available at https://www.opensocietyfoundations.org/publications/casting-shadows-war-crimes-and-crimes-against-humanity-1978-2001. The Human

Rights Watch report *Blood-Stained Hands: Past Atrocities in Kabul and Afghanistan's Legacy of Impunity* (2005) focuses on events in Kabul from April 1992 to March 1993 and is available at https://www.hrw.org/reports/2005/afghanistan0605/.

For a discussion on the 'Amnesty Law', see Sari Kuovo, 'After two years in legal limbo: a first glance at the approved "Amnesty law"', Afghanistan Analysts Network, 22 February 2010, https://www.afghanistan-analysts.org/after-two-years-in-legal-limbo-a-first-glance-at-the-approved-amnesty-law; 'Afghanistan: repeal amnesty law', Human Rights Watch, 10 March 2010, https://www.hrw.org/news/2010/03/10/afghanistan-repeal-amnesty-law.

Additionally, on how the events of this era link to Afghanistan after 2001, see Anand Gopal, *No Good Men among the Living: America, the Taliban, and the War through Afghan Eyes* (New York: Metropolitan, 2014). M. Hassan Kakar's *Afghanistan: The Soviet Invasion and the Afghan Response 1979–1982* (Berkeley: University of California Press, 1995) has vivid descriptions of the urban protests against the Communist government, drawn from the author's journal.

Lady Sale's Afghanistan: An Indomitable Victorian Lady's Account of the Retreat from Kabul during the First Afghan War (Leonaur: 2009) provides an insider's view of the key events of 1841–42. Florentina Sale published her journal when she returned to England in 1843, which recounted the battle near Bimaru Hill in Kabul, the infamous retreat, and months of being held hostage.

4: MAP OF MOVING IMAGES

Ethnomusicologist John Baily discusses the 'saving' of the RTA music archive – an account that bears resemblance to the Afghan Film archive narrative. 'It was a nice story but surely not the whole truth,' he concludes, in *War, Exile and the Music of Afghanistan: The Ethnographer's Tale* (Abingdon: Routledge, 2017), pp. 153–4.

A group of Afghan filmmakers and artists protested the decision to move the film archive to the Arg, arguing that it should be housed in an accessible, dedicated centre.

Kabul seemed to be full of international consultants in the years after 2001. But even during the 1970s, Xavier de Planhol writes, Afghanistan was home to the highest number per capita of foreign 'experts', westerners and Soviets in approximately equal numbers: see 'Kabul ii. Historical Geography', *Encyclopædia Iranica*, http://www.iranicaonline.org/articles/kabul-ii-historical-geography.

Italo Calvino's *Invisible Cities*, translated by William Weaver (New York: Harcourt Brace Jovanovich, 1974) comes to mind in Kabul often.

5: WALKING WITH THE DJINNS

T-walls as security hazards for ordinary Afghans are discussed in Jelena Bjelica and Kate Clark, 'The new Kabul "Green Belt" security plan: more security for whom?', Afghanistan Analysts Network, 25 September 2017, https://www.afghanistan-analysts.org/the-new-kabul-green-belt-security-plan-more-security-for-whom.

Ann Jones' *They Were Soldiers: How the Wounded Return from America's Wars – The Untold Story* (Chicago: Haymarket, 2013) maps the impact of the Afghan war on US troops.

6: VEILED CITY

The 2012 Afghanistan National Urban Drug Use Survey found that Kabul represented 13 per cent of the nation's population and over half of the total urban population. Several of these migrants to Kabul from other parts of the country were fleeing internal conflict and hunger.

The economic impact of the ISAF presence and subsequent withdrawal is examined in Matthieu Aikins, 'Kabubble: counting down to economic collapse in the Afghan capital', *Harper's Magazine*, February 2013, https://harpers.org/archive/2013/02/kabubble; and in Jonathan Goodhand, *Contested Transitions: International Drawdown and the Future State in Afghanistan*, NOREF, November 2012. Also see 'The economic disaster behind Afghanistan's mounting human crisis', International Crisis Group, 3 October 2016, https://www.crisisgroup.org/asia/south-asia/afghanistan/economic-disaster-behind-afghanistan-s-mounting-human-crisis.

Additionally, anthropologist Julie Billaud channels the voices of the young women living in the National Women's Dormitory of Kabul University in 2007 in *Kabul Carnival: Gender Politics in Postwar Afghanistan* (Philadelphia: University of Pennsylvania Press, 2015).

Songs of Love and War: Afghan Women's Poetry, translated by Marjolijn de Jager (New York: Other Press, 2010) contains *landay* or anonymous 'songs' collected by Afghan intellectual and poet Sayd Bahaodine Majrouh. '[T]he great originality of this popular poetry is the active presence of women. If, as everywhere else, she is the inspiration for male poets, here she imposes herself above all as creator, as the author and subject of innumerable songs,' he wrote in the introduction. Majrouh himself was murdered while living in exile in Peshawar, in 1988.

7: RETURNS

The international aid that flowed into Afghanistan from 2001 was in many ways ephemeral. Thomas Barfield in *Afghanistan: A Cultural and Political History* points out that a significant part of it was 'swallowed up by the expenses of providing it. The Agency Coordinating Body for Afghan Relief estimated that in 2008, of the $15 billion in reconstruction assistance given to Afghanistan since 2001, "a staggering 40 percent has returned

to donor countries in corporate profits and consultant salaries'"
(p. 316). Foreign capital was also carried out of the country by
members of the Afghan diaspora, who had returned after 2001
to participate in the reconstruction project. 'Afghanistan's
central bank estimated that $4.6 billion in cash left the country
legally through Kabul International Airport in 2011 alone,'
wrote Matthieu Aikins in 'Kabubble' (*Harper's Magazine*,
February 2013, https://harpers.org/archive/2013/02/kabubble).

By 2017, US Embassy employees in Kabul were using a
helicopter to cross the street, according to the *New York Times*
(Rod Nordland, 'US expands Kabul security zone, digging
in for next decade', 16 September 2017, https://www.
nytimes.com/2017/09/16/world/asia/kabul-green-zone-
afghanistan.html).

For the official website of Kabul New City see http://www.
dcda.gov.af/.

On lost kingdoms and loneliness, Jolyon Leslie's *The Garden
of Exile* (Ostfildern: Hatje Kantz, 2012) describes Kabul's most
famous refugee, the emir of Bokhara. On cities outside and
within cities, see Darran Anderson, *Imaginary Cities* (London:
Influx Press, 2015). On the nature of time in Afghanistan, see
Anna Badkhen, *The World Is a Carpet: Four Seasons in an Afghan
Village* (New York: Riverhead, 2013). On fantastic journeys,
see Ghalib Lakhnavi and Abdullah Bilgrami, *The Adventures of
Amir Hamza: Lord of the Auspicious Planetary Conjunction*,
translated by Musharraf Ali Farooqi (New York: Modern
Library, 2007). On women mapping invisible spaces, see Alice
Albinia, *Empires of the Indus* (London: Hodder & Stoughton,
2009); Sara Suleri, *Meatless Days* (Chicago: University of
Chicago Press, 1989); Ismat Chughtai, *The Quilt and Other
Stories* (London: Women's Press, 1991).

INDEX

Abdullah (driver) 73–4, 76, 96, 129, 144, 145, 169, 217, 221, 222, 234, 235

Abdur Rahman Khan, Amir ('Iron Amir') 9, 53, 57, 76, 131, 144–5

Afghan Film Organisation 119, 126–39, 185, 190

Afghan Institute of Archaeology 100

Afghanistan: 'Amnesty Law' (2007) 91; Anglo-Afghan Wars *see* Anglo-Afghan Wars; Bonn Conference (2001) and 5, 112; British and 2–3, 4, 9, 10, 32, 52, 53, 55, 63, 65, 72, 73, 74–7, 78, 79, 80, 81, 84, 99, 126, 229, 230–3; Buddhism and 96, 98–9, 100, 102–6, 137, 228; civil war (1992–96) 11, 12, 13–14, 23, 24, 43, 50–1, 62, 64, 84, 85, 86, 87, 88–92, 108, 128, 146, 155, 156–7, 158, 159, 171, 185, 193, 223, 226; constitution 10, 60, 144; constitutional monarchy ('democracy decade') (1963–73) 60–1, 83; coup (1973) 12, 60–1, 102, 135; coup (1978)/Saur (April) Revolution 12, 26, 61, 81–2, 133, 134, 210; declaration of independence from British 10, 231; Communist era (1978–92) 12, 24, 26, 29, 46–7, 57, 78–9, 81–2, 84, 85, 87, 92–3, 118, 122, 126, 127, 128, 133–4, 144, 150, 178, 210, 218, 222; economy 6, 24, 25, 26–7, 195, 216, 220; elections (2004) 5; elections (2009) 140; elections (2014) 216; kings/amirs of *see individual ruler name*; maps of xv, 50, 63–4, 110, 183; modernisation of 9–10, 39, 53, 65, 83, 131; origins of 8, 9; Soviet–Afghan War (1979–89) 12, 29, 61, 78–9, 80, 84–5, 93, 118, 122, 126, 127, 128, 133, 134, 144, 184, 222; Taliban rule *see* Taliban; Transitional Authority 5; TV channels 120, 136, 137; US-led war in (2001-) xii, xiii, xv, 5, 6, 7, 12, 13, 14, 38, 80, 90–1, 121, 129, 140–1, 155, 178, 195, 216, 220, 221, 222, 228; withdrawal of NATO troops from 220–3

Afghanistan Independent Human Rights Commission (AIHRC) 73, 90

Afghanistan Justice Project 90

Afghan National Police (ANP) 140

Afghan Red Crescent Society (ARCS) 144, 145, 147

Afshar Hill 144

Aga Khan Trust for Culture 43–4 aid agencies/workers 3, 5, 6, 7, 13,

19, 24, 25, 26, 27, 28, 30, 40, 41, 73, 80, 81, 84, 85, 164, 195, 220, 221, 224, 235 *see also individual aid agency name* Alauddini, Agha Sahib, *ziyarat* of 167–8

al Qaeda 5, 90

Alexievich, Svetlana: *Zinky Boys* 78–9

Aligarh, India xiv, xv, 3, 17, 18, 19, 33, 34–5, 36–8, 40, 41, 48, 51, 52, 58, 71, 108–10, 111, 112, 141, 142, 179–80, 181, 182, 186, 187, 188, 190, 196, 213, 218–19, 226, 230, 235–6

Amanullah, Amir (1919–29) 9, 10–11, 39, 56, 60, 73, 99–100, 107, 126, 163, 210, 229, 231, 233, 256

Amin, Hafizullah 82, 84, 133, 217–18

'amnesiac city' xiv–xv, 98

Anglo-Afghan Wars: First Anglo-Afghan War (1839–42) 63, 74–5, 79, 126; Second Anglo-Afghan War (1878–80) 73, 74–6, 79; Third Anglo-Afghan War (1919) 9, 74–5 *aqeedat* (devotion) 72

archaeology xiv, 98–106

architecture xiii, 9, 18–19, 23–5, 33, 73, 191

Arg complex 9, 93, 125, 138

Ariana Cinema 125, 126

Arify, Ibrahim 129, 130, 132, 134, 135, 136, 137, 138

Asheqan-o-Arefan, *ziyarat* of (the Shrine of Lovers and Mystics) 95, 157–8, 162 Asmai, goddess 49

attari (apothecary) shops 49

Baba (author's maternal grandfather) 16–18, 21, 34–5, 36, 41, 44, 48, 51–3, 58, 69, 179–81, 229, 230, 235, 236, 237, 238

Babur, Zahiruddin 8, 18, 41–4, 45, 52, 63, 65, 96, 131, 238; annexes Kabul (1504) 8; *Baburnama* 18, 41–3, 44, 63, 96; mausoleum of 43–4, 131 Bagh-e-Babur 131

Bagh-e-Bala 144

Bagh-e-Qazi 157

Bagh-e-Zenana (Women's Garden) 156

Bala Hissar (High Fortress) 8, 72–3, 75, 101, 155

Balkh, Afghanistan 52

barfi, custom of 164

Barikot cinema 107, 108, 112, 187

Barmak, Siddiq 108, 111, 112, 116, 117, 119, 127, 128, 156

batin (hidden or implied) xv, 191

bazaars vii, 8, 15, 27, 38, 42, 54–5, 68, 75–6, 94, 111, 157, 177, 196, 206

beauty salons 113, 197–201, 204, 206

Bedil, Abdul Qadir 48, 51, 52, 64

Behzad cinema 111

Bimaru Hill 126, 138

bin Laden, Osama 178

Bollywood films 108, 109, 111, 112, 113, 114, 115, 117, 125, 200, 202, 203, 211, 212

Bombay (now Mumbai), India 16, 63

Bonn Conference (2001) 5, 112

book market, Ju-e-Sheer 48–51, 107

bookshops 44–8, 51

Bostan Serai (Orchard Garden) palace 53

bridge (*pul*), origins of Kabul and 1, 216

British Cemetery 74, 76–8, 79, 80–1, 126

British Embassy 81

British Empire 2–3, 4, 9, 10, 32, 52, 53, 55, 63, 65, 72, 73, 74–7, 78, 79, 84, 99, 230–4

Buddhas of Bamiyan 98–9, 100, 105, 137, 228

Buddhism 96, 98–9, 100, 102–6, 137, 228

Bush Bazaar market 38

Calcutta (now Kolkata), India 36 chador (large cloth) 167, 168, 189, 201

Chahr Chatta bazaar 54–5, 75

chaikhanas (tea houses) 27

Chaman-e-Wazirabad (meadow) 40

charahi (crossroads) 7, 45, 56

Charahi Malik Asghar 56
Charahi Sadarat 45
Chardeh, valley of 44, 229
Chicken Street 110, 113
China 24, 78
Cinema Bakhtar 112
Cinema Kabul 111
cinemas 31, 37, 107–15, 125–6, 128,
        153, 187
civil war, Afghan (1992–96) 11, 12,
        13–14, 23, 24, 43, 50–1, 57, 62,
        64, 76, 84, 85, 86, 87–92, 105,
        108, 126, 128, 146, 155, 156–7,
        158, 159, 171, 185, 193, 223, 226
coffee shops/cafes 40–1, 46, 186,
        187–9, 219, 228
Cold War (1947–91) 12, 84, 144
counter-culture movement 78

Daoud Khan, Muhammad 12, 25, 26,
        61, 81, 133, 134, 135
Dari (type of Persian spoken in
        Kabul) 22, 34, 51, 60, 61, 110,
        116, 120, 184, 213
Darulaman (planned administrative
        capital) 10
Darulaman Road 153
Dehburi 13–14
Deh Dana 165
Deh Mazang roundabout 107, 131
Delhi, India 16–17, 32, 43, 57, 68,
        127, 177, 187, 216
depression 143, 150, 162
djinns 120, 141–2, 148, 151, 152, 153,
        154, 161, 163, 164, 165, 166,
        169, 170, 173, 174, 175, 176
Dost Mohammad Khan, Amir 75
drug addiction 142, 148, 153–62,
        170–6
Dubai 20, 25, 38
Dupree, Nancy: *An Historical Guide to
        Kabul* 22, 40, 68, 75, 144
Durand Line 4–5
Durrani Empire 8

Eid, festival of 118, 185
evil eye 25, 54, 159, 176

Facebook 186, 224
faith healers 143, 147, 153, 163, 164
Farkhunda 163, 164
Ferghana 8, 42
film/cinema 107–39
Firdausi, Abul Qasem: *Shahnama* 48,
        52, 64, 67, 180
First World War (1914–18) 229, 230
French Archaeological Delegation
        99–100
funerals 92, 93, 164

Gandhi, M. K. 50, 51
gardens xv, 1, 8, 11, 19, 21–2, 29, 28, 30,
        31, 40, 42, 43–4, 53, 56, 59, 69, 87,
        88, 92, 94, 126, 138, 144, 145, 157,
        187, 188, 217, 220, 225, 227, 235
Ghalib, Mirza Asadullah 48, 64
ghareeb (state of being away from your
        own land) 34–5
Godard, André 10
graveyards/graves 43–4, 70–3, 74–5,
        76–81, 83, 84, 87, 88, 92, 93–8, 101,
        131, 146, 157, 164, 168, 171, 233
'Great Game' (19th century
        diplomatic confrontation) 75
guest houses 18, 19, 20, 38, 39, 40,
        120, 218, 220, 227–9
Gulistan Serai (Rose Garden) palace 53
gulkhana (conservatory) 18

Habibullah Kalakani (Bacha-e-Saqao)
        11, 39, 57–8, 111
Habibullah, Amir 9, 229, 230
Habibzada, Dr Haroon 147, 148, 149,
        152
Hadda, Afghanistan 100, 105
Hafiz 59
hall weddings 193–5, 204, 225
Hamahang, Ustad 156–7, 191
Hazrat Tamim Jaber-e-Ansar, *ziyarat*
        of 95, 101
Hephthalites ('White Huns') 99, 103
hijrat migration (exodus of Muslims
        from India to Afghanistan)
        (1920) 230–4
Hilai 164–6, 167, 168, 169, 170

Hindu Kush 8
Hindus 49, 96, 99, 157, 231
Human Rights Watch 90

India xii, xiv, 5, 8, 16–17, 20, 43, 44,
    46, 51, 52, 53, 54, 60, 63, 64, 65,
    66, 68, 77, 100, 102, 108, 111,
    112, 113, 119, 127, 148, 156,
    170, 187, 196, 197, 200, 205–6,
    226, 230–4, 237; author's
    childhood in xiv, xv, 2, 3, 36–8,
    71, 108–10, 111, 131, 181–2,
    188, 190, 218–19; Babur and
    43; Bollywood films and 108,
    109, 111, 112, 113, 114, 115,
    117, 125, 200, 202, 203, 211,
    212; British rule 3, 32, 53, 65,
    230–4; *hijrat* migration (1920)
    230–4; Mughal rule 8, 42;
    Pathans and 2, 3; Persian
    language in 50, 52, 53, 77;
    Persian poetry and 48, 64, 65;
    weddings in 204
International Security Assistance
    Force (ISAF) 5, 7, 26, 46, 79,
    110–11, 127, 216, 221, 223;
    British Contingent of 79;
    headquarters 127; withdrawal
    from Afghanistan 220–3
internet 32, 34, 120, 135; cafes 186,
    219, 228
Iqbal, Muhammad 35, 48, 64–6,
    237–8; *Javed Nama* 66; *Musafir*
    (*Traveller*) 65–6
Iran 5, 45, 46, 48, 52, 84, 112, 150,
    154, 158, 159, 170, 173, 203, 204
Iranian Embassy 45
Iraq 5, 57
Islam 47, 58, 96, 97, 102, 141, 155,
    163, 230–1
Ismail Sahab 20, 21, 22, 27, 31, 40, 220

jaali (latticework screen) 44
Jada-e-Maiwand 83, 86, 111, 157, 173
Jalalabad, Afghanistan 11, 75, 85, 100,
    112
Ju-e-Sheer ('river of milk') 49, 107

Kabul, Afghanistan: Afghan civil war
    (1992–96) and 11, 12, 13–14,
    23, 24, 43, 50–1, 57, 62, 64, 76,
    84, 85, 86, 87–92, 105, 108, 126,
    128, 146, 155, 156–7, 158, 159,
    171, 185, 193, 223, 226; airfield,
    first 73, 126; 'amnesiac city'
    xiv–xv, 98; archaeology in ix,
    98–106; architecture 9, 18–19,
    23–5, 33; bazaars xii, 8, 15, 27,
    38, 42, 54–5, 68, 75–6, 94, 111,
    157, 177, 196, 206; beauty
    salons 113, 197–201, 204, 206;
    book markets 48–51, 107;
    bookshops 44–8, 51; British in
    see British Empire; capital of
    Afghanistan, first becomes 8;
    cinemas 31, 107–15, 153;
    climate 42, 43, 50, 71, 106;
    coffee shops/cafes 40–1, 187–9,
    219; counter-culture movement
    and 78; djinns and 120, 141–2,
    148, 151, 152, 153, 154, 161,
    163, 164, 165, 166, 169, 170,
    173, 174, 175, 176; drug
    addiction in 142, 148, 153–62,
    170–6; dust 1, 39, 45, 49, 68, 71,
    94, 148, 178, 203, 219, 228, 235;
    elites 6, 24, 31, 39, 50, 59, 61,
    63, 73, 84–5, 101, 112, 126, 156,
    192; film/film-making and
    107–39; gardens in xv, 1, 8, 11,
    19, 21–2, 29, 28, 30, 31, 40, 42,
    43–4, 53, 56, 59, 69, 87, 88, 92,
    94, 126, 138, 144, 145, 157, 187,
    188, 217, 220, 225, 227, 235;
    graveyards/graves 43–4, 70–3,
    74–5, 76–81, 83, 84, 87, 88, 92,
    93–8, 101, 131, 146, 157, 164,
    168, 171, 233; growth of 11, 13,
    19, 22, 23–4, 27; guest houses
    18, 19, 20, 38, 39, 40, 120, 218,
    220, 227–9; hillside settlements,
    informal 14–15; houses/homes
    1–2, 33, 40, 132, 217, 223–4;
    infrastructure 12–13, 14–15, 24,
    33, 140, 222; internet

Kabul, Afghanistan (*Continued*)
cafes 186, 219; kidnappings in 6,
170, 200, 218; love in 177–215;
marastoon (place of assistance)
143–51, 175; martyrdom/
martyrs in 71, 90, 92, 94, 163;
mausoleums 8, 43–4, 57, 102,
131; mental health in 140–53,
162, 175; name 1; newsreels of
126, 128, 130–5, 190; old city
xiii, 11, 83, 86, 88, 95, 111, 155,
157, 158, 175, 184, 185, 191,
229; origins of 1, 8, 216;
orphanages 145–6; patron saints
72, 157; picnics in 15, 16, 42, 94,
144, 188; poetry and 18, 35, 48,
53–4, 58–60, 61–3, 64–9, 120,
180–1 *see also* poetry; poppy
palaces 24–5, 31, 73, 156;
population numbers 23, 67, 85,
178; poverty in 35, 148, 155,
160, 163; power cuts 20–1, 31;
real estate prices 24–5, 73, 94,
219; reconstruction of 19, 22,
23–4, 40, 84, 88, 216, 220;
refugees and 5, 13, 14, 26, 30–2,
62, 64, 84, 97, 119, 147, 173,
203, 223, 226–7, 229, 230, 236–
7, 239; 'Ring of Steel' (police
checkpoints) 140; 'shadow city',
as xv, 72; sky 2, 4, 30, 181, 184,
186, 221; spy balloon 129, 223;
streams 7, 42, 49, 121, 122, 123;
suicide bombings 6, 22, 67, 129,
140, 202, 221; taxis 4, 7, 45, 53,
73–4, 86, 113, 129, 144, 169,
217, 218, 221, 222, 234, 235;
traffic 7, 40, 45, 56, 63, 67, 108,
129, 140, 153, 161, 164, 169,
178, 186, 193, 222, 227, 228;
trees 44, 45, 94, 96, 145, 146,
223, 225–6, 239; walls 1, 94, 107;
weddings in 14, 191–215, 225;
zoo 107; women in *see* women;
*see also individual place and area
name*

Kabul City Centre shopping mall
15, 20
Kabul International Airport 4, 217,
219, 234, 235
Kabul Intercontinental Hotel 193
Kabul New City 222
Kabul Polytechnic University 144
Kabul Public Library 55, 56–8, 60,
61–7, 127, 158–9
Kabul River xii, xiii, 8, 9, 11, 50, 51,
53, 83, 107, 111, 175
Kabul Serena Hotel 56, 112
Kabul University 14, 55–6, 65, 100,
177, 178, 190–1
Kabuliwala (a trader from
Afghanistan) 36, 69
Kandahar, Afghanistan 29, 60,
78, 84
Kanishka, King Kushan 99
Karmal, Babrak 84
Karte Parwan 144, 202
Karte Seh 7, 50, 86, 113, 187, 225
Karzai, Hamid 5, 112, 140, 228
Khair Khana 23, 197, 228
khak (native soil) 93–4, 97, 103
Khalid (Kal) (friend of author)
25, 26, 27, 28, 29, 30, 81–3,
92, 93, 112, 134–5, 138,
183–4, 187, 197, 217, 226,
227
Khalq (Masses) faction 82
Kharabat 95, 155–6, 157, 160, 170, 191
Khushal Khan Mina 13
Khyber Pass 65, 233
kidnappings 6, 170, 200, 218
Koh-e-Asmai xiii, 8, 11, 48–51,
107–8
Koh-e-Sher Darwaza xiii, 8, 43, 94,
155
Koh-e-Zamburak 94, 101
Kolola Pushta 7, 18, 27, 39, 196, 218,
220
Kucha-e-Kharabat 156, 157

Lycée Esteqlal 56
Lycée Mariam market 29

maajun (a mix of opium and other substances) 42–3
Mahru, Bibi 126
Maiwand, Battle of (1880) 84
'Maiwand Memorial' 84
Mandayi bazaar xii, 235
marastoon (place of assistance) 143–53, 175
martyrdom/martyrs 71, 90, 92, 94, 163
mausoleums 8, 43–4, 57, 102, 131; Abdur Rahman Khan 57; Babur 43–4, 131; Nadir Shah 102; Timur Shah 8 mental health 142–53
Microrayan 87–92, 114, 132, 210, 219
Minar-e-Ilm-wa-Jahl ('Monument to Knowledge and Ignorance') 107
Ministry of Defence 73
Ministry of Interior 81
Ministry of Public Health 143
Mughal Empire 2, 8, 42, 43, 68, 94, 144
muhajirin (migrants) 232–3
mujahideen (holy warriors) (Afghan guerrilla fighters) 12, 29–30, 46, 47, 57, 84, 85, 90, 108, 118, 119, 128, 146
Mumbai, India 50, 51, 77, 114, 116, 117, 123, 127
Murad (friend of author) 224–7, 229
Muradkhane 175
'*murgh-hai-ye Francewi*' ('French fowl') 56

Nadir Khan, 11
Nadir Shah, King 65, 66, 102
Naheed (murdered girl) 87–93
Najibullah, President 12, 85, 112, 128
Nasruddin, Mulla 51 NATO 3, 5, 30, 195, 220, 222, 224
Nauroz festival 20, 28, 126
nazarband (sealed off from harm) 176
Nazira (friend of author) 55–6, 64, 88–9, 92, 129, 130, 132, 144, 145, 148–9, 152, 167, 187–91, 202, 219, 220
Nejat (organisation) 155–62, 170, 171–2, 173, 174

NGOs 25, 39, 40, 80, 153, 154, 227
Northern Alliance 5, 121
nuqls (sugared almonds) 192

Omar, Mullah 76, 145
opium/heroin 6, 24, 42, 153–61, 170–1, 173
Osman, Akram: *Mardara Qawl As* 184–6, 191; 'Real Men Keep Their Word' (Akram Osman) 184–5
Ottoman Empire 163, 230

Paghman mountains xiii, 44
Paghman, province of 161
Paiman, Zafar 98, 99, 100–2, 103–6, 157
Pakistan 4, 5, 14, 23, 24, 26, 55, 84, 88, 89, 112, 125, 147, 154, 157, 158, 166, 170, 178, 199, 203, 223, 226
Panj-e-Shah, shrine of 96
Panjshir, valley of 59
Parcham (Flag) faction 82, 84
Park Cinema, Shahr-e-Nau 110–11, 112
Pashto 47, 50, 60, 102, 125
Pashtunistan Square 125, 133, 134
Pashtuns (called Pathans in India) 2–3, 4
patron saints 72, 157
People's Democratic Party of Afghanistan (PDPA) (Afghan Communist party) 12, 26, 29, 46–7, 81–2, 122, 210, 218
Persian: language 17, 22, 51, 52, 60, 64, 77, 92, 107, 112, 116, 124, 130, 181; literature xv, 16, 17, 18, 34–5, 48, 50, 51, 52, 53, 64–7, 180–1, 183, 191, 213; poetry xv, 18, 34–5, 48, 53, 64–7, 180–1, 183, 191
Peshawar, Pakistan 24–5, 50, 102, 158, 202
picnics 15, 16, 42, 94, 144, 188
pir (spiritual guide) 97
Pir-i-Baland, shrine of 144–5

poetry xiv, xv, 16, 18, 32, 34–5, 47, 48, 50, 52, 53–4, 55, 58–60, 61–3, 64–9, 120, 141, 156, 180–1, 183, 191, 238; Kabul and 18, 35, 48, 53–4, 58–69, 120, 180–1, 238; Persian xv, 18, 34–5, 48, 53, 64–7, 180–1, 183, 191; Sufi 52, 58–9, 156; Urdu 16, 32, 183

Pohine Nindare (Screen of Learning) cinema 31

poppy palaces 24–5, 31, 73, 156

PTSD 143

Pul-e-Charkhi 137

Pul-e-Sokhta bridge 173–4

Qabre Gora ('Graveyard of Foreigners') The 72–3, 74, 76–80

Qala-e-Fatahullah 27–8, 164, 167, 183, 217, 236

Qala-e-Musa 116, 117, 119

Qargha 16, 144

Qasr-e-Darulaman 10, 11, 97–8, 165, 167, 170, 219

qaseeda (panegyric) 68

Qol-e-Hashmat Khan 94, 102

Quran 23, 163, 192

Radio Ahmad Zahir 74, 234

Radio Kabul 136

Rahimullah (caretaker for the British Cemetery) 76–7, 81

Rais, Shah Muhammad 46–8, 49, 134
  Once Upon a Time There Was a Bookseller in Kabul 48

Rampur, India 2–3

Rattray, James: Scenery, Inhabitants & Costumes of Afghaunistaun 63

real estate prices 24–5, 73, 94, 219

refugees: Afghan 5, 14, 25, 30–2, 62, 64, 84, 85, 97, 119, 140, 147, 154, 173, 199, 202, 223, 224, 226–7, 229, 236–7, 239; Indian Muslim 230–4

'Ring of Steel' (police checkpoints around central Kabul) 140

Rohilkhand, India 2

Rohilla Pathans 2–3

Rudaba (fictional princess of Kabul) 180–1, 213

Rumi, Jalaluddin 48, 52, 58–9;
  Masnavi 59

Russia 9, 75, 99, 229, 233 see also Soviet Union

Sa'adi of Shiraz 48; Shirazi, Sa'adi:
  Bostan 53, 59; Gulistan 53, 59

Safed Koh (White Mountain) range 4

Sa'ib-i-Tabrizi 68–9

saints 72, 95, 97, 98, 144, 145, 157, 163

Saleem (lover) 177–9, 189, 190

Samarkand 42, 54 Saratan Road, 26 135

Sardar (wedding videographer) 201–3, 204–5, 206, 207, 208–9

Sar-e-Chowk 173

Sar-e-Kotal 23

Sarzameen-e-Dilawaran (Land of the Brave) (film) 120–4

Saudi Arabia 12

Saur (April) Revolution (1978) 12, 26, 61, 81–2, 133, 134, 210

Sediqa (salon owner) 198–201, 207

'sha'ir mega' ('the poet says') 54

Shaam-e-Paris ('An Evening in Paris') wedding hall 194

Sahab, Doctor 30–2, 33, 57, 83, 84, 94, 95, 97, 98, 157, 217, 228, 238

Shah-e-do-Shamshera, (the Saint of Two Swords), ziyarat of 163

Shaheed-e-Naheed (martyred Naheed) 92–3

shaheeds (martyrs) 71

Shaheen Films 119, 120

Shaheen, Saleem 115–25

Shahi kings, Hindu 49, 99

Shah M Book Co 44–8, 49

Shahrak-e-Aria 219 shahr ashob verses 32

Shahr-e-Kohna (old city) xiii, 11, 83, 86, 88, 95, 111, 155, 157, 158, 175, 184, 185, 191, 229

Shahr-e-Nau (new suburbs) xiii, 11, 15, 18, 22, 24, 26, 27, 38, 45, 81–2, 110, 117, 167, 184, 187, 193, 196, 203

Shahr-e-Nau Park 112
Shams al-Nahar (Morning Sun) 60
Shekast Qalbaha (The Defeat of Hearts)
    116
Sher Ali Khan, Amir 60, 72–3, 156
Sher Ali Khan Road 45
Sherpur 72–3, 74, 75, 76, 156, 217
shola ghorbandi (roadside food) 82
Shor Bazaar 111, 157
Shuhada-e-Saliheen (graveyard of the
    'Pious Martyrs') 94–9, 157
Shuja, Shah 75
Sikhs 49, 157
Silk Road 77, 99
Silo (granary and bakery) 13
Sipahi Gumnaam (tomb of the
    Unknown Soldier) 83–4, 86
Soraya, Queen 10–11, 193
Soviet Union 12, 13, 24, 29, 61, 78–9,
    80, 84–5, 87, 93, 100, 118, 122,
    126, 127, 128, 133, 134, 144,
    178, 184, 222
'*spand*' (small seeds), burning
    of/*spandi* children 54, 55, 158–9,
    176, 190
spring of Khizr 96
spy balloon 129, 223
Stein, Aurel 77
Sufi Islam 47, 48, 52, 54, 58–9, 156
suicide bombings 6, 22, 67, 129, 140,
    202, 221
Suleman, Dr Tariq 170, 171, 172–3,
    175

taaq (niche in house) 33
Tagore, Rabindranath 36
Taimani 157, 164, 194, 211, 217, 223,
    227
Taliban: book burning 47; Buddhas of
    Bamiyan destroyed by 98–9;
    films and entertainment,
    aversion to 108, 113, 114, 119,
    128, 129, 130, 136–7; Kabul,
    gains control of 12, 55, 62, 90,
    119, 159; Kabul infrastructure
    and 12, 24, 33; Kabul Public
    Library and 64; Kabul traffic and

74; marriages and 193, 210, 212;
    overthrow of xii, 5, 6, 47, 80,
    100, 102, 112, 113, 114, 130,
    142, 154, 178; poppy cultivation,
    ban on 155; refugees flee 5, 55,
    62, 88, 161; resurgence 6, 140,
    220; rule of (1996–2001) xii, 5,
    12–13, 14, 33, 46, 47, 55, 62, 64,
    74, 76, 80, 87, 88, 90, 96, 98–9,
    105, 108, 113, 114, 119, 121,
    128, 129, 130, 136–8, 140, 145,
    155, 159, 161, 190, 210, 212,
    220, 224; US-led air strikes
    target 13; vineyards burned by
    121; women and 114, 190
Taraki, Noor Mohammad 82, 133,
    134
Tarzi, Mahmood 9–10, 60, 231
taveez (charm) 174–5
Tepe Maranjan 101–2
Tepe Naranj (Orange Hill), Buddhist
    monastery at 98, 101–6, 130, 157
Tepe Zamarrod (Emerald Hill) 101
Timur Shah 8 Town Aces
    (grey minivans) 7, 86 T-walls
    140–1

United Nations (UN) 5, 25–6, 90,
    221, 223; Office of the High
    Commissioner for
    Refugees (UNHCR) 237;
    Office on Drugs and Crime
    (UNODC) 154
United States 12, 13, 23, 26, 28, 38,
    80, 84, 90, 127, 128, 129, 132,
    136, 140, 144, 155, 178, 216,
    220, 228; Afghan refugees in 23,
    26, 28; aid to Afghanistan 128;
    Soviet war in Afghanistan and
    12, 84; war in Afghanistan
    (2001–) xii, xiii, xv, 5, 7, 12,
    13, 14, 38, 80, 90–1, 121, 129,
    140–1, 155, 178, 216, 220, 221,
    222, 228
Urdu 4, 16, 17, 32, 35, 51, 58, 60, 117,
    183, 199; poetry 16, 32, 35, 183,
    235–6

'Voice of Shariat Radio' 136

warlords 23, 24, 87
Wazir Akbar Khan 126–7, 178
weddings 14, 27, 74, 113, 164,
    191–215, 223, 225
Wojodi, Haideri 58–60, 61–3, 67–8
women: education of 10, 55–6, 177,
    178, 190, 226; cinema/film and
    108–11, 112, 114; clothing 15,
    27, 88, 109, 131–2, 145, 234;
    crimes against 85, 87–90, 91–3,
    163–4, 221; drug addiction and
    155, 159, 161, 162; love/
    romance and 187–93; mental
    health and 143, 146, 147, 148,
    149, 150–3, 158, 159, 161, 162,

175; newsreels of Kabul and
    131–2, 133; rights of 6, 131;
    weddings and 27, 191–215
World Bank 26; World Development
    Indicators 220
World Health Organisation (WHO) 143

Yakub Khan, Amir 75
'Yeki bood, yeki na bood' ('There was
    one, there was no one') 1

Zahir, Ahmad 74, 96–7, 129, 144, 169,
    234
Zahir Shah, King 11, 12, 60, 66, 83,
    102, 144
Zarnegar Park 53, 56, 131
Zoroastrians 49